To Michael
with love
from Fran
Xmas 1989

Ale &
Beer

A Curious History

ALAN D. BUTCHER

M&S

Canadian Cataloguing in Publication Data

Butcher, Alan D.
Ale and beer : a curious history

Bibliography: p.
ISBN 0-7710-1797-9

1. Ale – History.   2. Beer – History.   3. Ale –
Anecdotes.   4. Beer – Anecdotes.   I. Title.

TP573.A1B87 1989   641.2'3'0207   C89-094743-0

Cover and text design by T. M. Craan
Illustrations by Jack Butcher
Cover photograph by Michael McDonald
Cover author photograph by Gerard Gotzman

Printed and bound in Canada

McClelland & Stewart Inc.
The Canadian Publishers
481 University Avenue
Toronto, Ontario M5G 2E9

For
Gisèle

Contents

Preface

Writing a book about beer is like writing about a well-loved dog. We like to talk about it, the wonderful things it does – this with a certain pride – and also, with feigned irritation, the bad things it does. But even these bad things we redeem with a wry humour. Same with beer. Beer lovers like to drink it, talk about it, point out the good things about it, and recall with a smile its eccentricities.

You'll find a lot of beer eccentricities here. And humour, heartbreak, fact and fancy, and a lot of plain and simple idiocy.

So many people frowned on beer you have to wonder how it survived. The puritans became stiff with outrage at the very mention of the word "beer"; militant temperance movements worked diligently to suppress it; drinkers themselves did terrible things to their brew, ostensibly to improve it; and some of the most ridiculous laws in the history of the legal profession were enacted to control it. Yet despite these frenetic efforts to destroy it, beer still lives, and this book is the story of its life.

I like to think I wrote this book myself, but a glance at the bibliography will show you what a laughable conceit that is. No one can produce a book entirely by himself. Apart from the technical assistance of printers, typesetters, artists, and designers, there is the priceless encouragement of family and friends, not to mention the nontechnical yet invaluable moral support of a good editor. I have been fortunate in all these areas, and to fail to recognize the fact would be unforgivable. To Roy Minter of Vancouver I must acknowledge the greatest debt; without his initial push nothing would have happened. The enthusiasm of my wife Gisèle and daughter Jean supported me during the years of research in ways that could never be measured. My son Jack's illustrations have given the book a dimension I could not have achieved alone. In the early stages of the book's development Mrs Mariliese Lehwaldt, head librarian at Labatt Breweries in London, Ontario, provided invaluable assistance. The libraries of Metropolitan Toronto were, as always, unfailing sources of guidance and wise counsel cheerfully given. And, ultimately, to my editor Dinah Forbes I can only say: Thank Heaven you were on my side. The book would have suffered without your firm and intelligent guidance. To these and the many others who gave freely of their time and expertise, I cannot offer sufficient thanks.

One last point: The story of beer is a long one, filled with sound and fury (a lot of fury), and more than just the occasional guffaw. No one person could recount the whole story, and a history that resounds to such constant conflict generates a world of violently divergent views. In the end I must, like the historian Ibn-Khaldun, "pray that men of ability and learning will examine my work with goodwill, and when they find faults will indulgently correct them . . . one should always be able to count on the courtesy of his colleagues."

And on that note, I think I'll have a beer.

A.B.
Toronto
June, 1989

Ale & Beer

1

Beer and Brewing

When the first fish came ashore from the primordial swamp it must have been dragging a mash tub, because beer has been with us since day one. As far back as records go there are references to brewing.

When we think about the origin of beer, its discovery doesn't at first surprise us. The process is, after all, absurdly simple. Take malted barley, add warm water, drain off the water, add yeast, and – *voilà* – you have beer. Nothing to it. Yet, as with so many apparently simple procedures, the right thing has to be done in the right order. It's like riding a bicycle: a simple matter of balance, turning the wheel the right way at the right time, correct weight distribution to make the turns, and all that; easiest thing in the world. Try telling that to a kid who keeps falling off. It's the same with the beer: just don't forget to steep the barley in the warm water; if you add yeast to water but overlook the malted barley you're not going to have much of anything.

In the case of the first "brewer," maybe fifteen thousand years ago, the discovery of beer had to be accidental. Unsophisticated, half-animal, our cave dweller was concerned only with survival. The principle of fermentation was an unwritten book. Perhaps some barley was allowed to germinate. Perhaps the cook added water and placed the bowl on the fire to soften the grain and make it more edible. Perhaps the water was then drawn off into another container. Chance may have brought airborne yeasts to settle in the barley water. Later, a thirsty prehistoric man scooped up a mugful, raised it to his lips – and took the drink that changed the world.

History does not record this first beer. Even the origin of the word beer is obscure, though its ties with barley

1

are fairly obvious. Beer was once the English name of both the plant and the brew. With the passage of time the plant's name became barley (*beer-lec*, or "beer plant").

That first prehistoric mugful may not even have been beer. Ancient poets tell of Circe, the enchantress who lived on an island in the Mediterranean. Men who drank from her cup turned into swine (the women of today might shrug and say "What else?"). Perhaps, as the ubiquitous poet, Anon, claimed, its ingredients were "red wine, and in it barley-meal and cheese and honey, and mighty drugs withal, of which if a man drank he forgot all that he had loved."

Circe's use of honey in her magical beverage may have been simply a reflection of the poet's own taste; the earliest fermented drink could have been mead, fermented honey and water. The origin of mead lies beyond the beginnings of recorded history. Ancient Sanskrit writings document its existence thousands of years ago. Its very simplicity, and the ease with which its ingredients could have come together – some watered honey left for a day or two, then sampled, and . . . hey, not bad! . . . followed by a pleasantly altered state of mind – would indicate that its origins probably date from our earliest days.

Cider, too, could claim to be the first fermented drink. The birth of cider is also obscured by time, and for the same reason: ease of discovery and production. Someone merely left the juice of wild apples to ferment, which it did voluntarily and without additives or assistance of any kind, and in a twinkling there was a glass of pretty good stuff. In 55 BC, Julius Caesar found Britain's Celts enjoying a flagon or two (or five) as a regular thing; these same Celts even paid homage to an apple god.

Mead and cider, however, have never enjoyed the same devoted press as barley. When history began, malted grain was already the big thing. The Egyptians brewed beer enthusiastically thousands of years BC; hieroglyphs and murals of five thousand years ago clearly show the people of the day gathering grain, malting, brewing, and drinking beer. They made it from a barley mash and added fragments of fermented bread. Filtration was pretty rudimentary. The nobles consumed beer from a vat, using long straws to penetrate the surface scum. The very noble drank through straws of gold.

In Egypt, the popularity of beer, or *hek* as it was called, was such that around 2,000 BC there was concern about the number of alehouses – or rather *hek*-houses – that existed. There was a great movement to close them and prohibit *hek* consumption throughout the land. This is one of the earliest recorded instances of prohibition (and about as successful as any other, as it turned out).

Egypt and Asia were the birthplace of beer, but we must add the qualification, *as far as we know*. In dozens of areas in Asia and Asia Minor there is evidence of brewing that takes us back thousands of years. In southern Turkestan (east of the Caspian Sea) more than six thousand years ago – some authorities say nine thousand – barley was cultivated. That almost certainly means someone was brewing beer.

Assyrian records of two thousand years ago list beer as an item on Noah's shopping list; Noah, too, knew what was good for you, especially if you were embarking (whether you liked it or not) on an ocean voyage. For the sake of consistency, the beer was probably a pair of twelve-packs.

By the time people first moved out of their caves and took the initial steps toward the development of centres of social activity, where groups of families formed small settlements, they were brewing beer from cereal grains. This was the dawn of brewing (specifically beer) among the early Germanic peoples, the Gauls, and the Britons. Though, until the advent of agriculture and planned sowing and harvesting, the production of beer, in the sense of being an organized activity, existed only where wild cereals were available. More than eight thousand years ago, villages in Turkey cultivated grain, and there is ample historical evidence to support the belief that where people grew grain, they were inclined to brew beer before they baked bread.

As far back as can be remembered, the Nubians (Nubia was an ancient region in northeast Africa) brewed a drink called *bonga*. (Nice sound, *bonga*. Makes you want to snap your fingers, laugh, and do a little dance.) It's a malt brew made from barley, and somewhat like a light German beer of today.

In India, three thousand years ago, they made an alcoholic beverage from the juice of plants of the asclepius genus (the same genus as milkweed). The Indian brewers mixed water with the plant's juices, strained it, added malt and warm milk, and left the mixture to ferment. Milk? To each his own, I suppose, but it doesn't sound like the kind of thing with which I would want to spend an evening. Yet the Indians held these plant juices in almost religious veneration. Among the earliest gods of India was the *soma* plant. Its intoxicating juice brought happiness and penetrating insight to its devotees, much like a case of beer today.

Africa, too, had its adherents to beverages made from plant juices. Livingstone found Africans drinking a toddy made from palm tree sap. "The men . . . trust to their wives for food, and spend most of their time in drinking the palm toddy. This toddy is the juice of the palm-oil tree, which, when tapped, yields a clear, sweet liquid, not at all intoxicating when fresh, but when allowed to stand until the afternoon causes inebriation." The idea of the men lounging around, guzzling toddies, beer, or whatever, while the women did the work was not new. Will Durant tells us that in the first century AD the Germans, like Britain's Celts, spent most of their time fighting the Romans. The men used any time left over gorging themselves on great haunches of meat "and drinking rivers of beer," while the women worked around the home.

You would expect these "rivers of beer" to produce noteworthy hangovers, and you would be absolutely right. The morning after one of those Gallic bashes was not the time for meaningful philosophical remarks like "Good morning." Yet, remarkably, ale as a relief for severe hangovers has gained wide acceptance. The Romans and Greeks, however, who apparently would believe anything, sought to prevent the drunkenness that was the *cause* of hangovers by using cabbage. Did they eat it themselves, or hang it around the necks of incipient lushes?

When the Romans arrived in Britain they were greeted by a fairly ragged bunch of natives. Naked and garishly painted, the island's inhabitants were a pretty unsophisticated lot. The beverages of the early Britons reflected the simple and uncomplicated character of the people themselves. Their drink came from materials ready at hand, and required little knowledge or imagination to prepare. These, as we have seen, were mead and cider. Simple liquor, nothing fancy. The Romans, however, brought civilization and a knowledge of agriculture. Within a short time, while the Celtic hordes to the north continued to scoff their mead, those farther south – flourishing, in a manner of speaking, under the aegis of the Latin conqueror – graduated to ale.

Pliny (61-113 AD) tells us that the Gauls spent much of their time drinking "barley wine" and called it, as the Romans did, *cerevisia* (a word derived from *Ceres*, the Roman goddess of agriculture, and *vis*, meaning strength; our word cereal comes from the same goddess). With time the name changed to the Gallic *cervoise* (sehr-*vwahz*), which remained in popular use until the end of the thirteenth century, when hops were introduced into ale. For the next 150 years *cervoise* as a name went into decline in France (though Spaniards still call their beer *cervesa*), and by the mid-1400s the term *bière* had come into official use.

If you frown on all the beer drinking you see, and feel you have to blame someone, blame the Danes. When the Vikings swarmed into Britain they came with a sword in one hand and a flagon of ale in the other. Before the coming of the Norsemen the original Britons called their own ale *cwrw*. This name was supplanted by the Danish *öl*, which in time became "ale" in English. (Not surprising; try saying *cwrw* after you've had a couple. Indeed, try saying *cwrw* when you're sober.) The Britons acquired a taste for the strong Danish *öl*, and its consumption became even more widespread than before. This occurred in the time of Britain's King Edgar (tenth century), but these things don't happen overnight; the Danes may have introduced their mighty *öl* into Britain and made it national in scope, but its equivalent had been part of Britain's life long before the Danes arrived. As early as 616, laws existed governing the *eala-hus* (alehouse) of King Ethelbert's time. Ine, king of Wessex (688-726), a kingdom that extended from London west to Cornwall and south to the Channel, also issued laws to control the proliferation of "ale-booths" and "ale-stonds."

To the west, in the wild lands of the Welsh, singing and painting their bodies represented only two of the natives' activities. They also excelled in the art of brewing. During the time of the Anglo-Saxons, Wales was renowned for the quality of its ale. A barrel of Welsh ale always brought premium prices. In these Saxon days, the Welsh king's steward received ale as his daily pay, the amount of ale being determined by the steward himself: he thrust his middle finger into a cask and took home ale to the depth of that finger.

The profusion of early beer laws illustrates that medieval Britain took a dim view of brewers and alehouses that produced and sold inferior ale. Offending ale-wives – brewing was woman's work in those days – suffered a vigorous ducking. The authorities made it a public ceremony, with a special stool that tipped the offenders into a large trough of water. The poor of the town received the bad ale, no charge. This seems not only rough on the alewife, though she deserved it, but also pretty hard on the poor, who were left to drink the ale that nobody else wanted.

Until the Middle Ages the brewing of beer was exclusively the province of the woman in the household. Old laws even went so far as to state that the vessels used in brewing were her personal property. But this arrangement did not originate in Britain. As far back as 2,000 BC, Mesopotamia (part of modern Iraq) acknowledged women as brewers, in an industry that even then was held in the highest regard. In Babylon, female brewers (or brewsters, feminine, just as baxter and spinster are the feminine forms of baker and spinner) were priestesses in the temple, giving the industry an ecclesiastical flavour that continued to the monastic breweries of medieval England.

The mention of baxter and baker is not an idle one. The connection between beer and bread – the two walk hand-in-hand throughout history – is found in the root of the word "brewing": the Old English *breowan*, from which also comes the word "bread." The Germans saw the same relationship develop: the old German *briuwan* (brewing) also gave them the word *brot* (bread).

Much of medieval brewing in Europe was carried on in the local monasteries, those noble fountainheads of learning, piety, and triple x. Not incidentally, the symbol "x," signifying the purity and strength of the brew, indeed the monastery's imprimatur as it were, originated in these clerical establishments, and first were in the form of a crucifix, which is logical enough given the ecclesiastical inclination of the brewers. Over the years it's not unlikely a few lopsided crosses appeared – and I'm not suggesting for a moment that the monks were into their own sauce to a secular and impious degree, but it's well known they put away a fair amount – one lopsided cross led to another, and the x became a standard mark, strength increasing with each x. Triple x (xxx) was a good strong ale.

During medieval times, monasteries began brewing beer on a larger scale; gradually women's involvement in the brewing process diminished and finally came to an end as the man became more and more the brewer in the home.

When men took over brewing, things changed. What was once a simple wifely art, performed with skill and a quiet pride, evolved, through male ego, into a convoluted, mysterious, and almost religious act. Brewing guilds formed and grew powerful. As far back as 1493 the Bavarian brewers guild required that all brewers complete an apprenticeship of three years and that they be of lawful birth. Also, no moonlighting. The same guilds strictly controlled the brewing and the retail sale of beer. As certain beers gained in fame, the methods of their brewing became even more secret, almost sacred. Man, as usual, could not leave well enough alone; even the simple term "brewing" was too inadequate for male self-esteem. In 1575, for example, it was referred to as "the Divine and Noble Gift of the Philosophical, Highly Honourable and Wonderful Art of Brewing." This was the "Wonderful Art" that in the seventeenth century Hanover saw one in every three people directly involved in the brewing trade; earlier, in England, the same ratio applied throughout the country, indeed in rural areas almost all men were engaged in brewing, producing ale for their family's use.

To discourage fraud in the dispensing of ale in the various alehouses and inns, every medieval locality had its official ale-taster. His function, one of considerable substance in the community, consisted in not only monitoring the quality of the ale sold, but also guarding against short measure. He would circulate around the local drinking places, slupping up the beer – thumbs up, thumbs down, as the case may have been – and anyone who did not abide by the accepted standards was in trouble. Malefactors suffered outright corporal punishment. The ale-taster also provided the drinking places with vessels of standard measure, "sealed quarts," bearing the ale-taster's seal or mark, as official measures of capacity. Some alehouses suspended these pewter vessels above their doors as a promise of good ale within.

In all times beer has been the subject of great concern; laws have invariably levied stiff punishment on those who tried to profit from unethical methods of brewing and sale. In Babylon, centuries before Christ, death was the penalty for any irregularities in the selling of beer. Brewers, being human, were prey to the same shortcomings that afflict all of us; greed, more than anything else. Business was business in those early days, too, and if unchecked, business tends to maximize profits by . . . well, by just about any method that maximizes profits.

When the barons of England forced King John to sign the Magna Carta in 1215, such was the concern over ale that a clause was inserted regarding standards to control its sale. If you have even a mildly cynical mind you will infer that there must have been many sellers of ale who needed such control. And you are right. Laws were enacted, taxes laid on with a liberal hand, and if a brewer tried to evade them he was in deep trouble. Even so, thirteenth century penalties imposed on those who dodged the beer tax seem, today, to have been excessively harsh. The authorities chopped off the offender's right hand, destroyed his house, and banished him for a period of five years. Of the various punishments, banishment was probably the most welcome; the brewer was undoubtedly glad to be far away from guys who went around chopping off hands.

The year 1295 (according to one historian) marked the first recorded mention of brewing at Burton upon Trent, England. That year the monastery at Burton listed an annual pension of sorts awarded to a member of the community, specifying that it should include "two gallons of the convent beer." On the other hand, with the exasperating perversity that history and historians often exhibit, *Cups and their customs*, a small volume published in London in 1869, claims that the first brewery in Burton opened its doors in the year 1002. A difference of a mere 293 years.

When Richard I was king of England (1189-1199), the abbey at Burton upon Trent was already well known for the quality of its ale, due in part to the high gypsum (calcium sulphate) content of the well water in the area. Also, *Britannica* tells us that a Benedictine monastery was founded there in that year, and knowing the monasteries' habit of starting to brew before the cement on the cornerstone was dry, I'm inclined to go along with the 1002 date.

In the days of Peter the Great of Russia (1682-1725), Imperial banquets always included dark foaming oceans of Burton ale. The richness of these grand ales was universally recognized. "If some was spilled on the table the glass would stick to it." The fame of Burton ales rests on the brewing practices of the ancient abbey; monasteries across the land observed similar methods and from them came many of the outstanding local ales of England.

9

The Abbot of Burton brewed good ale
  On Fridays when they fasted,
But the Abbot of Burton never tasted his own
  As long as his neighbour's lasted.

Today, the term beer means just about any malt beverage, other than porter and stout. In the sixteenth century
the appellation "beere," current in Anglo-Saxon times
but long dead, came once more to differentiate between
"ale" and "hopped ale." Samuel Johnson, in his monumental dictionary of the English language (1755),
defined beer and ale, and noted the fundamental
difference between the two. Ale: "A liquor made by
infusing malt in hot water, and then fermenting the
liquor." Beer: "Liquor made from malt *and hops*." The
hopped variety, beer, was more expensive because people thought it was better than straight ale. Four hundred
years later the situation has been reversed, and ale has
now acquired a universal, and largely unwarranted,
cachet.

The date of the first use of hops in beer is hazy. The
Benedictine monks of Freising, Germany, grew hops in
768, and though there is no indication they were used in
the brewing of the abbey's beer, it seems likely, as mention is made in medieval German public documents (822
AD) of hops and beer, suggesting that hops were used in
brewing at that time. Direct association of the two
appears in the writings of the Abbess Hildegard of
Rupertsberg in 1079: "If one intends to make beer from
oats, it is prepared with hops."

The same Abbess Hildegard also mentions the preservative qualities of hops. The Germans were the first to use
hops in beer, and until the English adopted the custom,
German beer was the only brew that could be exported,
thanks to those same preservative qualities of the hop.
The ability of the plant to maintain the life of a brew over
longer periods was quickly perceived by the brewers of
Hamburg, who were among the first to use it. Much of
the city's heavy export trade was overseas, thus the brew
and the city benefited from the hop.

Humulus lupulus, the botanical term for hops, comes
from its Roman name *Lupus salictarius* – *lupus* meaning wolf. In its wild state the hop often grew among
willows and had a destructive effect on the trees; early

records describe its effect as "like a wolf among sheep," thus the Roman term *lupus*.

The hop's resins and oils lend beer its bitter flavour. Czechoslovakian hops particularly are held in high regard wherever beer is produced. In Bohemia, formerly a kingdom in the western part of modern Czechoslovakia, hops were grown as far back as 859 AD. The romantically inclined Czechs claim their Bohemian hops are superior because they are still gathered by the hands of beautiful young girls.

In the first part of the 1300s hops were used in the brewing process in Holland, whence, a hundred years later, the plant appeared in England. There are records of the use of hops in French beer in the year 1268 during the reign of Louis IX of France, where laws controlling brewing stipulated that "Nothing shall enter into the composition of beer but good malt and hops." That yeast was, to a certain degree, controlled by the brewer, and that fermentation was not left to the vagaries of airborne wild yeasts, appears in further clauses of the same laws: "No beer yeast shall be hawked about the streets, but shall be all sold in the brew-houses" and "Beer yeast brought by foreigners shall be inspected before it is exposed to sale."

By the mid-fifteenth century, most western European countries had welcomed the hop; Finland had even legislated against its importation and encouraged local farmers to grow it. At the same time – early fifteenth century – the hop was being grown in England, and was encountering the violent reaction that was to plague it for a century.

Toward the end of the Hundred Years' War (1337-1453) between France and England, hops were introduced into English beer for the first time. An English manuscript, *circa* 1440, carries the earliest mention of England's use of hops in brewing, making the distinction between ale and beer. Ale, it said, was to be drunk new, while beer was aged. To preserve the beer during its maturation, hops were added. Hops, according to some authorities, arrived in England in 1520. "From Bohemia comes this goodly vine ... with its aid is made that good drink that we call Brunswick Mum. But the [Germans] call it 'bier,' for it is made from the bere or barley plant." The year 1520 seems a bit off the mark. In the previous century England's Henry VI (1422-1461, 1470-1471) banned the use of the hop in brewing, considering it an adulterant, and enacted laws to check its use. More than a hundred years passed before the "wicked weed" was accepted and its beneficial properties recognized; beneficial not only in that it helped to preserve the brew, but also added an agreeable flavour.

In the early 1400s immigrants from Holland settled in Kent (a county in southeast England), planted and culti-vated hops, and used them in their beer as they had done in their homeland. These Flemish newcomers soon became famous for the quality of their hops.

As with anything new, the introduction of hops in the brewing of beer was resisted bitterly (if I can use that expression), usually as a result of the self-interest of those who saw the hop taking the place of whatever plants they themselves were growing and supplying to the breweries – and in the early days they used all man-ner of plants in brewing as flavouring agents. In ancient Egypt they used the evergreen rue to lend a bitter flavour to their beer. Rosemary, that glorious herb that does so much for sauces, was used in sixteenth century England. In some parts of Norway and Sweden juniper is still used to flavour beer. Resistance to the hop was also a matter of old-fashioned inertia: ale had always been made with-out hops, why change?

The characteristic tolerance of the English was shown in the fifteenth century in Henry VI's insistence that the Flemish settlers in Kent be allowed, by law, to continue using hops in their beer, even though the people of the region frowned on the practice (this, remember, was the king who had earlier banned hop's use; we all change with time). Kent is still famous for its hops. Mr Jingle, in Dickens' *Pickwick Papers*, says "Kent, sir? Everybody knows Kent – apples, cherries, hops, and women." And that's as good an accolade as any area can ask.

In the early 1500s, England's Henry VIII felt that hops were an adulterant to good English ale, and issued an injunction against the use of the plant in the brewing of beer, but the duration of the edict was short. His succes-sor, the young Edward VI (1547-1553), and his counsel-lors gave brewers the freedom to add hops to beer. The tastes of the public, too, became more tolerant toward hop's use. "Hopped ale" – beer – was here to stay.

12

Beer and ale acquired many names down through the centuries. "Barley broth" and "oil of barley," for example; common terms in everyday conversation three hundred years ago. John Taylor, poet of the Thames and keeper of an alehouse in London, flourished in the time of Charles I (1600-1649). "Ale," said Taylor, "is the warmest lining of a naked man's coat." A bit obscure, but it illustrates his views on ale. Around the same period you would have heard the expression "Wine is but single broth; ale is meat, drink, and cloth." The expression itself won't keep you warm on a winter's night, nor will ale. But ale helps.

On the other side of the Atlantic the Incas, Aztecs, and Mayas, too, were brewing beer before the Spanish conquest, using corn instead of barley. Columbus was the first European to sample this brew when he arrived in Central America on his last voyage (1502). Shortly thereafter the first brewery in the new world was established in Mexico by the king of Spain.

Ale has always had a lot of friends. No less than three saints are patrons of beer: St Augustine, St Nicholas (our old friend Santa Claus), and St Luke, a physician who knew what was best for you. St Thomas à Becket, though not a patron saint of ale, nevertheless knew a good thing when he saw one: In 1158, when he first went as an envoy to France for Henry II, he took along seven barrels of English ale. Nothing like a barrel of ale (or seven) to resolve differences of opinion.

While politically useful, strong English ales wrought wonders on the battlefield, too. Shakespeare tells us (King Henry V, act iii, scene 5) that Henry's victory over the French at the battle of Agincourt prompted the Gallic commander to gnash his teeth in fury and frustration. "Where have they this mettle?" he fumed. "Can sodden water . . . their barley broth, decoct their cold blood to such valiant heat?"

Even before Oliver Cromwell came to power in post-reformation England and gave a certain cachet to the brewer's art (being a brewer himself, following in the noble footsteps of William the Conqueror whose father had also been a brewer), the brewmaster held a position of circumstance in the king's household, higher in importance than even the royal physician himself.

Thinking for a moment on this royal brewmaster and the state of the brewing art of the time, you can understand that skill in brewing was only one of his talents. He would also have been a fair-to-middling fast talker to justify to the king the occasional brewing disaster caused by incomplete knowledge and control of fermentation. Early ales were left to the mercy of spontaneous fermentation, the result of airborne yeasts; not the most reliable guarantee of a good brew. A "dyetary" written *circa* 1542 by Andrew Boorde nevertheless speaks of pure ale as being nothing more than malt, water, and yeast – the yeast being added by the brewer, indicating that at least by the mid-sixteenth century fermentation was no longer left entirely to chance.

Beyond the pleasures of consumption, ale has had other applications. Perhaps the strangest use to which ale has been put occurred in the Middle Ages. During the years when the economic power of the Hanseatic League extended throughout northern and western Europe, great fleets of ships exported Hamburg's beer. Such liquid wealth drew numerous pirate attacks on the busy port. At one time the furious citizens manned the walls and poured thousands of litres of boiling beer down on the attackers, a tasty though not very refreshing twist to the medieval use of boiling oil.

Good, substantial ale, like St Thomas à Becket's seven barrels of political goodwill, has always had the ability to banish differences between friends. Many a cordial *entente* has been achieved hob-nobbing over a tankard or two. The expression "to hob-nob," meaning to be on friendly terms with, generally in the sense of drinking together, may have come from the time of the lusty, four-gallon-a-day maids of honour in the days of Henry VIII. Occasionally they preferred a warm beer and would have their tankard placed on the hob of the grate in the fireplace. Thus their host asked "From the hob or not from the hob?" Another possible source for the term comes from the Saxon *habban* (to have) and *ne habban* (to have not), which with usage became "hab-nab" and today "hob-nob."

Elizabeth I, Henry VIII's daughter, knew the stout maids of honour of her father's court and grew up with the same tastes. John Bickerdyke, writing in 1889, quotes one of Elizabeth's contemporaries: "Her own bere was so strong as there was no man able to drink it." Other writers refer to this same comment on the Queen's taste and capacity, but it's out of context and misleading. The source is certainly the Earl of Leicester. In June of 1575 the Earl was with Queen Elizabeth at the town of Kenilworth (central England). In a letter to Lord Burghley, dated the 28th, he remarked on the strength of the ale available in the town. "[Had to send to various places] where ale was, her own here [in Kenilworth] was such strong as there was no man able to drink it. It did put her far out of temper." The reference, in context, clearly relates to the strength of the Kenilworth brew, not Elizabeth's taste for super-strong ale as some writers imply. (In justice to Dickerdyke, his term "her own bere" can only be a typesetter's error; see Leicester's letter: "her own *here*".)

Sixteenth-century concern over ale quality prompted the formation in England of citizen's groups that many villages empowered to seek out the major crimes of treason, rebellion, murder, and robbery – and, just as important, to see that no brewer "made ale and beer hurtful to man's body." Brewing substandard ale was right up there with treason.

Government regulations have always been with us, but rarely have they been as onerous and downright unfair as in the time of Elizabeth i. A beer drinker of famous proportions, she was paranoid when it came to governing the brewers. Sometimes she allowed them to brew, and sometimes not, and the decision was an arbitrary one. She kept a jaundiced eye on beer quality, and Heaven help the brewer whose product fell below her rigid standards: offenders suffered back-breaking fines, at best; some were flung into prison. Elizabeth determined the selling price of beer, and the brewer was compelled by law to continue brewing even when the queen's retail price was less than the brewer's cost! But if you were smart you didn't fool around with short-tempered Elizabeth. You swallowed your loss, in the knowledge that "time changes all things," as it invariably did.

In 1606 a law was enacted in Britain which frowned on crafty brewers who delivered their beer in carts. The springless metal-shod wheels and the rough streets gave the beer a good shaking. When opened, the casks, of course, appeared full, but "when they are settled, they lack some gallon of beer, to the enriching of the brewer." They're a cunning bunch these brewers.

In the mid-seventeenth century England's Charles II staggered the Restoration beer industry with a 20 per cent tax on the price of a barrel of beer. Later, during the period when England was killing itself with gin, the English government (in 1795), to encourage the consumption of beer instead of spirits, relieved the brewing industry of all taxes. This, in the manner of governments everywhere, was followed four years later by a *retail* tax on beer. The government giveth, and the government taketh away – only, as usual, it was the guy on the street that got taken.

The four centuries that followed the first Elizabeth witnessed drastic fluctuations in the number of brewers in Britain. In 1550, London had twenty-six brewers operating in the city; within a century the number had increased almost eight-fold to 199. Other centres saw the same growth; by the mid-1800s there were 133,000 licensed brewers in England. In the eighteenth century there were around three hundred breweries in the city of London, alone.

With growth came prestige and wealth for the brewers – but were they really happy? The answer, of course, is yes, very happy. Well, most of the time. There *were* periods – under Elizabeth I, for example – when the brewers got the short end of the stick; times were tough, and a tear could be seen in their eyes. But most of the time, like Liberace, they cried all the way to the bank.

As the brewer grew richer he bought land, built estates, yearned for status, and through the power of his money saw himself as a gentleman, a man of prestige, and conducted himself accordingly: he dressed in fine clothes, dined well, called the great by their first names and considered himself their peer. John Taylor, the seventeenth century alehouse proprietor and poet of the Thames, tells the story of the brewer whose coachman, William, was a slave to drink. Exasperated, the brewer finally had to fire William – I mean, a drunken coachman, after all; think of the neighbours – and replace him with a non-drinker. The brewer went so far as to point out to poor William that, had he been a sober man, he would have kept his job. "Let that be a lesson to you,

Billy old chap, and stick to water," he probably said. William was understandably bitter:

> "Drink water," cried William; "had all men
>   done so,
> You'd never have wanted a coachman, I trow.
> They are soakers, like me, whom you load with
>   reproaches,
> That enable you brewers to ride in your coaches."

By the late seventeenth century, brewers everywhere were growing more affluent; the local village brewer faded into memory as breweries became large family businesses, increasing in size and wealth. A brewery established near Vienna in 1632 and bought by the Dreher family in 1796 became one of the great breweries of the Austro-Hungarian Empire. By 1900, after a century of Dreher guidance, it had expanded its market into Bohemia and Italy. According to a journalist writing at the turn of the century, the Dreher breweries represented the largest business conducted under one management in all of continental Europe.

Often with wealth and fame came a sense of responsibility, of *noblesse oblige*. Many brewers earned reputations in philanthropy. The statue of the "Little Mermaid" in the harbour of Copenhagen was a gift to the city from the Carlsberg brewery, a firm noted for its liberal assistance in the arts and sciences.

The success of some brewers just shows what you can accomplish in your spare time. In the neighbourhood of Burton upon Trent, England, in the year 1723, a man operated a small carrying firm, and as a sideline, sold a home-brewed ale he made himself in his off hours. The demand for his brew was so great he sold his carrying company and entered the brewing business. The man's name was Bass. Today the firm of Bass Charrington is the largest brewery in the U.K., and exports its product all over the world. One of their symbols, the Toby Jug, used since its acquisition in 1933 for their Toby ale, was first adopted by the Red Lion Brewery, London, a firm established in 1492. Another prominent Burton brewing family is Allsopp. The Allsopps have been in beer since the time of the Crusades. One member, Hugh de Allsopp, marched to Jerusalem with King Richard Lion-Heart (1189-99).

Across the Atlantic, the American War of Independence disrupted the domestic production of beer, and for fifty years thereafter brewing reverted to the cottage industry that existed in early England. The availability of English ale and porter in America was, of course, severely limited for a long period after 1776. Yet, less than a hundred years later, breweries had sprung up in cities like Philadelphia and Milwaukee, whose large German populations drank, in Philadelphia, 180,000 barrels annually, while Milwaukee's consumption was a substantial 70,000-plus. Within a century Philadelphia supported ninety-four breweries. But time (and competition) changes all things: today that number has been reduced to two. The same shrinkage (or expansion if you happen to be the surviving brewery) is seen everywhere.

Canada's brewing history goes back to the mid-seventeenth century. Jean Talon, the intendant of New France in 1665-1668 and 1670-1672, built Canada's first brewery at Quebec City in 1668. At the time of its construction the colony spent 100,000 *livres* annually on imported wines and spirits. To encourage self-sufficiency in the colonists, Talon restricted importation to a mere 1,200 hogsheads, the rest of the demand to be met in beer from his brewery. His plan worked. The brewery began production in 1670, and the following year supplemented the meagre importation with 2,000 hogsheads of ale, and at the same time shipped a further 2,000 hogsheads to the West Indies. This commerce, among its many benefits, not only refreshed the colonists, but at the same time consumed 12,000 bushels of surplus grain. But when Jean Talon returned to France the restrictions on alcoholic importations into New France were relaxed, at the cost of Talon's brewery, which closed in 1675.

The reason for the brewery's closing can only have been a political one – office politics was as rife then as it is now – because certainly the market was there, in spades. A Jesuit spokesman in the year 1636, describing the diet of the common man in New France, noted "they are given . . . a quart of beer [a day]." While much of the beer consumed was the product of home brewing, there would still have been a clamorous market for Jean Talon's 2,000 hogsheads (at least half a million quarts).

In 1876 Louis Pasteur discovered, during his studies on pasteurization, that the occasional yet costly failures in the brewing process were often caused by airborne "wild" yeasts. Until then, knowledge of yeast and how it worked was incomplete; Pasteur's microscope revealed the living world of the micro-organisms that caused fermentation, and soon control and protection of the yeast was achieved, to the joy of brewers everywhere.

Yeast is the catalyst that turns the wort (pronounced "wert"; the strainings from the malt-and-hot-water mash) into beer; in the course of its action it converts the sugars from the malt into alcohol, carbon dioxide, and other substances like vitamins and minerals, which together give beer its character. In pasteurized beers – and today most of them are when they leave the brewery – the familiar sparkle is enhanced by adding carbon dioxide, often the same CO_2, recovered and retained by the brewer, that was given off by the action of the yeast that created the beer in the first place. A nice happy cycle.

Elizabeth I's reign had been a dark period, financially, for many brewers. But closer to our own day, toward the end of the nineteenth century, there was another bleak interlude for the brewers, a brief season that illustrated the adage that the shoemaker should stick to his last. An excursion into areas other than brewing proved disastrous. In the late nineteenth century, around two thousand of the seven-thousand-odd London pubs were owned by breweries. There was at that time little incentive for them to increase their holdings. Most public-house purchases were financed by a loan from a brewer on the unwritten understanding that the new pub would buy its beer from the brewery that advanced the money (step out of line and the brewery would call in its loan). This arrangement had worked well until, in the 1880s, an economic slump brought a drop in beer consumption. Publicans saw their revenues fall, but costs continued to rise and profits suffered. Many pub owners, to reduce losses, diluted their beer. The breweries threatened to take back their loans if there was any more of that sort of thing, and rapidly the pub-brewery relationship deteriorated. Pub owners began to seek other sources of financing that would free them from the London breweries.

The brewers of Burton saw an opportunity to seize a larger share of the London beer market, and magnanimously offered to assist the struggling pubs. The London breweries swallowed convulsively; Burton ale was their most powerful competitor, and the idea of Burton securing a bigger piece of the lucrative London action wasn't an attractive one. But the glorious golden ales of Burton caught the public taste, and sales of London's porter dropped. The London brewers fought back with pale ales of their own, but the damage had been done; they saw their hold on the city's pubs slipping through their fingers as Burton's market share grew. In desperation, many of the London breweries went public to raise the necessary funds to buy more public-houses and thus ensure outlets for their beer.

The 1890s quickly became *the* time to sell a public-house. Pub prices skyrocketed. A public-house which twenty years before had sold for £2,000 went for £86,000. The London breweries went on an orgy of buying. One brewery's pub-buying budget increased 11,000 per cent between 1892 and 1896; in the last four years of the century another brewery, Allsopp's, committed £3.2 million to the purchase of pubs.

The breweries were not the only ones who got deeply into pub buying. Shrewd publicans dealt in pubs as they dealt in pints: one after another. The spiralling market was inebriating; buy today, sell tomorrow, double your money. The money tree seemed to bloom perennially. Somewhat the same euphoria flourished on Wall Street in the autumn of 1929.

As with all orgies, there comes the morning after, the painful hangover, and the agonizing self-reproach: "Why did I do it?" The brewers must have looked around at their newly acquired pubs and recoiled at the thought of what they had done. The prices they had paid would be considered madness even in today's inflated market, and prices today are ten times what they were at the turn of the century.

In 1899 the crash came. A London pub that scarcely a year before had sold for £33,000 was lucky to fetch £12,000. Within a year the golden market was swept away on a wave of bankruptcies.

The breweries must have felt that Someone up there didn't like them, for as we have seen, the breweries were the creditors of many of these pubs; faced with bankruptcies on every hand, the breweries were left with a lot of fairly useless paper. Of course, there was the positive side (though the breweries might have argued over the term "positive"): the failures left them with a lot of pubs. By 1915 brewery ownership stood at 95 per cent. "But," the brewer might well have asked, "95 per cent of what?" The pubs, for which he had paid millions of pounds sterling a few years before, were selling (if they could find a buyer) for a tenth of that in the turn-of-the-century market. And, to add a twist to the knife in the brewer's heart, the authorities went on one of their periodic anti-drink binges and assiduously closed pubs and refused to renew licences. Many brewers lay awake nights, staring at the ceiling.

Rather than reproduce page after page of brewing production statistics for every beer-drinking country in the world, a glance, perhaps a paragraph or two, will be enough to illustrate that beer production – and that means beer consumption; the breweries aren't going to make it if no one's going to drink it – hasn't dragged its feet in the face of world population growth. Volume-wise, it's still firmly in second place; the Pacific Ocean is first.

In 1900, Denmark, home to some of the world's great names in beer, brewed 247 million litres, compared to 296 million in Sweden; probably the first, and last, time Sweden ever exceeded Denmark in beer production. At that time 520 breweries were operating in Sweden. Of all the beer-producing countries of the world, however, the U.S.A. is number one, brewing close to 20 *billion* litres annually. This figure exceeds the total production of both West Germany and Britain, themselves numbers two and three respectively.

In 1900 there were almost 2,800 breweries in France, and this, remember, is a country whose predilection for wine is legendary, yet there it is: 2,800 breweries, all brewing like mad, and someone out there must have been drinking it. Even the tiny Grand Duchy of Luxembourg (pop. 350,000) has six domestic breweries, despite being cheek by jowl with two of the world's great beer-brewing countries, Germany and Belgium. Belgium itself has 150 breweries to serve 10 million people. By comparison, there are only around sixty breweries in the U.S.A., brewing for a population of over 250 million.

Nineteenth century England's 133,000 brewers almost disappeared overnight as a result of an 1887 law that prohibited farmers from giving beer to labourers as part of their wages. In effect this virtually eliminated the small householder as a brewer. By 1894 only 9,600 brewers remained, a number that dropped to 1,400 by 1906. Brewers became fewer, and bigger, and richer. By 1936 the number had dropped to 450, and in 1967 seven brewing firms produced 73 per cent of England's beer.

In 1985, in all of England, there were only eighty breweries, and of their product almost 80 per cent was sold on draught, proof of the enduring popularity of the public-house.

Not all countries have seen a reduction in the number of breweries or production figures. At the beginning of the twentieth century there were over a thousand breweries in Russia. Three-quarters of a century later the number is substantially the same. Soviet beer production is estimated at 5.4 billion litres, though a Russian news agency claims the real figure is in excess of seven billion. If the latter figure is correct, Russia ranks third in world production comparisons, ahead of even a thirsty country like Britain (6.3 billion litres). Japan, too, has not stood still. In 1900 there were perhaps a dozen breweries in Japan, brewing 26.5 million litres for domestic consumption, or slightly more than half a litre per capita. Obviously, beer was no big deal in Japan at the turn of the century. Today, however, beer from Japan has an international profile, and claims accolades from beer drinkers all over the world.

In some countries beer is simply a business, in others it seems a way of life. West Germany boasts around 1,600 breweries (1982); but that figure changes every week, through closures and mergers. A decade ago there were over 2,000; five years ago, only 1,300. More than two-thirds (68 per cent) of West Germany's breweries are situated in Bavaria, the southernmost state. Notwithstanding the number of German breweries, the trend, throughout the world, seems to be: fewer breweries, more beer.

2

The Brews

Looking at beer from a technical viewpoint is perhaps not the most entertaining way to look at it. Nevertheless, as beer enthusiasts we should be aware of the facts. A strong beer can have an alcohol level as high as 10 per cent, though most beers today run between 4 and 5 per cent. Thomas Hardy's Ale, at 12.48 per cent alcohol, is the strongest in Great Britain, but falls slightly behind Zurich's Samichlaus Bier (Brauerai Hurlimann) which claims the laurels in the *Guinness Book of World Records 1987* as the world's most alcoholic at 13.7 per cent. Eldridge Pope of Dorset produced Thomas Hardy's Ale in the 1960s as part of the first Hardy Festival to celebrate the writer and his work. The brewery suggests that the ale be put down for at least three years, preferably five, before consumption. A further recommendation urges us to keep it for twenty-five years for optimum improvement.

The average bottle of beer contains 90 per cent water, 4 to 5 per cent alcohol, 4 per cent carbohydrates, plus minor bits and pieces of salts, proteins, vitamins, and so on. Colour and strength have no relation; a darker shade results from the longer roasting of the grain during the malting process.

Attentive Chemistry 101 students know of the incompatibility of oil and water; some of the less attentive learned this through practical experience in the neighbourhood tavern. Even those students who spent all of their time in the tavern, and missed chemistry classes entirely, learned the hard way that the life of the beer's head will depend on the oil on your skin. Watch out for lipstick; never wear it if you plan to do any beer drinking or you'll sit there, horrified, as the head on your beer is reduced to an oily swamp.

Glasses are important. Whatever glass you decide to use for beer, that's it: beer only. In the case of your favourite glass or mug – and though the philistines might sneer, we all have a favourite, and it *does* make the beer taste better – don't let the kids use it. There isn't a kid in the world who doesn't want to drink out of your special glass. Don't let the little monster *near* it! In the twinkling of an eye he'll have it full of milk, or orange juice, or some other poisonous mixture, and you'll have to cure the glass all over again.

But (sigh) it happens. So here's how you cure the vessel – in fact, do this with any new glass, mug, pot, or whatever, that you introduce into your beer-drinking pattern. Give it a good protracted scrubbing with salt and hot water – a little water, lots of salt (half a teaspoon). Rinse well in hot water. Let it cool. Or, if you're thirsty, rinse in hot, then gradually in warm, cool, then cold; wise beer drinkers will not pour ice-cold beer into a steaming hot glass. After every use rinse well in hot water, nothing else. No soap. Periodically give the glass the salt cure to keep it fresh.

Okay. You now have a great new well-cured glass you're dying to try, and you have a fridge full of beer. What do you do next? Right. You pour yourself a glass of beer.

Now, there are those who maintain that to get a good head on your beer you pour the beer straight into the middle of the glass. They then recommend that if the head builds too quickly – and unless the beer is frozen solid it will build too quickly – you change tactics, in mid-stream as it were, and pour down the side of the glass.

Frankly, these yahoos shouldn't be allowed to *drink* beer, let alone pour it. By their own admission, they control the head by pouring down the side of the glass. So why not do that from the outset? Down the side of the glass, and leave the little games to the immature. What you want, after all, as a serious beer drinker, is a drink of beer, not twelve fingers of foam. Who wants to fight their way through mountains of foam? You could drown. And while there are worse ways to go, that's not the point.

So. As a mature, sensible beer pourer you have filled your glass – with a delicate hand sensitive to every nuance of timing – and have arrived at a head that suits your taste. The Dutch claim a two-finger head is ideal, and I agree; an attractive adornment to a golden glass. According to the Guinness company, three-eighths of an inch represents the perfect head on a glass of Guinness stout. Good ale, poured gently down the side of the glass, will give you that satisfactory head.

The head should be dense, perhaps a bit rocky and uneven, indicating natural fermentation. Long, continuous chains of small bubbles should rise from the bottom of the glass throughout the time it takes you to drink it, a sign that the brewing has been done with the loving attention that you want lavished on your beer. As you drink, the foam should stick to the sides of the glass, forming a lacy pattern, another indication that knowledgeable care has been taken with your brew.

In the early 1800s, an itinerant medic named Alvin W. Chase roamed the northeastern part of the U.S.A. and Canada, peddling groceries and medications to the pioneers. As he travelled he gathered recipes, household hints, cures and treatments used by the country folk, and ultimately put them all together in a book entitled *Dr Chase's Recipes, or Information for Everybody*. The book swept the country like a brush fire. Students put themselves through university selling copies door to door. At one time in the 1850s sales of the volume in North America were exceeded only by the Bible. Among the hundreds of recipes it contained was a method of brewing ale. I'll let the doctor tell you himself:

> The following formula for the manufacture of a famous home-brewed ale of the English yeomanry will convey a very clear idea of the components and mixture of ordinary ales. The middle classes of the English people usually make their ale in quantities of two barrels, that is, 72 gallons. For this purpose a quarter of malt (eight bushels) is obtained at the malt house – or, if wished to be extra strong, nine bushels of malt – with hops, 12 lb; yeast, five quarts.
>
> The malt, being crushed or ground, is mixed with 72 gallons of water at the temperature of 160° F., and covered up for three hours, when 40 gallons are drawn off, into which the hops are put, and left to infuse. Sixty gallons of water at a temperature of 170° F. are then added to the malt in the mash-tub,

and well mixed, and after standing two hours, sixty gallons are drawn off. The wort from these two mashes is boiled with the hops for two hours, and after being cooled down to 65° F., is strained through a flannel bag into a fermenting tub, where it is mixed with the yeast and left to work for 24 or 30 hours. It is then run into barrels to cleanse, a few gallons being reserved for filling up the casks as the yeast works over. When the yeast is worked out it must be bunged [presumably the cask, not the yeast].

If half a pint of this was taken each meal by men, and half that amount by females, and no other spirits, tea nor coffee, during the day, I hesitate not in saying that I firmly believe it would conduce to health. I know that this which a man makes himself, home made, are all that any person ought to allow themselves to use in these days when *dollars and cents* are the governing influences of *all* who deal in such articles.

It's sad to note that in Chase's time, too, people held the manufacturer in the same jaundiced regard they do today.

Dr Chase's seventy-two gallons of beer sounds like the kind of thing you'd put together for a sales convention – it's a lot of beer – but in mid-nineteenth century America, in the area that Chase covered, you couldn't drop around to the beer store on Saturday morning for a dozen pints. Your nearest neighbour, let alone beer store, might have been two hundred miles away. Worse, your nearest neighbour might have been a band of Indians who were arguing the toss whether you should even *be* there.

At least Chase's brew was a trifle more sophisticated than the operation conducted by the peasantry of southwest Russia, in the region between the Black and the Caspian seas. At the time Chase was circulating among the pioneers, the Russian peasants still observed rites of worship accompanied, as in ancient times, by foaming tubs of beer. The term "beer" is used generically more than anything else; their brew was pretty basic. They boiled crushed barley for a couple of days, non-stop, then filtered the brew through wool sacks into hollowed-out stumps of trees. They then tossed in some wild hops, covered the stump, and left the mixture to fester for a week, at which time it was ready to drink. Sounds like pretty rough stuff, the kind of brew you'd have to drink with a straw to penetrate the surface scum, much as the early Egyptians did.

Many beer-drinking countries of the world produce a bock beer of sorts, varying in quality from what appears simply an ordinary beer coloured a dark brown, to some of the magnificent bocks of Germany. One of the origins of the name "bock" derives from the attempt in Munich in 1614 to duplicate the popular beer of Einbeck (beck, bock; a rather tenuous connection, but there it is). The imitation was so well received that Munich beers, hitherto considered of dubious merit, gained a reputation that is now worldwide.

Compare the pure and unadulterated delight of bock to an early description of a brew called Brunswick Mum. Brunswick Mum, a strong ale, and a pretty democratic brew, had just about *everything* in it. Brewed from wheat malt, with the addition of oatmeal and ground beans, it also supported a farmer's market of vegetable matter, such as the tops of fir and birch, marjoram, thyme, elderflowers, cardamom seeds, barberries, watercress, parsley, and, if your taste leaned that way, "six handfuls of horseradish"; and in the end, just before closing the hogshead (or rather *forcing* the lid down on all that garbage), the brewers tossed in a couple of fresh, uncracked eggs, and left it for two years to mature. In 1673 a petition to Parliament in London classed it, quite rightly, as "detrimental to bodily health" and, in England, it fell from whatever favour it might have enjoyed.

And yet, when have we ever arrived at a consensus on beer and beverages? On the one hand we see Parliament knocking Brunswick Mum, but we learn from the 1613 edition of a book by the physician Dr Jacobus Theodorus Tabernamontanus that half a century before it fell from favour Brunswick Mum was considered to be a fairly thick, clear, bitter beer, of pleasant acidity and "many other good qualities." Christian Mumme of Brunswick created the beer in 1492, and in northern Germany it has been held in high regard ever since.

So there you are. Who are we to believe? Next time you're passing through Brunswick (Braunschweig) try a glass and judge for yourself.

The story of beer is filled with these hallucinating mixtures, some simply strange, others frankly dangerous as in the later Brunswick Mum. "Why?" is a question we constantly ask. If our ancestors sought an extra kick they had no need to look any farther than the common ale on their own tables. Mighty ale ruled in the Elizabethan days, when the everyday brew of the common man "would make a cat speak." Even in the late 1700s, the standard day-to-day ale of the ordinary people earned accolades. "[It was] as strong as the strongest ale brewed today"; this from an elderly gentleman called Dyche in the mid-nineteenth century, who recalled his time in the brewing industry of that earlier period.

But apparently these monumental ales weren't enough. Some warped need drove men to invent numerous weird concoctions. Strange, because from all reports they loved simple ale to distraction. Yet history shows them compounding odd, sometimes frightening, recipes. Even the Romans added unlikely things to their wine, perhaps for variety, or to give it a different flavour as we do with spirits in cocktails, or to dilute its strength; some classical wines could be cut as much as twenty to one with water and still be drinkable, a commentary on the harshness of Greek and Roman wines. Roman additives included such surprising and temperance-encouraging items as pepper, poppies, milk, wormwood, chalk, or tar! They even smoked their wine in a kiln in the belief that this improved its quality.

To induce a restful night's sleep our forefathers of three or four centuries ago would occasionally whip up an Ale Posset. They'd heat up a pot of ale to which had been added sugar, ginger, and nutmeg, then match the ale with an equal amount of boiling milk. All mixed together, you understand. The stomach lurches. As a variation on the posset, a popular eighteenth century drink called Syllabub consisted of a large bowl of strong ale, spiced with nutmeg and sugar, into which you then milked a cow. The connoisseur used a firm hand in the milking because a good froth was *de rigueur*.

Other liquors sometimes replaced the ale in possets, the rest of the recipe remaining unchanged:

Then my wife and I, it being a great frost, went to Mrs Jem's, in expectation to eat a sack-posset [sack: a white wine of Spain or the Canary Islands].

– Samuel Pepys, 5 January 1660.

The term sack comes from the Spanish *saco*, the skin in which these wines were imported. Another possible derivation of the word sack is *vin sec* – dry wine. Sack seems to have had a fairly broad meaning: it referred to dry sherry – the original sack, according to social historian Frederick Hackwood – and to white wines in general. Shakespeare's Falstaff enjoyed sherry sack.

Possets are pretty revolting, but they seem comparatively civilized lights in the dark tunnel of history where horrible pseudo-beers appear to have been the normal (or abnormal) thing. Take, for example, a poisonous-sounding eighteenth century amalgam called Cock Ale. Here it is:

Take four pounds stoned raisins, half a pound sliced dates, two ounces each of nutmeg and mace which have been infused in a quart of canary (wine) for twenty-four hours, and add them, including the wine, to a cask of twelve gallons of ale. Then take a six-month-old cock, boil it to a jelly in a gallon of water until the gallon is reduced by half. Press the bird well and add the resulting liquor to the cask of ale. Add a few blades of mace. Then add a pint of yeast and leave it for two days. Says an eighteenth century writer: "If it proves too strong, you may add more plain ale to palliate this restorative drink, which contributes much to the invigorating of nature." Yes, I'm sure it does.

The name Cock Ale came from the spiritous regimen of England's eighteenth century fighting cocks. The aggressive birds scoffed this mixture while they were training for a fight. The trainers themselves, I understand, joined the cocks round the merry cup. Just one big happy sports-minded family.

Boswell has left us a brief picture of the cock-fighting establishment of eighteenth century London. The room was circular, surrounded by tiers of benches that rose from the central pit. "The uproar and noise of betting is prodigious. The cocks, armed with silver heels, fight with amazing bitterness and resolution." Understandable, I suppose, after having shared a couple of belts of Cock Ale with the boys before the match.

Still, Cock Ale assumes the appearance of a kindergarten coffee break compared to Egg Ale, a sulphurous brew that undoubtedly helped fuel the English longbows at Crécy and Agincourt. Egg Ale was a *living organism*. Take a quart or two of this before you ask the boss for a raise:

To twelve gallons of fermenting ale add the gravy from eight pounds of beef. Then place the beef itself in a linen bag along with twelve eggs and a pound of raisins, oranges, and spices. Leave these in the ale until it has ceased fermenting. Add (as if an additive were needed!) two quarts of Malaga sack (wine). After three weeks, bottle, adding a little sugar.

A bottle or two of that of a morning will get the old eyes open, by George. A bit dicey shaving, perhaps, but nothing compared to the creative driving you'll be doing on the freeway.

Not all the adulterations were nightmares like Cock and Egg ales. Some were as lively and appealing as their names. There was Tewahdiddle (the children will want some of that, certainly! Don't give it to them): Take a pint of ale, slide in a tablespoon of brandy and a teaspoon of brown sugar, grate in a little nutmeg or ginger, and add a curl of lemon peel. Serve ice cold on a hot summer afternoon. Delightful! Er . . . serve one only.

The Parting Cup, which has a sad sound to it – good-byes always seem sad, especially when good friends have gathered – was guaranteed to leave you with overnight guests: Take a bowl, put two slices of very brown toast in the bottom, sprinkle over them a little nutmeg, pour in a quart of ale, then – here comes the overnight guest part – add two-thirds of a bottle of sherry. Just before drinking, add a bottle of soda water. Let's hear it for the soda.

The name "porter" comes from the popularity that brew enjoyed among the porters in the London markets. Originally a mixture of ale, beer, and "twopenny" (the last being "small beer," the second or third strainings from the mash, strong beer was the first straining), this blend, called "Three Threads," became in the early 1700s a specific brew called porter. (The term "stout" signifies a strong porter, and derives from the expression "stout ale," an ale of vigorous authority.)

Three Threads enjoyed considerable popularity, but for the tavernkeeper it was a pain in the butt. He had to draw the ale from one cask (or butt), beer from another, and twopenny from yet another. And you can bet someone always complained. "Here, George, what the devil are you playing at? This glass hasn't quite the right balance." (Takes substantial mouthful.) "Too much twopenny." (Drinks half the glass; gazes at ceiling.) "Yes, entirely too much twopenny. Do be a good chap and add a bit more of your best ale . . . "

In 1722 an enterprising London brewer named Harwood saw an opportunity and decided to produce casks of pre-mixed Three Threads, which he called "Entire" ("entire butt" beer, in the sense that it came from a single butt or cask). This may easily be the first instance of pre-mixed pre-packaged booze. After a brief period of usage, the term "Entire" gave way to porter.

The alehouses that sold porter were called porter-houses, hence the name for a select steak served there. John Mariani, however, writing in *Harper's Bazaar* in

March 1986, claims the term "porterhouse steak" originated in New York. In 1814 Martin Harrison opened an eating-house there that became renowned for its superb beef and porter, from which came the name porterhouse steak. But let's just think about that for a minute. By the time Harrison's steak had gained its fame, Londoners had been eating beefsteaks in porterhouses for a century, and they, too, had undoubtedly called them porterhouse steaks, probably before Harrison was even born.

While porter is not my idea of a good time – a little too heavy for my taste – the panegyrics it engendered in the past, amounting almost to adoration, attest to its goodness. In the middle of the nineteenth century, the Persian ambassador to England left London to return home. Among his retinue many broke down and cried, shattered by the realization they were leaving porter forever. One claimed his idea of Paradise was to remain in London, birthplace of "the most universally favourite liquor the world has ever known," stretch out under the trees and drink gallon upon gallon of porter.

Porter was first brewed in London in 1722. Two hundred and fifty years later, in 1973, the last bottle of porter in all of Britain and Ireland was brewed in Dublin. Its place has been taken by stout. Happily, many other countries of the world still produce a porter-style brew.

Happy ale, smiling companion at many a friendly gathering, had its darker side. At Tyburn Tree, London's infamous place of execution, the condemned of the eighteenth century were refreshed for the last time with a great bowl of ale. The ultimate pause that refreshes. As an example of how beneficial it is to take the time to enjoy a pot of ale, there is the story of a criminal who, when offered that final ale beneath the shadow of the gallows, became so sick with fear he refused the draught and thus went dry into the Hereafter. Yet – bitter irony – hardly had he stepped into Eternity than his reprieve arrived. If he had paused for a, literally, life-giving bowl of ale, he would have lived to enjoy many more.

The distressed, the down-at-heart, the sad, the hopeless, all have sought and found solace in beer and ale. Far from a current fad or fancy, this has been the case, not only for centuries, but for millennia. Mary Queen of Scots lightened the gloomy days of her captivity with more than a drop or two of Burton ale. Hugh Latimer, one-time bishop of Worcester, and one of the larger movers in the swing toward the Reformation, calmed his spirit with a cup of ale at supper on the night of 5 October 1555; the following day he was burned at the stake. While Latimer found repose in ale the night before his death, Sir Walter Raleigh apparently felt the need of it closer in time to the actual event: on the morning of 29 October 1618, scant yards from the place of his execution, Sir Walter composed a few words of self-justification, lit a final pipeful of tobacco, drank deeply from a large pot of ale, and took with a lighter heart the final steps to oblivion.

The same ale that infused the bowman's arm with such vigour at Agincourt also warmed the heart and fed fond memories of friends. Ale and poetry conjoined. Inscribed centuries ago upon the death of John Dawson, a treasured butler of Oxford University, these lines still live:

> Weep, O ye barrels! that John may float
> To Styx in beer, and lift up Charon's boat
> With wholesome waves . . .

Poets were never at a loss for words when it came to ale. When they picked up a pot they picked up a pen and put their hearts on paper, telling of both the joy and plain common sense of drinking ale. Hundreds of years ago this quatrain pointed out the monetary advantages of good ale:

> He that buys land buys many stones,
> He that buys flesh buys many bones,
> He that buys eggs buys many shells,
> But he that buys good ale buys nothing else.

The common beer drinkers, and the authorities, were always concerned over quality, and watched the brewers and retailers with a stern eye. Unremitting devotion to purity was the only acceptable quality, and adulterers suffered the full weight of the law. Sounds great. But "pure, unadulterated beer" didn't figure too prominently in early mixtures. In the annals of beer, strange recipes abound for some of the most unlikely beverages imaginable (the term "beverage" was current in the English language in the fifteenth century, and came from the Norman *bever*, which denoted a light nosh, a snack, or a drink between main meals, though if I know the Britons of that early period you can bet your life it was a drink). These weird mixtures illustrate that human beings are congenitally unable to produce a simple beverage; there must be odd twists of method, and wildly improbable additives. Often one or more of the components seem superfluous. The recipe's name, too, sometimes misleads us, as in this one for Irish Moss Ale: Irish moss, one ounce; hops, one ounce; ginger, one ounce; sugar, one pound; water, ten gallons; boil, ferment, and bottle. *Voilà*! Irish Moss Ale! (Irish moss is a dried seaweed, carageenan, sometimes used to clarify today's beer.) The recipe is reminiscent of the legendary chef who claimed he could make soup from a stone. Put a stone in a pot, add water – and a few incidental ingredients like meat and vegetables – boil, and what have you got? Soup! From a stone!

Odd mixtures aside, ale was (and still is) looked upon as a promoter of good health.

> Ye doctors, who more execution have done
> With bolus and potion, and powder and pill,
> Than hangman with halter, and soldier with gun,
> Or miser with famine, or lawyer with quill,
> To dispatch us the quicker, you forbid us
> malt liquor
> Till our bodies grow thin, and our faces
> look pale
> Observe them who pleases, what cures all diseases,
> Is a comforting dose of good Nottingham Ale.

In the same vein, you will remember the story about

> A man to whom illness was chronic,
> When told that he needed a tonic,
> Said, "Oh, doctor, dear,
> Won't you please make it beer?"
> "No, no," said the doc, "that's teutonic."

Though surpassed by ale, mead still endured in many areas as a popular drink. The Anglo-Saxons drank it, the diarist Samuel Pepys drank it, and as late as the nineteenth century in Abyssinia (now Ethiopia) they distilled a form of brandy from mead. There have been other names for mead: meathe, metheglin, hydromel, methegle, or metheglum – the seventeenth century Irish called it *miodh* – all basically the same honey and water, with sometimes a spice or a herb added.

> . . . and I, drinking no wine, had metheglin.
>
> – Samuel Pepys, 25 July 1666.

Recent history has seen mead and cider superseded by beer and ale, but while mead has slipped into obscurity cider is, if not in vogue, still widely used. In the early days of the American west the taverns served cider (though tavern customers habitually demanded whisky, and every tavern catered to the pioneer taste for hard liquor. The whisky usually came from a distiller, but not always; the taverner sometimes made his own from corn, rye, or barley). The abundance of wild or cultivated fruit formed the basis of numerous interesting ciders; one, an apple variety, when allowed to become semi-frozen produced a concentrated cider that undoubtedly ensured the customer a good night's sleep. Or an all-night party.

We've seen the ease with which mead and cider came into being. Now let's look at how beer is born. History delights in paradoxes, and beer rates high on the list: a glorious beverage, yet so simple to prepare. Admittedly it now lacks the simplicity of earlier days, a result of the current demand for consistency and reliability.

But consistency costs money, a fact of life reflected in the retail price at the beer store. Many maintain that you can beat the system by making your own. Home brew; it's the only way to go. Difficult? Not at all. Want to brew up a couple of quarts? Just give me sixty seconds of your time.

Now, before we start this beer, you might be pleased to learn of the economies of home brewing. A beer enthusiast back in 1965 looked at the costs of all the ingredients that went into the production of a batch of home brew, and estimated that a twelve-ounce bottle of respectable ale shouldn't cost more than a few cents. Today, it might cost you as much as thirty cents. Makes it all worthwhile, doesn't it? So let's get on with our brew.

Got a large tea kettle? Right. Now, this is a nineteenth century recipe, so if it blows up in your face don't blame me. Okay, pour a quart of malt into your kettle. Add a quart of hot (not boiling) water. Let it stand for half an hour, stirring occasionally. Pour off the liquid into a four-quart pan. Repeat the process (with the same malt) a second time, and a third. You now have a pan containing three quarts of malt liquid. Onto the stove with it, add maybe an ounce of hops. Boil for two hours. Let it cool, perhaps to a level a little below blood heat. Add a pinch of brewer's yeast. Leave it for an hour. Skim off the top. Underneath that foam is bitter beer. Wait three or four hours, then bottle it. Cap the bottles and put them in your cellar. Three days later put your feet up, relax, snap off a cap, and enjoy a pure, unadulterated beer.

Now, that recipe is pretty basic; you can't get much simpler than that. After discussing methods with other home-brew enthusiasts you might wish to introduce a few personal wrinkles. Go ahead, and the very best of luck to you. You will, after all, simply be illustrating what we said earlier: man detests simplicity. He has to add something, change it, make it his own. Man is the most insecure animal on earth, and nowhere is it more revoltingly exemplified than in his drink. Take stout. Grand beverage. Just the thing as a bedtime drink. Calms the nerves, soothes the spirit, promotes restful sleep. Right. Well, here's a mixture that falls (or staggers) into the same "bedtime drink" classification: a grisly piece of work called a Beer Nog, which tastes like rum-flavoured Milk of Magnesia (with profound apologies to the manufacturers of that well-known remedy). It is without a doubt one of the best ways of ruining rum and beer. Here it stands, in all its simple horror: one and a half pints of stout, a cup of rum, half a cup of sugar, four eggs. Mix up everything but the eggs. Boil, then simmer for five minutes. Remove from heat. Beat eggs and add slowly, stirring. Chill for a couple of hours. Just before drinking (ecch!), beat it with an electric beater. Serves two or three people.

Why would anyone want to play such horrible little games with a brew as noble as stout? But it takes all kinds, I suppose. For those who can't leave well enough alone, you might try:

Black Velvet: Half and half, champagne and stout. Supposedly created to celebrate the death (1861) of Prince Albert, consort to Queen Victoria. George Ade, a newspaperman in the early 1900s, remembered a vicious combination called simply "Velvet" that was "guaranteed to put dead bodies all over the rugs": half and half, champagne and porter.

Top Hat: Stout and ginger beer. The 1935 movie "Top Hat," starring Fred Astaire and Ginger Rogers, inspired

this mixture, though it appears little more than a variation on a shandy or shandy gaff (ale and ginger beer).

Shandy: Stout and lemon-lime soda (can nothing stop
these madmen?). As previously noted, a shandy frequently refers to a flagon of ale and ginger beer. The
louts who enjoy these mixtures are nothing if not incon-
sistent.

Calcutta Cup: Stout and tonic water. This at least
provided a measure of quinine to the stalwarts who
upheld the Empire in India, back in the good old days,
though I don't know why anyone would feel the need of
it in London or New York.

Midnight: Stout and port wine. Gets worse as we go
along, doesn't it?

Black and Black: Stout and blackberry liqueur. Admittedly, the blackberry appears only as a dash, but the very
idea is appalling.

Black and Tan: Half and half, stout and ale. Well, that's
civilized at least.

Mention of Calcutta Cup, above, brings to mind the
origin of the term "punch." Punch derives from *paunch*,
a Hindustani word meaning five, the number of basic
ingredients in the mixture – spirits, water, sugar, lemon,
and spices. East India traders introduced it into England
in the late 1600s. The ingredients noted may have suited
the drinkers of India – they even added little toasted
biscuits – but the English didn't play around with
effeminate spices and childish additives like biscuits,
and very quickly these items disappeared from the
lineup.

> Whene'er a bowl of punch we make
> Four striking opposites we take –
> The strong, the weak, the sour, the sweet,
> Together mixed, most kindly meet.
> And when they happily unite
> The bowl is pregnant with delight.

Calgary Red-eye (beer and tomato juice) and Callibogus are dubious drinks from the Canadian west and
east, respectively. I've never been able to understand
why anyone would deliberately alter a glass of good beer
by mixing it with tomato juice. Even the name itself has
an unsavoury past. As far back as the turn of the century
the term "red-eye" meant a cheap whisky, a vile product
that Robert Service called "red paint." Meanwhile, out

east, the smouldering concoction known as Callibogus – rum, molasses, and spruce beer – must have them lining up outside the emergency wards.

Spruce beer I'll go along with, if you happen to like that sort of thing. Like beer and ale, it's healthy and straightforward. Take young shoots of spruce, boil, strain, add sugar (or molasses if you prefer), yeast to suit, and let it ferment. In the old pioneer days it prevented scurvy. In the early trade with the Indians it was also the first firewater, quickly replaced by the sturdier demon rum, and numerous other deadly mixtures like high wines (alcohol and flavoured water).

High wines, as we see, bear no resemblance to actual wine. Their simple composition – alcohol and water, plus the flavouring of your choice – made them an inexpensive and thus favoured currency in dealings with Indians during America's pioneer days. The Indians, if they'd had the chance, would have agreed with the anonymous eighteenth century poet who cried:

> Deceitful wine! embrewed with mixtures dire,
> By the curs'd vintner's art for sordid pelf.
> O! grant me, Heav'n, to live with health and
>   ease,
> My books, a sober friend, small beer, and
>   sense:
> So shall my years the smiling fates prolong
> And each auspicious morn shall see me happy.

Around the house, a century ago, beer or ale (if there was any left over) acted as an excellent furniture polish.

A nineteenth century recipe book lists ale as a component in a reliable glue:

> Take ale one pint; best Russian isinglass two ounces. Put them in a common glue kettle [Glue kettle? What's a glue kettle? Having foreseen this, the writer said if you do not have a glue kettle, take an oyster can – which doesn't put us that much farther ahead, really. Oyster can? What's an oyster can?] and boil until the isinglass is dissolved, then add four ounces of the best common glue, and dissolve it with the other; this will not take long; then slowly add one-and-a-half ounces of boiled linseed oil, stirring all the time while adding the oil and until well mixed. When cold it will resemble India rubber. When you

38

wish to use this, dissolve what you need in a suitable quantity of ale to have the consistence of thick glue. It is applicable for earthenware, china, glass, or leather.

The handyman will undoubtedly welcome the news that ale sometimes took the place of water in the mixing of cement to lend the mortar greater strength. The proportion of ale to mortar remains unknown, but it was probably along the lines of "a pint for the cement, and a pint for me . . . "

In emergencies, ale appeared in ecclesiastical functions. Mid-nineteenth century records tell us of a church in a remote part of India where, for a brief period due to an absence of wine, they celebrated communion with bottled beer.

Considering the volcanic Brunswick Mum mentioned earlier, the one abhorred by Parliament, you wonder, really, why anyone would place these hallucinating mixtures ahead of a glass of good, sound ale. In Canada we find fly beer, for example, an item from the Maritimes and one of the countless variations on the standard beer theme. The brew comes from potatoes and hops, a pinch of yeast, molasses, and water. While this brew might be highly esteemed on the east coast of Canada, can it really match a world-renowned name like Pilsener, the glorious Czechoslovakian beer? The people of Pilsen have brewed their famous lager (meaning aged; stored beer, from the German *lager*, to store) since the thirteenth century. King Wenceslas II of Bohemia (1278-1305) first produced Pilsener in 1292. Its outstanding qualities have become the world standard against which other lagers are judged.

We've talked about possets as a restful drink before bed. But there are those who claim, and I'm one of them, that few pre-bedtime drinks beat a simple pint of ale. Very relaxing. Drink two if you like, but stop at two or you'll have friends in and might not get to bed at all. Others, oriented toward gourmandise rather than DTs, prefer a mug of hot chocolate. Well, okay, to each his own; chocolate lovers are a race apart anyway. Someone once told me that the caffeine in chocolate will keep you awake. Reputable sources, however, claim the caffeine content of chocolate is negligible, so I expect it's much like any product containing potentially harmful substances: it depends on how much you consume. Drink fifty cups of hot chocolate and you will lie awake all night, guaranteed.

Ale appeared in many recipes compounded to relieve discomfort. Egyptian pharmacists, 3,500 years ago, produced a list of 700 prescriptions, of which 100 had beer as a component. Medicated ales played a large role in pharmaceutical dispensations in the Middle Ages. *Cerevisia oxydorica* benefited eye afflictions, and for head problems the medieval pharmacist might have prescribed *cerevisia cephalica*. (*Cerevisia*, you will remember, was the Latin, or Roman, name for ale.)

The strength of the Saxon ales naturally led to their use medicinally, and contributed to the belief that they had powerful curative properties. One remedy against "fiends" was to mix herbs, garlic, and a splash of holy water in a horn of ale, sing a handful of masses, then scoff the ale. The application of another ale mixture on the limbs brought relief(?) from stiff joints. Animals, too, benefited from malt liquor: sheep were bucked up immeasurably with a tankard of strong ale.

Ale's use in veterinary medicine, though perhaps not supported by the vets as enthusiastically as it once was, is still seen in our own day. Back in the nineteenth century, a horse belonging to an English brewery fell ill; influenza, or something dire like that. All attempts to cure it failed. In desperation they gave the animal a draught of stout. Let's hear it for stout, the vet's friend. The horse lapped it up with gusto. After two weeks on stout alone, the horse was reborn the very picture of vigour and vitality. A bit red-eyed, perhaps, and kept people awake at night with ribald songs, but very healthy.

Herbalists and medical men of the past also used beer, and particularly its additive, hops. The ancient Jews brewed a drink from barley in the period of the Exodus, and there is basis for the belief that it, too, contained hops, as the drink was held to prevent leprosy, and hops, in the eighth century BC, were also said to prevent that disease. Many early physicians acclaimed the hop's almost miraculous curative powers. They used the plant variously to purify the blood, to combat scurvy, to bring relief in cases of gout, and to banish pestilential fevers, "hysterical affections," and other abstruse maladies too numerous to mention. It seems to have worked, too; "hysterical affections," for example, have been completely eradicated. At night a pillow filled with hops apparently soothed England's George III in his periods of madness. Invalids were encouraged to spend an entire day wandering around in a field of hops, in the belief that the surrounding air was beneficial.

Walking around in a field of hops might have been all right for the invalids, but most people of the day got their hops the old-fashioned way: by the quart. And it didn't take much to convince our ancestors that if one quart was good for you, *two* quarts were *twice* as good for you. Simple mathematics, right? Now, if you accept that mathematical progression – and what thinking person wouldn't? – it follows, logically, that *twelve* quarts are *extremely* good for you. The drinkers of the day agreed and began setting consumption records that had the recordkeeper's eyeballs spinning like a lathe. Consumption became the national pastime.

3

Consumption

In the mid-1600s, when the population of England was five million, the annual consumption of imported wine was perhaps 7.5 million gallons, or 35 million litres. Add this to the 13 million barrels of beer consumed each year and we see that each citizen drank, annually, a mere seven litres of wine (less than an ounce a day, 30 mL), but a staggering 440 litres of beer.

In Bamberg, Bavaria, the inhabitants drink over 200 litres of beer a year, almost double that of the rest of Germany (who are not doing too badly at around 140 per capita). But these figures pale before Dutch consumption in the seventeenth century. In those days the Hollander drank over 300 litres a year; even children drank 150. Of course, in those days, youngsters also smoked pipes. Food consumption, too, was prodigious. Excess seemed the byword during that period, so we can believe almost anything. Today's figures are, comparatively speaking, more modest, yet it's interesting to note the difference in beer consumption between the northern and southern Netherlands: in the north the average is around 75 litres per capita annually, while in the south they drink in excess of 100.

At the beginning of the twentieth century an anonymous writer, examining the history of beer in *One Hundred Years of Brewing*, claimed "there is something in the composition and effect of malt liquors which supplies a want in the national characters and physiques of the most intellectual, vigorous, and progressive countries of the globe."

This gives all of us the opportunity to feel intellectual, vigorous, and progressive because beer is enjoyed in every country of the world. However, a glance at some representative consumption figures shows that some of

43

us are more int, vig, and prog than others. Canada appears a little slow in the int/vig/prog department. Annual per capita beer consumption in Canada amounts to around 86 litres, compared to over 140 in Germany, around 100 in England, and approximately 90 in the U.S.A. Figures for 1986 indicate that the world produces close to 580 million barrels of beer annually. This means that yearly consumption is around 95.4 billion litres, or more than 260 million litres a day. France, a predominantly wine-drinking country, would be expected to rate low on the beer consumption scale, and it does; the current national average is a modest 28 litres per body, annually. Yet toward the end of the nineteenth century, France showed some startling regional differences. Rouen's per capita consumption was a mere four litres a year; even Paris drank only nine litres per head; but Lille's 160,000 inhabitants' annual average was 381.

This was a thirsty time. Many countries witnessed mounting consumption figures. The last fifteen years of the century saw Belgium jump from 162 litres per capita to 219. In 1900 there were over 3,200 breweries in that country. Germany, too, has always been big on beer. In 1900 there were 18,800 breweries in Germany, producing over seven billion litres (125 litres per capita). Then as now, Bavarian breweries were predominant, numbering over 10,000 at the turn of the century. Bavarian consumption at that time was 255 litres per person. In Munich, 170 breweries produced 429 million litres to slake Bavarian thirsts. In 1889, the city of Munich itself consumed 156 million litres of beer, a record 511 litres per head.

At the same time, the gold-seekers in Dawson City, up in the frozen Yukon of Canada, were doing their best to be number one in beer drinking, but they were restricted by simple economics. There just wasn't any percentage in trying to transport a case of beer hundreds of miles over impossible terrain, for what? Maybe five dollars a bottle? Still, they made up for it: in 1898 Dawson City imported 120,000 gallons of liquor – more than five gallons a head for every man, woman, and child of the city's 23,000 population.

While some countries have national consumption rates that are hardly worth noting, often localities within those countries exhibit vast thirsts. Czechoslovakia drinks its share, but does not startle the world, yet the inhabitants of Bohemia in western Czechoslovakia, home of glorious Pilsener, consume over 160 litres per capita (West Germany, as noted, presently leads the world's countries, consuming 147 litres per person annually). Australia, too, has a well-founded reputation as a beer-drinking country, but its national average doesn't even approach that of Darwin (on the north coast, a stone's throw from Java). Darwin has a heavy reputation: beer-consumption capital of the world, drinking an estimated 230 litres annually per capita.

Any examination of beer consumption, though it may start with a scholarly look at consumption in general, must unavoidably slope off into excess. Ribald songs, naked dancing girls, orgies, the whole sordid intemperate story. Sad to relate, but that seems to be the way of things; if there is a deep end, we will go off it.

For centuries after the Roman occupation of Britain, wine supplanted to a great extent the native mead drunk by the early Britons. The Romans brought wine to the island, and planted vines with modest success in southern Britain. Within a century of William the Conqueror's arrival in 1066, the wines of Bordeaux were sold in London. The Norman conquerors, unlike the Romans, had checked the inhospitable skies of England and felt the chance of establishing a domestic wine industry was small.

Even in those years the Britons drank to excess – an early example of the taste for intoxicating liquor that was to plague the island over the centuries. This tendency toward alcohol has drawn considerable bitter criticism, like Marchant's rather cynical commentary on the British Empire: At the time of the Indian Mutiny of 1857, if the English had indeed been pushed out of the country, "the only relics of their rule would have been gigantic piles of pale ale bottles."

Records from the sixth century indicate that monks were obliged to perform fifteen days' penance if they were "in drink" to the point where they couldn't speak. The existence of the penance proves the need, and illustrates that monks were at least occasionally speechless from ale. It's not a particularly pleasant picture, a monk growing maudlin over his ale, and religious derivation of the term "maudlin" doesn't make it easier to accept (maudlin: from the French *Madeleine*, which in turn comes from the Latin *Magdalena*, a reference to the weeping Mary Magdalen). And while we're on the subject of alcoholic derivations, occasioned by the intemperate monks, the expression "boozing it up," both clerical and secular, comes of course from "booze." The term "booze," noun and verb, has its origin in the Old English word *bousen*, meaning to drink. The noun, in today's usage, carries just the slightest inclination toward hard stuff rather than beer, though "boozing it up" is a pretty general phrase for getting bombed on whatever refreshment takes your fancy.

But back to the jolly friars. Clerical laws in Saxon times ordered monks to avoid drinking in public places where ale was sold. Now, ostensibly, this could be seen as a curb to ecclesiastical excess. In reality, though, it mustn't have been too hard to bear. The monastery provided its inmates with two drinking horns of mead per day (two *Saxon* drinking horns, the big ones, which could have amounted to three or four quarts), "and on festival days, of which the calendar was nearly full, twice a day also with wine." Certainly a well-lubricated day.

St Boniface (eighth century) found, sadly, that the clergy in England, from the bishops down to the local priests, all drank to excess. Along with the people, they caroused in the very church itself. "Men sit up by night and drink to madness within God's house." Writing of the practice, one contemporary was horrified to see that "the people fell to lechery and songs, and dances . . . and also to gluttony and sins, and so turned the holiness to cursedness."

Things didn't improve with the coming of the Norsemen. England under the Danes became a country of debauchery, with heavy drinking being the normal way of life. Later, in the eleventh century, this tendency was to have serious, historically far-reaching, and for King Harold, terminal consequences. When the English met the Norman conquerors on the field of Hastings in 1066, the English, as usual, had been more than a little drunk the night before. Their revelry had been loud and brave. Confidence flowed from their cups, and cries of "Wassail!" and "Drinc-hail!" sounded throughout the camp into the early hours. As a result, the following morning the English, red-eyed and hungover, fell easily before the Normans. Ale had changed the course of history.

The frequently ludicrous, though entertaining, part about drinking to excess is the stories it generates. Hyperbole, fine; a little exaggeration adds piquancy to a tale, but I mean, sometimes, *really*. They tell the story of a military friend of the gastronome Brillat-Savarin, a certain General Bisson, who habitually drank eight bottles of wine with breakfast (*breakfast*?). Now hold it, just a minute; admittedly beer, wine, and food went down those ancient gullets without touching the sides, but *eight* bottles?

Along the same Munchausenesque lines is the story of William Lewis of Wales, who died on 30 November 1793 at the very moment he was downing a cup (a forty-ounce flagon) of ale. Well, there are worse ways to go. A man of upright habits, he read the Bible every morning and drank eight gallons of ale every night (*thirty-two quarts!*). It was said of him – almost a eulogy, you might say – that in the course of his obviously happy life he consumed sufficient ale to float a seventy-four-gun ship. Can you ask for a better epitaph?

Both beer and wine were contemporaries in ancient Egypt. But even then, beer was the drink of the common man and wine that of the nobility; the pharoahs and their high-born associates would sip a glass of wine while the seething mass of the unwashed would guzzle beer.

Wine for the nobility, ale for the rabble. The Normans, too, perpetuated the division of drinking habits. William the Conqueror brought wine with him when he landed in England, and as it was the Norman's habitual drink, they continued to import it from France. Because all of Saxon Britain had drunk ale, from the kings and earls to the lowest serf, now only the conquered were ale drinkers; the rulers – the Normans – drank wine, and maintained the old distinction: wine for the rich, ale for the poor.

This is not to say the nobility didn't drink beer. The Earl of Eglinton, certainly, never lacked refreshment, and we have it in writing. Can you imagine one of your servants painstakingly recording everything you drank during the day? Could you ever really come to love such a servant? But there it is: 26 November 1646, the living record of the Earl of Eglinton's intake: Morning draught, one pint; lunch and after, eight pints; at four o'clock, one pint; then another pint; supper, three pints.

George Washington, the American revolutionary general and first president of the new republic, was a great lover of porter. Yet we can't help but wonder how he made out during and immediately after the War of Independence. We know that in 1776 the American revolutionary Congress declared that each soldier would receive a daily quart of spruce beer. Did George, too, settle for spruce beer? I wonder. The spruce routine mustn't have excited the patriots, who were used to the good English ale that until then had been shipped from England. Britain was still shipping ale, but not to the newborn U.S.A. In the eighteenth century more Bass ale, for example, was shipped to Russia than was consumed domestically. *Piva Burtonski*, as it was known at the Imperial court, was in great demand. Catherine the Great of Russia consumed vast quantities of Burton ale, and her court was not far behind her. "Imperial Russian" stout, another of Catherine's favourites, was brewed in London. This beverage is one of the strongest in the world. "Imperial Russian," produced in England by the Courage Group, weighs in at a substantial 10.5 per cent alcohol. A small 170 mL bottle (half a Canadian bottle) contains as much alcohol as a jigger (45 mL) of scotch. This stout enjoyed Russian patronage from 1770, when it was first brewed, to the time of World War I. The brew matures in the bottle for a year, and will keep for at least five years.

The Americans quickly established their own beer industry, of course, and examples of its grand scale abound. Within a century of Washington's spruce beer, Adolphus Busch, the American beer baron, had laid the foundations of the vast Anheuser-Busch brewery, the world's largest. In the 1870s, during his visit to Budweis in Bohemia, the brew of the Budvar brewery so impressed him that he introduced a similar beer into the U.S.A. in 1876. Now almost a household word, Budweiser is the world's largest seller. Busch did things in style. In the age of opulent private railway cars he indulged his taste – with, perhaps, a little public relations thrown in for good measure – by fitting out his own rolling palace with piped-in beer in every compartment. Now *that's* hospitality, especially if we look back through the centuries to the hospitable Armenians of 2,500 years ago. They refreshed themselves and their guests from a large communal bowl of malt brew. The thirsty used a hollow reed, thrust it into the bowl and sucked merrily away. Okay, maybe it doesn't carry the same weight as the efforts of Adolphus Busch – the bucks make a difference – but, hey, it's the thought that counts.

Mexico does not consider beer an intoxicant, and since 1931 the law has so classified it, officially. Indeed, government advertising campaigns encourage the drinking of beer (when your alternative could be tequila, who needs encouragement?). Frankly, I think the Mexican government is going a bit far; I like their sentiment, and if more of the three-double-gins-before-lunch fellows were influenced by the government's view it would be a better world, but beer as a non-intoxicating beverage? Well . . .

Most of us sensible fellows, of course, need no encouragement. But for the few who do, certainly among the best reasons for drinking a cool ale were those put forward by the poet Henry Aldrich (1648-1710):

> . . . being dry,
> Or lest we should be by and by,
> Or any other reason why.

As sound as these reasons are, there were still deaf ears even in Aldrich's thirsty times. Jonathan Swift, Irish poet and wit (1667-1745), charged that "persons of high rank declare they could learn nothing more at Oxford and Cambridge than to drink ale and smoke tobacco." Well, there's nothing like a classical education. Absolutely nothing. The poet John Dryden (1631-1700), in one of his clumsier couplets, tells us frankly:

> In college you scorn'd the art
>   of thinking,
> But learned all moods and figures
>   of good drinking.

You may find your tongue stumbles a bit over the last lines, but the point is nevertheless there.

Coming from fellows who've never lied to us before, that's quite a knock, and one not restricted to the halls of higher learning. Ben Jonson, in his play *Bartholomew Fayre* (1614), points to the sordid courts and lanes around London's Trafalgar Square, home to whores, vagrants, and other unsavoury yahoos, and asks "and how doe they entertain the time, but with bottle-ale and tobacco?"

Even in our own day there are those who seem to frown on beer drinking, and strive to make it more expensive and difficult to obtain, and they're not Temperance types, either; ironically they are the very ones who stand to profit most from beer's consumption: the tax men. In England the working man consumes 30 million pints of beer every day (1985). Excessive beer taxes thus weigh most heavily on those least able to support them. Nevertheless, beer is invariably the happy hunting ground when politicians seek to raise taxes, thereby penalizing citizens who, frequently, find their only pleasure in a glass of beer after a hard day's work.

Across the centuries, the story of beer consumption is one of steady, largely uninterrupted guzzling; a vast sea of beer, subject to continuous consumption and continuous replenishment; regular, placid, unending. From this broad sea there projects the occasional pinnacle of truly outstanding consumption, the work of real heroes. H. L. Mencken remembers a typesetter in the composing room of the Baltimore *Herald* at the turn of the century who reigned as the champion beer drinker of the area. Mencken claims to have seen the man drink thirty-two bottles of beer in succession. "Perhaps you have seen the same," said Mencken, "but have you ever heard of a champion who could do it *without once retiring from his place at the bar?!*"

Often there are those who, rather than choosing to consume, have conspicuous consumption thrust upon them in spite of themselves. In October 1814, in one of London's breweries situated in the squalid Tottenham Court Road area, a giant vat of porter burst. Now, on the surface at least, this would appear to be just another of life's contretemps. Messy, but not much more than that. However, this vat contained 20,000 barrels of porter, almost 750,000 gallons. The resulting tidal wave swept down on the crowded tenements, flooding some, knocking down others; eight persons died – smiling as they expired.

When the talk turns to beer consumption, the Germans – who else? – have the last word: "It takes beer to make thirst worthwhile."

Many a happy group will drink to that. Thirst generates consumption, and consumption, given the right time, place, occasion, and company, promotes good times, laughter, and generally innocent merriment. In the past, however – and not too distant past, either – the forms that merrymaking took would not be considered, today, to be very funny. At least not funny-ha-ha; rather funny-odd, if not downright funny-psychopathic. Good times, accompanied by drink, have a tendency to show us the inner man, with all the warts – *in vino veritas* – and to illustrate once again that it sure takes all kinds.

4

Merrymaking

Drink because you are happy, never because you are miserable.

                   – Chesterton.

Ale and merrymaking go hand-in-hand, each seeming to encourage the other. Notwithstanding Chesterton's injunction, ale *can* help to banish sadness, depending upon its nature and severity. "[Strong ale] driveth all sorrow from your hearts," said Francis Beaumont, a seventeenth century poet and playwright. Yes, well, poets do tend to get carried away on the subject of ale. The important thing is, while a pot of ale might not drive *all* sorrow from our hearts, it *tries*, if you see what I mean; there's that quality about ale that's so positive, so ebullient, so ready to join you in gaiety and the rejection of all things negative.

Legend claims the Greek Terpander of Lesbos (seventh century BC) as the inventor of drinking songs. This is a bit hard to believe; looking back beyond the birth of history, when man lifted his first glass, you can bet your life that three hours later he was singing of its glories. Terpander, though, gets the nod from legend, and earns a place in drinking history through the irony of his death: While Terpander was belting out one of his songs at a drinking party, a disgruntled listener tossed a fig at him; it caught him in the mouth, lodged in his throat, and Terpander expired at the very height of his form.

"Though sore ills oppress," intoned Thomas Wharton (1748), "heart-rejoicing ale cheers the sad scene, and every want supplies." Part of cheering the sad scene were the jokes and games that a glass of ale generated in any gathering. One amusing pastime was the candle caper. Understand, now, I'm putting this forward purely and simply as an example of some of the games played that involved beer; I wouldn't suggest you try this next time friends drop by for an ale.

In olden days, in the south of England around harvest time, a popular amusement – just a barrel of laughs – was to place a lighted candle in a glass of beer, then drink. By skilfully using the tip of your nose to keep the candle in position you could drink the glass and win the bet. If the candle rolled off your nose you were in trouble. Double trouble, actually, because if you failed you had to go through the whole procedure again. And again, and again, until you either succeeded (and it became understandably more difficult with every partially drunk glass) or ended up under the table. As I say, just a barrel of laughs.

Chug-a-lug is another alehouse pastime, generally practised by the younger drinker, to win a bet, or prove something, or whatever, and consists of downing a glass of ale non-stop; a short-term variation on the theme of the drinking marathon. An example of the *real* marathon occurred in England in 1762, when a man undertook to drink an entire butt of beer within two weeks. Reports claim he won the bet. Figure it out: a butt contains 108 gallons. That's 432 quarts, or more than thirty quarts a day (that's over twenty-eight litres); or around fifty ounces of beer (four standard bottles) per hour twenty-four hours a day, for fourteen days straight. Right; I don't believe it either. Consider: at the end of the first twenty-four hour period your reluctant body would contain the alcohol equivalent of four bottles of whisky. And that's only the first day; there are thirteen more to go.

Good times in the early American west often had the exaggerated aspects of a bad western movie; and the reality was sometimes more hallucinating than Hollywood's imagination. Take fighting for example, which usually took place in or in front of the saloon. In the movies, we have all watched the hero and the villain punch each other from one end of the bar to the other, in the course of which they manage to break every piece of furniture in the place. Pretty unbelievable. But the reality was even more so. The harsh conditions of the American west, and the lack of the more sophisticated amusements of the east, bred some frightening pastimes. Eye-gouging was a common way of passing an afternoon. After pounding your opponent cross-eyed with your fists, you grasped his hair with your fingers (for leverage), stuck your thumbs into his eyes and – gouged them out. You had to be on your toes, however, because a quick turn of the head and your opponent could have your thumb in his teeth, and eye-gouging victory could be turned into thumbless defeat. Good moves drew appreciative applause from the onlookers, for eye-gouging was a spectator sport, combining all the footwork, timing, and body contact of modern-day football, though without the complicated scoring system; in eye-gouging the scoring was simple: You won, or you lost.

Slightly more socially acceptable were the balls that were held in the frontier tavern, involving fifty or sixty men and perhaps two or three women. An observer would see the men dancing (often with each other), wearing their hats tipped at a jaunty angle, pistols and hunting knives prominently displayed at their hips, cavorting to the music of a banjo that went unheard over the roar of the drinkers at the bar and the shouts of the card-playing gamblers. The dancers' already clumsy steps would become more and more blundering as the whisky flowed. These *soirées*, if indeed *"soirée"* is the term I want, were always a great success, with everyone getting bombed out of their minds, but all very happy and sociable; as a witness remarked of one such affair, "very good natured ... there were only a few shots fired."

In England's alehouses a popular form of entertainment (or not so popular, depending on your taste, or lack of it) was the music box. A forerunner of a later generation's juke box, the music box of the 1890s was just as ornate, but without the flashing lights. As with the later juke box, the public-house customer simply dropped a penny in the slot and enjoyed (or was subjected to, if it was someone else's penny) one of the songs or instrumentals then current. A contemporary advertisement for one model, the Polyphon (there was also a Symphonion), called it the "Greatest Sensation wherever seen and heard," and they were seen and heard in such unlikely places as the ice-bound saloons of the Yukon. In the opening stanza of *The Shooting of Dan McGrew* Robert Service recalls

> A bunch of the boys were whooping it up
>   in the Malamute saloon;
> The kid that handles the music box
>   was hitting a jag[rag?]-time tune ...

If every public-house in the 1890s had a coin-operated music box, and if indeed it was a "great sensation" and played "over 1,000 tunes and is popular everywhere," and as the manufacturers claimed "in public places it can be very profitable," then perhaps we have stumbled across the *real* reason why the turn of the century marked the decline of the Victorian pub.

Put two beer drinkers together and right away one is going to tell a joke. "Have you heard the one about ... ?" Generations ago the following joke really cracked them up:

Two guys meet and one says, "I always find beer makes me lean."

"Lean?!" says his friend. "I always thought beer makes folks fat!"

"Well," says the first fellow, "it makes me lean – against a lamp-post."

They were great ones for the snappy rejoinder back in the old days. That bit of dialogue undoubtedly had them rolling in the aisles. A real rib-tickler. It was the kind of sparkling humour you heard from the boys who were holding down the bench in front of the American frontier tavern. It was understandable, I suppose, as the range of amusements in that time and place was fairly limited. Drinking, smoking, telling jokes, chewing tobacco, and spitting would seem to cover it; also a good amount of swearing, and a bit of putting the feet up perhaps. But spitting was the big item.

> They sat in all the different ways
> That men could sit, or ever sat;
> They told of all their jolly days,
> And spat in all the different ways
> That men could spit, or ever spat.

And it went everywhere: the floor, the walls, your shoe, their *own* shoe – sometimes it never made it past their chin; no one seemed to care, except the effete easterners who turned away in disgust.

Hey, how about beer *à la régalade*! Sounds interesting? Okay, put your bathing suit on. That's right, bathing suit. Actually, strip right down if you happen to be in the right company, because beer *à la régalade* means pouring it straight down the old throat without touching the sides. Frankly, this isn't my speed. I like to take my ale by the mouthful, savouring it. But younger, stouter readers might consider it an amusing way of spending a (very short) evening. But off with the clothes, okay? Because there'll be a lot of splashing, foam and gargling, and a fair amount of gasping for air, which means a lot of spraying, so be dressed for it – or *un*dressed for it. The bottle, according to those in the know, is held at least six inches from the mouth, which means head back, throat open, and the best of luck. Actually, it's a Temperance drink, because most of the beer splashes all over you know-who. Still, naked, in tolerant mixed company, it can provide a lot of laughs.

Sports, both active and sedentary, always formed part of the alehouse scene. In London in the latter half of the nineteenth century, billiards was insanely popular and many public-houses in and around London added a billiard room to their establishments. Other sports, while not enjoying the same all-consuming vogue as billiards, also centered around the pub. Many public-houses catered to pigeon clubs; cross-country runners wisely started from one pub and ended at another (a pint to get you going, and a gallon to cool you off); boat-racing enthusiasts assembled at one riverside inn and rowed like madmen to the finish line, where providentially there was another pub.

The term "piss artist," denoting one who drinks to excess, probably had its origin in the entertaining and competitive practice of pissing your name in the snow on a winter's evening. Dead easy if your name was Al or Joe. Humphreys and Alexanders had to really take on a load until they were blue in the face. In Montreal guys like Théophile, and especially Jérôme, had an extremely difficult time of it. Those bloody accents. You had to pinch off the stream, then quickly release it to splash the accent – accuracy was paramount, or you could end up with a comma, like Je,ro^me, – then continue on to the next letter. It required a lot of skill because the accent had to go the right way. *Accent grave* instead of *aigu* was not acceptable. Guys like François had to perform athletic prodigies to get that cedilla under the "c" without messing up the "o" that followed. Too often it came out Françzzmmm, and he'd have to go in for more beer. Next day you'd walk by and see about two dozen Françzzmmms scrawled up the side of a snowbank, with scuffed and increasingly irregular footprints leading to the bar.

In Babylonian times, about 2,000 BC, the traditional drink at wedding banquets was the "wine of the bee," or mead. It was the accepted practice that the father of the bride agree to provide his new son-in-law with all the mead he could drink for a full month after the wedding. Hence the term "honeymonth" or honeymoon.

Among the wedding guests there was always religious representation to solemnize the event. Yet nine hundred years after the birth of Christianity the Christian religion was still, among the German people, little more than a variation on their original paganism. Marriages and deaths were celebrated by dancing and merrymaking, and unbridled beer drinking, the duration of festivities depending upon the beer supply. Even the priests who officiated at these ceremonials joined in and tossed back a tankard or two, or five. In 852, Bishop Hincmar of Rheims placed a heavy interdiction on his ministers who spent entirely too much of their time in dice, dancing, and drink. Indeed, the merry, red-nosed medieval monks of Chaucer's day (fourteenth century) have become a cliché. We read of heavy ale drinking and much merrymaking in the monasteries. There are also reports claiming similar merrymaking went on in the nunneries. Records dating back as early as 1102 commanded priests to avoid drinking or carousing in any way, and commands like that are not issued unless there's a reason for them.

Certainly the ancients lacked a sense of moderation. Temperance advocates would have been stiff with outrage at the conduct of our Viking forebears. These warriors put together a vibrant brew called *aul*. After downing a bucket or two the Norsemen used to go berserk. The Icelandic *berserkr* was a warrior who fought with demonic fury. The word means "bare shirt," signifying without armour; after taking on a load of *aul* the Vikings were so feared they had no need of armour.

> King Hardicanute 'midst Danes and Saxons stout
> Caroused in nut-brown ale and dined in grout.

Nut-brown ale is a familiar term, but what's this grout? Grout, according to Hackwood, was a particularly stiff ale, the malt for which was toasted in an iron pot. You get the impression that in those days there was no such thing as a barrel of ale. Ale seems to have been drunk straight from the brewing vessel until there was no more left. Our ancestors' ale must have been wonderful stuff to have promoted so impatient a thirst. (We see more recent testimony in the old song "Roll Out the Barrel," whose popularity came from the passion for English ale that Canadian soldiers developed during World War II.)

With beer so much a part of merrymaking and happy get-togethers of all kinds, it's not surprising to learn that at a banquet for Elizabeth I in 1575, the guests consumed 23,000 gallons of beer. Yet, just a minute; 23,000 . . . that's over 90,000 quarts! And none of that 5 per cent stuff we endure today, either; the story goes that few could match Elizabeth in the strong ale department, so you can bet that those 90,000 quarts constituted four-square, robust, knock-'em-down-drag-'em-out *beer*. We'll have to be charitable, I suppose, and assume that there sure must have been a lot of people at that banquet.

On a more local and personal level, ales – in the sense of Bride Ale, Help Ale, and Church Ale, for example, meaning a community get-together, a friendly neighbourhood bash – were common in Tudor times (fifteenth and sixteenth centuries) and generally held under the aegis of the Church. A quantity of ale was brewed especially for the occasion, and the parishioners contributed food to augment the party, all of which was sold during the festivities with the profits going to the person or institution for whom the Ale was organized: the bride in the case of Bride Ale, the Church in Church Ale, and some local impoverished person in Help Ale.

Then came the Reformation. The swing from corrupt Catholicism to self-righteous Protestantism cooled the merrymaking; the more puritanical frowned to see so many people enjoying themselves so often, and all that ale, too; shocking. The Church was obliged to divorce itself from participation, and without a stern clerical hand at the helm the parties degenerated and became in reality what the puritans believed them to be: drunken debauches. This is not to imply that there was not a lot of excessive drinking done at the Church-regulated affairs, but at least the authority of the Church helped to curb any really *wild* excesses.

There was an ale – a neighbourhood party – for every occasion imaginable. In most instances their names and purpose are self-explanatory, like Church Ale, Bride Ale, Marriage Ale, Child Ale, Journey Ale, and Christening Ale. Add to the list the millions of saints' days – and every individual, community, village, and town had a favourite saint – and it's obvious there was no lack of excuse for a medieval brew-up.

The Anglo-Saxon *bredale*, or Bride Ale, was a prominent part of the marriage ceremony in those thirsty post-

Roman times. The bride's family brewed a special ale, and friends gathered to toast the betrothed. The term "Bride Ale" lives on in our present-day usage, bridal.

The term "Scat Ale" came from the Saxon *sceat*, a part, and meant a celebration where each participant paid his share of the party's cost.

After serving his time as an apprentice, a young man would give a Foot Ale for his friends, to celebrate his entry into his trade.

A Wake Ale recognized a saint's day; Clerk Ales provided financial assistance to church clerks; even former members of the community, long deceased, could be remembered fondly through a Give Ale financed by a bequest from the dear departed.

The idea behind the Bede Ale (or Help Ale) of medieval times was a warm-hearted one; considerate, socially conscious, and as magnanimous as you could ask. If a member of the community was in financial straits, his friends got together and drank him back to fiscal health. Ale was laid on and a part of the price for each drink went to aid the unfortunate one. Great idea! It was such a great idea it had to be abandoned: People began drinking each other back to financial stability every day of the week. George would spend all his money helping Tom, so the next day Tom would spend all he had gained to help George, then George and Mike would help Bill, then Bill and Tom would help George, then Ralph and Dick would –

Because of the frequency of these ales, the authorities attempted to place restrictions upon them and limit their financial burden. In the seventeenth century, Britain enacted a law that set the maximum charge for dinner at a Bride Ale at fourpence, so that guests obliged by family ties or close friendship to attend a number of these functions would not be destroyed financially. Not incidentally, this illustrates that wedding guests in those earlier days often subsidized the food costs at these affairs, an arrangement not unheard of at today's ethnic nuptials. Given this, it was natural that an enterprising tavernkeeper would offer to assume the responsibilities of organizing such festivities, deduct his expenses from the collected funds (making sure, of course, that the dinner charge more than covered those expenses), and smiling all the way to the bank, remit the remainder to the newlyweds to start them along the road of life.

Of all the reasons, or excuses, for drinking a large beer or two, nothing affords greater justification than a wedding. What other moment in a person's – or indeed a family's – life calls for more merriment and celebration? No question about it, and wedding parties have agreed for thousands of years; at least the guests have, though the parent who had to carry the expense undoubtedly stared, aghast, at the insatiable thirsts at work on every side. Sixteenth century weddings in England were certainly well-lubricated affairs. The period was marked by heavy drinking, and a contemporary observed: "Early in the morning the wedding people begin to exceed in superfluous eating and drinking, and when they come to the preaching they are half drunk, some altogether."

The popularity of fairs is undeniable, and given the often harsh daily grind that faced the common people of the nineteenth century, it's not surprising to see them embrace any excuse for diversion. Fairs, particularly, seemed to leap into being at the slightest provocation. Also, they appeared less structured than the highly organized productions of today, where the advertising often costs as much as the produce of the fair. In January of 1814, the city of London suffered the iciest frost it had seen for more than a century. The River Thames froze solid from bank to bank. Though pretty rough on the river's boatmen, who were denied a living for a month, it takes more than a record frost to deter the mercantile opportunist. The river had hardly frozen before tents seemed to sprout from the very ice itself and a month-long fair began. The city's populace flocked to the frozen fairground to indulge themselves. There were "fruit, oysters, perambulating pie-men, and purveyors of gin, beer, and brandy-balls, and gingerbread."

> At the punch bowl's brink
> Let the thirsty think
> What they say in Japan:
> "First the man takes a drink,
> Then the drink takes a drink,
> Then the drink takes the man!"
> – Edward R. Sill

That might be what they say in Japan, but it's not all they say in Japan. The poet Tahito (665-731) had a few thoughts on the subject:

> Instead of holding forth
> Wisely, with grave mien,
> How much better to drink *sake*,
> To get drunk, and to shout aloud.

(Shout aloud? There's another way of shouting? I've tried shouting silently; it doesn't work.)

Eight centuries ago, Japanese nobles discovered the healing properties of tea, and sipped it thankfully (and gingerly) the morning after an overly long night on *sake*.

"Sake," said the Japanese philosopher Kaibara Ekken in the seventeenth century, "is the beautiful gift of Heaven. Drunk in small quantities it expands the heart, lifts the downcast spirit, drowns cares, and improves the health ... Enjoy sake by drinking just enough ... and thus enjoy seeing flowers when they are just bursting into bloom."

Notwithstanding the wisdom of these thoughts, there's nothing to be gained by quoting them to a fellow the morning after. The damage has been done. If you want to avoid those noisy morning-after seltzer preparations – depending on your condition, they can sound like a boiler shop – here's the answer: take them the night before, if you can remember. It's common sense, really. Taken the next morning they are simply a case of locking the barn door after the horse has escaped. As I say, the damage has long been done.

It may sound suicidal, but a pot of ale following a night of debauch is a better cure for hangover than the common commercial remedies.

> Welcome to my lips, great king of frolic,
> Stern foe to headache, devils blue, and cholic;
> Thy sterner aid I claim, and ask thy might
> To quell the riots of that punch last night.

The Lion, an inn at Hampton, England, was a favourite drinking and dining spot for literary types like Dryden, Pope, Swift, and others. A famous (or infamous) evening of drinking engaged in by Joseph Addison and Alexander Pope, two of the eighteenth century's outstanding poets, left the latter with a hangover so great it's a wonder he didn't commemorate it in verse. Then again, maybe it's not such a wonder; hangovers have not produced many lasting literary masterpieces.

Both Addison and Pope could have profited from Finland's experience. In Finland they often brew in the sauna, where they also drink the resulting beer. This home-brewed beer, according to the Finns, won't give you a hangover. I find this hard to believe as it weighs in at up to 10 per cent alcohol. Perhaps the lack of a hangover comes from the leaching action of the sauna; maybe the Finns have long known one of the world's great humanitarian secrets: hangover-less drinking, enjoyed in the friendly, fragrant atmosphere of the sauna.

Nevertheless, if that grim morning-after does catch up to you, and your eyelids feel like rusty tin cans, and, like Hamlet, all the uses of your world seem stale and flat, it might help to remember the words of Robert Mitchum. In an address to a large audience, the screen actor once said: "There are, I believe, some of you who never touch alcohol. I respect your convictions. But I am sorry for you at the same time. Because when you wake up in the morning, that's as good as you're ever gonna feel."

Many of the drinking customs we practise today as a matter of course – toasting present and absent friends, drinking healths, round-the-table drinking, and so on – are also found among the habits of the ancient Chinese, thousands of years BC. The Romans, too, though they are portrayed as ardent wine drinkers, were not above taking a jar of ale now and then. The great general Julius Caesar raised a flagon of beer in toast to his officers when the army crossed the Rubicon in 49 BC (an act which, though contrary to his instructions from Rome, eventually gained him the laurel crown of Caesar).

To the humourless historical mind it may be difficult to picture Julius Caesar (noble Caesar!) carousing on a hilltop with a bunch of scruffy unshaven soldiers, raising a sloshing pot of beer, and perhaps singing something like

Come troll the jovial flagon,
  Come fill the bonny bowl,
Come, join in laughing sympathy
  Of soul with kindred soul.

The Romans, when drinking to the health of, say, the emperor or distant friends, would traditionally pass the cup from left to right, always with the right hand, each man toasting in his turn. This same tradition appears in the port ceremony, where, until the recent rise of feminism, the ladies left the dining room while the gentlemen remained and circulated a bottle of port, again always from left to right, but – interesting wrinkle – the bottle was passed and received with the *left* hand. This departure from the established Roman custom was born on the northwest frontier of India at the height of the British Empire. Such was the climate of native mutiny and rebellion that the men in the officers' mess always kept their right hands free to draw their pistols.

The Loving Cup gave birth to our modern toast – toast, that is, in the sense of raising your glass to someone in a gesture of recognition or tribute. When the Danes occupied much of England, an Englishman died on the spot if he dared to drink in front of a Dane without permission. This, naturally, slowed down the Englishman's drinking. From this there developed the custom of pledging the safety, the continued health, of the drinker while he drank (the Loving Cup had two handles; while the drinker drank his hands were thus engaged and he could not defend himself). Later, at official gatherings, the host filled a Loving Cup with ale and floated a piece of toast on top. The host drank, and the cup passed among all. When it returned to the host he finished it and ate the toast, this last as a gesture in honour of his assembled friends.

> Then hail, thou big and foaming bowl,
>   Hail, constant idol of my soul;
> How laughingly the bubbles ride
>   Upon thy rich and sparkling tide.
>   – Brasenose College Shrovetide Verses.

On the other hand, a seventeenth century critic damned the habit of toasting: "this hellish ceremony of beginning, seconding, and pledging healths." Quite right; makes for a rough morning-after, and is devilishly expensive, too.

Notwithstanding adverse views, raising a bumper or two to toast one's friends has an appeal, over and above the contents of the bumper, that will outlast all criticism. The ceremony entailed in the gesture touches some atavistic chord in the human character; people everywhere love pomp and ceremony. On the subject, the term "bumper" possibly comes from the French *bom-*

barde, a large drinking vessel. Then again, another (though dubious) origin has it that it's a phonetic twist to *au bon père*, a toast by monks to the head of their order.

But when it comes to toasts, or nightcaps (which almost always become toasts, to pleasant company and an enjoyable evening), few can match the *savoir-faire* of a Montreal brewer during the 1940s. Say what you like, the brewers of Montreal had class. After enjoying a night on the town, one well-known brewer took the entire orchestra and the chorus line from the Normandie Roof nightclub back to his brewery for a nightcap, which sure beats a cup of coffee and a peck on the cheek. ("Here, I'll just open the valve on this 50,000-gallon vat . . . pass me your slipper, my dear . . . ")

> Old Christmas comes to close the wanèd year;
> The shepherd to blazing hearth repairs,
>   and nut-brown beer.

Facets of our Christmas festival appear in Scandinavian and Roman lore, and lend to the tender sentiments of Christmas and its deeply felt Christian beginnings antecedents of a grosser nature. The Norsemen celebrated the winter solstice, the longest night of the year, as the great darkness before the creation of the world. The big deity in this festival was Yule, from whom we get our yuletide references. Among the Romans the pagan feast of Saturn – officially their god of seed or sowing, though in practice, feastwise, the deity of all-out licentiousness – occurred around the same time, in mid-December. The early Christians, very wise fellows, realized that to curtail these celebrations in the name of the new religion wouldn't do the Christian faith any good at all, so they brought in Christmas to replace the frowned-upon Saturnalia. The same thinking applied to the Norseman's yuletide festival: Don't rock the boat; the people enjoy the merriment, the feasting, the happy times with friends. Call it another name – Christmas, for example; give it another meaning, the birth of our Lord, and we'll gradually wean them away from the grosser aspects of the pagan rites. Just don't prohibit the good times. Bit of a calculated risk, actually; I mean, associating the Christ-child's birth with the really advanced partying that went on during Saturnalia . . . still, you play the cards you're dealt, and history shows they were right. Hardly any licentiousness at all at Christmas these days

Yule gave his name to the yule-cake, a delightful nosh that became part of the Christmas Eve festivities. Toasted slices of the cake were left to soak in spiced ale, then scoffed by all, with much shouting and general merriment, and a number of noggins of ale, naturally.

In medieval England, when the period known to the Norsemen as Yule came to an end, they celebrated the rebirth of the sun in feasting and drinking, and the burning of the symbolic yule log (a tradition that went into eclipse in the latter part of the nineteenth century with the coming of Queen Victoria's Prince Albert and his teutonic traditions of Christmas trees and Santa Claus). As the yule log was borne in, those assembled would begin

> To quaff brown ale foamed high
>   from tall stone jugs
> And pledge deep healths
>   in oft-replenished mugs.

Vortigern, a fifth century British tyrant who gained power on the heels of the Roman withdrawal, is part of the origin of the term "wassail" (though the spoilsport Oxford English Dictionary implies that fifth century references to wassail are anachronous. The earliest reference, according to the OED, occurs *circa* 1140 AD). At a feast in his honour, the Saxons presented Vortigern with a bowl of ale and the words *"Louerd king woes ho l."* ("Lord King, your health." For what it's worth, Hackwood claims the Saxon expression was *"Liever Kyning, Wass-hael!"*) Puzzled, he asked the meaning of the phrase. "It is the custom among the Saxons," his hosts replied, "that friend says to friend, 'Wassail,' and the other says 'Drinc hail.' " The term wassail came, with time, to mean drinking, feasting, and merrymaking in general, especially at Christmas, New Year, and on Twelfth Night. Early on New Year's Day, young people visited the houses of their friends and neighbours, holding high a bowl of spiced ale, singing and dancing and carolling yuletide verses.

The Oxford English Dictionary unequivocally records the pronunciation of the word "wassail" as *wah-s'l*, the accent on the first syllable. Pity, because on the second syllable, wah-*sail*, it acquires a much more festive ring. Sounds like you're really having a good time. But *wah-s'l*. Ech.

"I'm going to *wah*-s'l!"

"Well don't do it here, I've just washed the floor."

But change the accent:

"Let's wah-*sail*!"

"Right on! Move the chairs back!"

"Mary, where's the wassail-bowl?"

"Come on, Harry, let's have a song!" (Singing) "Deck the halls with boughs of holly . . . "

(Others join in) "Fa-la-la-la-lah, la-lah-lah-lah!" (Laughter and cries of "Wassail!")

Wah-*sail*. Much better. A happy word, full of innocent fun; a word that promises lots of ale for all, and merry times all round.

Wassail occupies a place at the very heart of Christmas, and not necessarily in its sense of drunken revels ("necessarily," however, is the key word; wassail has never been associated with Temperance). "An English gentleman, on Christmas Day, had all his tenants and neighbours enter his hall by daybreak. The strong beer was broached, and the black jack [a large leather beer jug] went merrily about with toast, nutmeg, and good Cheshire cheese."

In earlier days Christmas and the wassail-bowl were synonymous. Indeed, what a joy it was to arrive at a friend's home, and standing before the door with smoking breath rising in the winter night, catch the scent of the fragrant bowl within, and hear the cries of welcome before the merry door was opened! And once inside – Dickens himself there in spirit, along with Scrooge reclaimed – happy arms sweep you to the blazing hearth; with much slapping of backs and wishing of healths you pull off your mittens and warm your hands in the glow from the fire. And there the wassail-bowl holds court amid the culinary glories of the table. Your friends press a glass into your unresisting hand; a toast! a toast! You quickly think of something appropriate, keeping it clean because there are ladies present, then drink to the past year, the present yuletide season, and the wonderful year to come.

If you were smart, you did not – repeat, did not – have a couple of drinks before you arrived. These wassail-bowls, innocuous-sounding and equally innocent-looking, are nevertheless substantial pieces of work. Depending on the size of the company, they go something like this· In the bottom of the bowl you put a half-pound of sugar. Pour over this a pint of warm beer, and add some grated nutmeg and ginger. Pour in four glasses of sherry, and finish by adding five pints of beer. Stir it up and leave it for two or three hours. Just before serving, float three or four pieces of thin toast on top. Toss in a few slices of lemon. Some will add roasted apples; it's a matter of taste. It's a warm and friendly brew, but that sherry . . . try to restrict yourself to a single traditional glass, maybe two. Remember the song: "On the first day of Christmas my true love gave to me . . . seven glasses of wassail." If you really get into the wassail-bowl, believe me, you can cross off the remaining eleven days.

As an illustration of the tenacity of paganism, the heathen ceremony of the Jule (yule) festival was still observed in Norway as late as the tenth century. During that time the Norwegian king Hakon the Good decreed that Christmas and Jule would be held as a single feast. He also stipulated that the festivities should last so long as the beer held out. Merry Christmas, indeed.

The puritans deplored ale's high profile at Christmas. "It's *supposed* to be a *religious* festival, you guys," they would say, irritably gathering up yet another bunch of empty tankards. But they were in the minority; the supply of ale was a serious matter for those who felt that Christmas should be celebrated *comme il faut*. One yuletide, in Greenland, an apprehensive Eric the Red (tenth century) heard with relief that a ship had arrived from "home" bringing the necessary malt and accessories for a yuletide brew-up. Then, as now, Christmas just wouldn't have been the same for pagans without feasting, carolling, and oceans of ale.

Sir Roger de Coverley was a fictitious character described by Addison in *The Spectator*, a London magazine of the early eighteenth century. Incidentally, this was the same Addison who did much of his drinking at the Lion in Hampton, along with literary luminaries like Dryden, Pope, and all that bunch. Sir Roger de Coverley was the apotheosis of the English country gentleman. "I have often thought," he said, "it happens very well that Christmas should fall out in the middle of winter. It is the most dead, uncomfortable time of the year, when the poor people would suffer very much from their poverty and cold, if they had not good cheer, warm fires, and Christmas gambols to support them. I love to rejoice their poor hearts at this season, and to see the whole village merry in my great hall. I allow a double quantity of malt to my small beer, and set it a-running for twelve days for everyone that calls for it."

Thus we see an English Christmas in the seventeenth or eighteenth century, with the neighbourhood squire providing yuletide refreshments for his people. If he were reasonably well off, his festive board included wine, perhaps some brandy, but strong ale was the drink of choice. The historian Thomas Macaulay (1800-1859) confirms this: "As the habit of drinking to excess was general in the class to which he belonged, and as his fortune did not enable him to intoxicate large assemblies daily with claret or canary, strong beer was the ordinary beverage. It was only at great houses, or on great occasions, that foreign drink was placed on the board."

As late as 1900 the peasants of Norway celebrated Christmas with a great brew-up, producing quantities of strong ale with which to entertain friends and neighbours. Following in the footsteps of merry King Hakon, the party's duration depended upon the amount of ale available: if you had a lot of provident friends, why, you could still be celebrating Christmas in July.

Sir Walter Scott, too, recognized Christmas as the happiest of times:

> England was merry England when
> Old Christmas brought his sports again;
> 'Twas Christmas broached the mightiest ale,
> 'Twas Christmas told the merriest tale;
> A Christmas gambol oft would cheer
> A poor man's heart through half the year.

And a Merry Christmas to you, too, Walt.

An attractive yuletide beverage, popular in Anglo-Saxon times, was a compound called Lamb's Wool – though "yuletide beverage" is misleading; Britons enjoyed it at Christmas, certainly, but they also drank it regularly throughout the year. It consisted, generally, of brown ale, spiced with nutmeg, ginger, and sugar, with the addition of roasted crab apples that had burst in the roasting, the white interior mixing with the ale. Heated by the fire, the ale was borne in, steaming, to delight the happy guests, the carrier crying "Wassail!" and the recipients answering with Christmas songs.

Early in January 1667 Samuel Pepys brought one Christmas season to a happy close:

> At night to sup, and then to cards, and last of all to have a flagon of ale and apples, drank out of a wood cup, as a Christmas draught, which made all merry.

In the nineteenth century, in the north of England, it was customary to roast Christmas apples before the fire. Beneath the apples was a vessel of spiced ale. The apples, supported by a string, would fill the air with their sweet aroma and eventually drop into the ale, which lends a delicious new dimension to bobbing for apples.

On the subject of losing a few days at Christmas (and beer drinkers do, occasionally), in the early 1900s Yankee saloons offered their regular customers free egg-nogs and Tom & Jerrys (or is that Toms & Jerry?) over the Christmas season. According to newspaperman George Ade, after eight mugs of Tom & Jerry you could get out of bed the next morning (*if* you could get out of bed) and you would be able to *see* your breath. He tells the story of the happy fellow who spent all of New Year's Day drinking T & J. The next morning he walked by a butcher's shop and his breath caught on one of the meat hooks.

Beer is famous as an impetus to merrymaking for its own sake. Perhaps not as renowned is beer's role in the pursuit of loftier aims, especially creative ones.

> If with water you fill up your glasses,
>   You'll never write anything wise,
> For ale is the horse of Parnassus
>   Which hurries a bard to the skies.
>   – Thomas Moore.

Many a writer will applaud such sentiment, but then these same writers would probably drink a dozen quarts when writing something as creative as their name on the back of a rubber cheque, so can we really hold them up as examples of ale's contribution to creative genius? Would we instead be more justified in categorizing them not as drinking writers, but rather as drunks who also write, creative versions of Ben Jonson's sodden clods?

> Those that merely talk and never think,
> That live in the wild anarchy of drink.

Yet it seems a heavy knock to writers generally, and one that is largely unearned. To the puritans a single glass sets you irrevocably on the path to Inferno; what you create along the way doesn't enter into their thinking. But to the more sensible mind, what counts is the thing created; whether the artist is drunk or sober, sot or saint, isn't really germane to the question. But history's pages resound with the puritan's cries, and beer bears the brunt of their attacks.

The writer nevertheless writes on, and ale continues to lubricate his pen.

5

Beer and Literature

What is it about writers, particularly? Critics will look at these creative people and with little effort draw up a great sordid catalogue of drunks and weirdos. Frankly, I think "drunks and weirdos" is a bit strong; true, they do seem a thirsty lot, and inclined toward, er, originality, but I mean who's perfect after all?

Some friendly observers, such as Frederick Hackwood, claim that indeed the study of the drinking and eating habits of the great writers and poets can be illuminating and instructive. "To learn the tastes and diet of great men ... and the favourite dishes in which they indulged [is] to see their weaknesses as well as their greatness, and so to bring them nearer to ourselves." Well, perhaps. I wonder, though, if it brings us any nearer to a great man to learn that he regularly consumed, at a sitting, a gross of oysters, or knocked off eight quarts of ale with one hand. Still, I suppose it illustrates, as Hackwood says, that great men, too, can be by turns as sensible or as intemperate as we often are ourselves.

The poet Charles Lamb (1775-1834) sensibly gave his guests beef and porter, and when he ate at a friend's table considered the company as important as the menu: "Good company makes good food." Far from the substantial beef and porter of his mature years was the faint fare of his younger days at an English boarding school, where he gobbled tea and hot rolls in the morning, and snatched up a "quarter of a penny loaf, moistened with beer in wooden piggins [small wooden cups, made like barrels, with one stave left longer to serve as a handle], smacking of the pitched leathern jack it was poured from."

(The jacks he mentions were fairly common on boarding school tables. The inside was coated with pitch to make them watertight, which gave them their generic name, black jack, and not incidentally gave us the term "pitcher." These large leather vessels also lent their name to the thigh-length leather boots of the period: because of their similarity to black jacks they were called jack boots.)

Lamb, however, tends to justify the views of the abovementioned critics, as well as Hackwood's more charitable opinion. The poet's great liking for porter became, in his later years, a pronounced weakness. He was not alone. His contemporary, Robert Burns, too, loved porter's dark flavour, but his tastes were more eclectic: if it was malt, it was good; if there was lots of it, it was better. Brendan Behan, the Irish novelist, and no mean hand at a pint himself, once said about porter: "Porter is a lighter drink than stout and there's not all that much of it sold nowadays [Ireland, 1960]; but I recall my father telling me that before the First War, when it cost a penny a pint, it was so good that the glass it was used in used to stick to the counter."

Teetotalers frown on these hard-drinking creative types, but they should remember that while literary giants may have had a glass in one hand, they had a pen in the other, and rose above those of us who chose instead to have a glass in each hand.

Of us singleminded two-glass men, Samuel Johnson once said that few of us have the intellectual resources necessary to enable us to give up our ale and yet find something to do with ourselves between dinner and supper.

Thanks a lot, Sam.

The tendency when considering writers and ale-drinking is to slope off into a wild description of the unfettered alcoholic licence indulged in by artists everywhere, but this would simply substantiate the accusations of the critics. The trouble is, try to find an upright example; a writer, say, who drinks only a cup of warm milk at bedtime. Maybe I move in the wrong circles, but I don't know any. I haven't even *heard* of any. Take Dylan Thomas: poet, died young, great talent; I have a picture of him, pen in one hand, glass in the other, so we can't very well choose him, can we? Brendan Behan: an Irishman and a writer; deadly combination. "Give an Irishman lager for a month," said Mark Twain, "and he's a dead man. An Irishman is lined with copper, and the beer corrodes it." Well, anything you say, Mark, but Behan spent many years disproving that theory. True, he's no longer with us.

There are, of course, writers who have not established a reputation for heavy drinking, though none is known as the warm-milk-before-bed type. They might not advocate ale as a way of life, but you can often see where their preference lies. H. L. Mencken, erstwhile newspaper editor, writer, and vitriolic critic, had a word or two for hosts who gave dinners with nothing to drink: "They seemed to think that literary gentlemen were always glad to get a free meal. So they were – but not a dry meal." This from a writer who drank Pilsener from a five-gallon beer glass. Even during the last days of his life, Mencken found enjoyment in a foaming stein of imported Canadian ale, a brew he claimed produced an aristocratic belch.

When a man like Samuel Johnson says "The tavern chair is the throne of human felicity," you have a good idea what his feelings are, drinkwise. In later life Johnson gave up drinking, but still retained his appreciation of its contribution to social intercourse. Yet he had an enduring dislike, not to say contempt, for Bordeaux (called claret in his day). "Poor stuff," he said. "A man would be drowned before it made him drunk. No," said Johnson, "claret is the liquor for boys; port for men; but he who aspires to be a hero must drink brandy. Brandy will do soonest for a man what drinking *can* do for him."

Brandy as the measure of a man is one yardstick, but when it comes to separating the men from the boys one of the most effective separators is the following, advanced by the novelist Kingsley Amis: Take a twenty-ounce tankard and pour in one solid shot of dry gin (none of that jigger business; a well-rounded *slug* is what we're after here). Add ten ounces of stout – Guinness will do the trick. Fill the tankard with ginger beer. This, says Amis, "will certainly revive you ... or something." Three or four of these will conclusively separate not only the men from the boys, but also the *real* men from the men.

There exist as many yardsticks for measuring a drinking man as there are drinking men – from Johnson's brandy and Amis' gin and stout, to the teutonic subtlety of German dramatist Gotthold Lessing (1729-1781): "One can drink too much, but one never drinks enough." You can bet there was not too much tea drinking in *his* household.

In an ecclesiastical vein, if I can use the expression and avoid blasphemy, poets have given the effects of ale and liquor religious overtones. A. E. Housman maintains that

> . . . malt does more than Milton can
> To justify God's ways to man.
> Ale, man, ale's the stuff to drink
> For fellows whom it hurts to think.

Lord Byron takes a lighter view, expressing a juxtaposition the defenders of Temperance would abhor:

> There's nought, no doubt, so much
>   the spirit calms
> As rum and true religion.

The religious aspects of ale generated little attention among the actors and singers of the eighteenth and nineteenth centuries, who (a) were probably not that interested, and (b) had long known of ale's more practical and beneficial effects on the voice. Charles Macklin, whose portrayal of Shylock at Drury Lane in 1741 was hailed as a masterpiece, lived to be a hundred and habitually tucked away vast quantities of stout, usually in an alehouse called the Antelope in White-Hart-yard, Drury Lane. His career on the stage was a tempestuous one, and he undoubtedly needed stout's restorative properties. Fanny Kemble (1809-1893) had her debut at London's Covent Garden at the age of twenty in the role of Juliet, a part that established her reputation for the next forty years. She could frequently be found backstage, both during and after her appearances, getting outside a large pot of stout.

"Classics which at home are drowsily read," said Emerson, "have a strange charm in a country inn."

Keats, a man of more urban tastes, nevertheless leaned the same way, remembering a contented hour or two in his "Lines on the Mermaid Tavern":

Souls of poets dead and gone,
  What Elysium have ye known,
Happy field or mossy cavern,
  Choicer than the Mermaid Tavern?

"There is nothing which has yet been contrived by man, by which so much happiness is produced, as by a good tavern or inn." Samuel Johnson again; and a better authority would be hard to find. Johnson spent many of his waking hours in taverns, taking vast quantities of snuff which he carried loose in special leather-lined pockets of his waistcoat. Though his love of taverns was life-long, he did not drink to excess. Conversation was his forte. He claimed that drinking in a tavern "exhilarates my spirits, and prompts me to free conversation and an interchange of discourse . . . I dogmatize and am contradicted, and in this conflict of opinion and sentiments I find delight."

Johnson was always ready to visit a tavern. Early one morning in 1753, friends called on him at his rooms off Fleet Street in London. It was three o'clock; they had been carousing and wanted Johnson to come out with them. Johnson at this time was a young forty-four, so he set aside the heavy club with which he had met them at this door (thinking them thieves) and joined them "in joyous contempt of sleep." In a nearby tavern they called for a bowl of bishop (hot port wine, spices, sugar, and oranges or lemons), talked, and watched the dawn break over the Thames River.

Once, in an evening of conversation with his friend and future biographer James Boswell, Johnson had the opportunity to justify his views on taverns. "There is no private house in which people can enjoy themselves so well as in a tavern." Regardless of the grandeur and elegance of the private home, or the quantity of good things to eat and drink, there was always an element of anxiety present. The host would naturally be anxious to see his guests suitably entertained and their wants satisfied. The guests would take pains to be agreeable to the host, anxious lest their compliments sound false and contrived. Among the guests there would also be a certain constraint; you can hardly order people around in another man's home as freely as in your own. But in a tavern there is none of this anxiety. "You are sure you are welcome," said Johnson, "and the more noise you make, the more trouble you give, the more good things you call for, the welcomer you are. No servant will attend you with the alacrity which waiters do who are incited by the prospect of an immediate reward in proportion as they please."

To say that Johnson did not drink to excess in his earlier years is perhaps misleading; it has to be taken in context. In the mid-1700s Johnson and Boswell would often stroll along to the Mitre Tavern in Fleet Street, their favourite meeting place. It was the tavern where they were introduced to one another and where they had many suppers together, meals well-lubricated with port and conversation. During their evenings of supper and talk they customarily drank two bottles of port. Sometimes they waived the supper and just had the port. Half-hearted attempts at temperance generally failed, with Boswell painstakingly measuring the wine between their two mugs, while Johnson muttered, "Come, you need not measure it so exactly." In the end they usually said to hell with it and ordered a second bottle. "I think," said Dr Johnson, taking a lifesaving pull at his replenished mug, "two bottles would seem to be the quantity for us." Frederick Pottle, Boswell's biographer, points out that for their time both Boswell and Johnson were not heavy drinkers, even at a bottle apiece. Restricting themselves to a single bottle, says Pottle, "would have been regarded as abstemious by most of [their] acquaintances." (Try drinking a bottle of port. Don't do it alone; make sure you have someone to help you get home. It will give you an idea of eighteenth century capacities. It will also give you a monumental hangover.)

While there are stories of the violently alcoholic lives of many of history's literary figures, their *creative* lives were, by the very nature of their art, ones of solitude, and generally sober. You have to be missing a few cards from your deck if you can live violently while sitting alone at the typewriter. The breaches of peace and tranquillity that occurred were often caused by artistic problems – the sometimes vain search for the right word, the felicitous line, the colourful expression. Many sought ideas in a pot of ale. Some found them; others simply found refreshment, and struggled on. Usually the artist's creative life was, and is, a quiet and somewhat reclusive one, governed by fairly simple needs, and as Jerome K. Jerome said, simple things are often the best:

Let your boat of life be light, packed with only what you need – a homely home and simple pleasures, one or two friends worth the name, someone to love and someone to love you, a cat, a dog, and a pipe or two, enough to eat and enough to wear, and a little more than enough to drink; for thirst is a dangerous thing.

6

Alehouses

He goes not out of his way who goes to a good inn.
– Nineteenth century proverb.

So frequently did the poets sing of taverns and inns, and
the pleasures they found there, that you can't help but
wonder about the quality of their home life.

> Whoe'er has travell'd life's dull round,
>   Where'er his stages may have been,
> May sigh to think he still has found
>   The warmest welcome at an inn.
>
>   – Shenstone.

Within the tavern, men of wit and wisdom encouraged
the poet's intellectual freedom, and he embraced the inn
with expectation and satisfaction. You can sense the
poet's smile of pleasure in the lines – again by the
eighteenth century poet William Shenstone – from
"Written at an inn":

> 'Tis here with boundless power I reign,
>   And every health which I begin,
> Converts dull port to bright champagne;
>   For Freedom crowns it, at an inn . . .
>
> And now once more I shape my way
>   Through rain or shine, through thick or thin,
> Secure to meet, at close of day,
>   With kind reception at an inn.

Something about the alehouse seems to have reached
out to poets particularly. No matter how impoverished,
the bard blossomed in the warm embrace of the tavern.

Tavern, I love thee more and more;
　Mine every want dost thou supply;
I care not what's without thy door,
　Within, there's none so rich as I.
                              – Pierre Motin.

Some poets, like an anonymous twelfth century scribe, never wanted to leave:

For on this my heart is set:
　When the hour is nigh me,
Let me in the tavern die,
　With a tankard by me.

The poet may have loved the tavern, but then as now the tavernkeeper wasn't all that happy with poets. Most poets were (and are) long on drinking but short on paying. Since the tavern first opened its doors it was the businessman and the traveller the tavernkeeper sought to attract.

Periclean Greece (fifth century BC) had inns to serve the traveller's needs, but they were infrequent along the country's roads – though the term "roads" is pushing charitable expression to its very extreme: a dirt path was the best road in town. Even the use of the word "inn," as a place of rest and refreshment to which you would look forward with agreeable anticipation, is open to a lot of argument. They were, more often than not, the home of thieves and lice.

Five centuries later the Romans introduced taverns into Britain and there has never been a lack of them since, proof of the durability of the alehouse's welcome. The greatest concentration of taverns and inns was in the towns and cities that offered a large number of paying customers. London, for example, in the early 1700s had a population of 700,000 that supported over 6,000 outlets for drink (a little more than 115 persons per outlet). Even in the thirteenth century there were in London almost 1,700 alehouses and taverns industriously brewing and selling their own ale. Compare those figures with more recent ones: in 1985 only seventy public-houses, in all of Britain, brewed their own beer.

Samuel Pepys, the meticulous diarist who gave us such a detailed picture of London life in the mid-seventeenth century, spent many happy hours in alehouses and taverns, sampling the delicacies found there.

Oysters at the Angel in Westminster; ham and lobster at the Cock Alehouse in Fleet Street; off to the Bell in Westminster for leg of veal, bacon, a brace of capons, sausages, and fritters; herrings at the Dolphin in Tower Street; back to Westminster and a dish of anchovies and olives at the Black Dog; and away again to the Three Stags in Holborn for a venison pie; then a quick whip round to the Mitre Tavern for beef and marrow bones – all helped on its way by a pint or two of strong ale or a jar of sack. At many of these establishments reservations were necessary, illustrating that at the better eateries nothing has changed over the centuries.

The men of Pepys' time indulged a pleasant habit: the drinking of a morning draught of ale, or something substantial and alcoholic at least, much as we would start the day with a coffee and danish. Pepys refers to it frequently:

> Drank my morning draught at Harper's ... [3 Feb 1660]

> Waked in the morning with my head in a sad taking, through the last night's drink ... so rose and went out with Mr Creed to drink our morning draught, which he did give me in chocolate to settle my stomach. [24 Apr 1661]

> ... a morning draught of buttered ale. [Buttered ale: ale, butter, sugar, and cinnamon.] [5 Dec 1662]

> ... the Ship Taverne at the hither end of Billiter Lane ... I in there to drink my morning draught of half a pint of Rhenish [German] wine. [8 Apr 1667]

Seventeenth century London offered Pepys a stunning variety of alehouses in which to enjoy his morning draught. A tavern much frequented for centuries was the Devil and St Dunstan, or "The Devil" to use its more popular name, a usage that may have had something to do with the city's curt order to the tavern's owner in 1608, to alter his sign "and put the devil clean out of it and have St Dunstan alone." The tavern was very popular with the literary figures of its time. Samuel Johnson enjoyed supper there, and Alexander Pope considered it one of the better dining rooms; Goldsmith, Swift, and Addison could be seen there frequently. So great was Ben Jonson's affection for the Devil that he moved and took up residence nearby so he could more conveniently patronize his favourite tavern.

The Saxons never became *involved* with taverns to the same passionate extent as Samuel Pepys or Dr Johnson and his friends of a later era. Saxon amusements tended toward unsophisticated outdoor pursuits: lots of drinking and fighting, some rape and pillage, loud songs – simple things, group activities. As the Roman Empire fell, the wine of the Romans followed the Latin conquerors into decline, and with the advent of the Anglo-Saxons came the taste for strong ale. Our teutonic ancestors brought with them stirring tales of heroes who spent eternity in Valhalla, scoffing endless haunches of meat and drinking oceans of ale, served to them by the tall and beautiful Valkyries, buxom women who watched over a warrior in battle and joined his spirit in Valhalla if he was one of the unlucky guys that got killed. Fantasyland, to be sure, but it had an irresistible appeal to the rank and file who had to do the fighting. Temperance wouldn't have had a chance among the old Saxons and Danes.

Some say the Valkyries, involved as they were with the serving of strong drink, are the origin of the barmaid, a figure sadly underdeveloped in modern North America. Where they do appear they seem more intent on taking your money than supporting your fighting spirit or nourishing your soul. They wouldn't have been tolerated in Valhalla.

Class distinction seems a part of the human condition, and it reared its patrician head even in the realm of beer. When the Irish Benedictine monk St Gall built a brewery in Switzerland (612 AD) he produced three brews: the first was a regular, for the monks themselves; the second a weak brew of no special merit, for beggars and other such low-lifes; the third was a beer of superior quality for the biggies like bishops and the nobility that might happen to drop in.

Alehouses proliferated in the larger cities and towns of England, where the concentration of people provided them with profitable patrons. This was great for the cities, but outside the city's walls the countryside saw fewer places of refreshment. In thirteenth century England, the Archbishop of Canterbury Robert Winchelsey exemplified the extent of clerical charity and hospitality offered to wayfarers in those days when roadside inns were rare. Those inns that did exist were, after all, not quite the places you would recommend to your friends, so travellers sought the archbishop's bounty and he gave it freely. Winchelsey fed 5,000 of the poor every day, and those who for reasons of ill health were unable to come in person he provided for in their homes. Let's hear it for Bob.

Service and consideration was the motto of Archbishop Winchelsey's establishment. But Winchelsey was one of only a few democratic islands in a vast sea of class distinction. Beer and ale, served at the long dinner table of a great lord, came in a variety of vessels. The sixteenth century English baron, observing the distinction between noble and commoner, used cups of silver, pewter, horn, and wood. Three guesses who got the silver and who got the wood.

By 1600, inns were more frequent along the main roads of England, flourishing at the junctures of major thoroughfares and serving the important market towns and fairs. In most instances the hosts of these establishments were responsible publicans, and kept clean and orderly houses, though lamentably some of their staff operated hand-in-glove with the local highwaymen.

Following the Reformation, when many of the Catholic abbeys were obliged to close, the English clergyman assumed the mantle of hospitality once borne by the monasteries: that of providing wayfarers with ale, much as an alehouse did. While he did not appear to have the right, by law, to *sell* ale, nevertheless if his church was in a sparsely populated area, and his house the only source of good ale, it seemed only right and hospitable to refresh the traveller, and the vicar could hardly be expected to do it for nothing.

The better roads of the eighteenth century, and the mail coaches that travelled them, gave birth to inns of a higher class. Coaching inns sprang up along the main roads. We see their happy activity, their trumpets and scampering dogs and rosy-cheeked coachmen in the charming prints of the period. The inn became a welcome stop along the route; a place of warmth, rest, refreshment, and an opportunity to exchange news and gossip as well as mail.

Gossip, as always, was more sought after than news or refreshment. At this time, the mid 1700s, there were two inns on the road south to London. One was called the Cock, the other's name was the Bull. They were staging points where the southbound coaches stopped to change horses for the last leg of the journey to London. While the stablehands saw to the horses, passengers relaxed for a moment in the inn's bar to exchange news of the day over a refreshing pot of ale. Landlords of staging inns were popular sources of information and gossip, and the publicans of the Cock and the Bull were enthusiastic retailers of the latest stories, scandals, and rumours. A little too enthusiastic, as the travellers learned later; most of the stories were gross fabrications. Word got around, and eventually news brought from the two inns was greeted with contempt. "Another Cock and Bull story," people would sneer. The expression is still current today, after two centuries of frequent use.

As English inns grew in number and quality, the taverns of their American cousins changed, too, though not quite along the same lines. "All tavernkeepers are farmers, and the best farmers are tavernkeepers," said a nineteenth century observer of the American midwest. A settler who began as a farmer often became a tavernkeeper *malgré lui*. Faced with the sketchy transportation facilities of the time, and the difficulties of getting his surplus produce to market, the wise farmer became a taverner, thus bringing the market to his produce, selling it to travellers who stayed at his inn, and not incidentally making two or three times the profit the market would have given him, without the effort and expense of having to transport it there.

As the pioneers moved west, living conditions in the taverns became harder, then harsher, then simply non-existent, until the term "living" was reduced to its most basic dictionary definition. Of civilization's amenities there was virtually none. In the tavern's "dining" area sanitary conditions were difficult if not impossible to maintain, and the pioneer tavernkeeper himself did little to alleviate the situation; primitive thinking seemed to go with primitive living. Watching preparations for supper could cause the sensitive guest to decide that fasting was good for the soul. Flies were everywhere, in the air and in the food. A pile of manure was outside the dining room door, and the open doorway let you know it was there, buzzing with the next generation of dining-room flies. Tablecloths were often bedsheets, and if the tavernkeeper needed a "clean" tablecloth (for the table) it was sometimes snatched unceremoniously from the sleeping body beneath. In one tavern a guest who complained about the filthy condition of the establishment's only towel was told, irritably, that "Two hundred men have wiped on that towel and you are the first one to complain."

But as more settlers moved west across the American plains they left settlements behind them. Yesterday's ragged vanguard became villagers, occupying a cluster of cabins that proudly boasted a street or two; the settlements grew in size, and so did the pioneer tavern/hotel. Bachelors and newlyweds lived in the town's tavern. Many of the town's functionaries who were not farmers – the lawyers, merchants, and clerks – also made their home in the tavern and were the establishment's "regulars." The problems of tavern growth were solved by simply building another log cabin beside the original one. More growth? More accommodations needed? Build another cabin. Like a Daliesque dream the tavern would spread: the hydra Hilton, blossoming on the road to the west. One "hotelier" in Michigan referred to his place as a "nine-storey tavern." It consisted of nine separate cabins, a sort of horizontal highrise.

In Saxon times every small community had its designated brewer who assembled the necessary materials and brewed for all. As a guide to those seeking the brewer he hung a bush above his door. Travellers would stop at the sign of the bush, sure of a friendly tankard of ale and all the latest news of the community. The passage of time standardized the display of the bush and it became an accepted sign. The brewer mounted it horizontally on a pole that extended from the front door out over the street. A law enacted in 1375 regulated its height above the roadway, as there had been complaints from horsemen who got bonked by the pole as they rode past. In later centuries a ship's figurehead, set at the door of an English inn, was a common sight, though it never came to serve as the recognized designation of an alehouse or inn as did the simple bush.

Even in those early days there *must* have been individuals with minds oriented toward advertising, though the term "ad exec" wasn't current in the Middle Ages. These innovative minds, attuned to public relations, soon realized that if all alehouses were identified by a bush it would be difficult to push the merits of a specific establishment.

"I can't get too excited about the bush concept, George."

"A bit too generic do you think, J.B.?"

"Entirely too generic. Completely lacking in product identification. I'm not knocking bushes *per se*, you understand; nothing wrong with bushes, or trees, or even forests. I mean, I don't want to get on the wrong side of the environmental people, but what we need here is brand recognition."

"Like a catchy brand name, J.B.?"

"Exactly, George. Something like – now I'm just thinking off the top of my head but something like . . . 'The
Red Lion' or 'The Pig and Whistle'."

The alehouse sign was born.

The evolution – not to say convolution – of English inn
and alehouse signs can strain the imagination at times.

> It even puts Apollo
> To all his strength of art to follow
> The flights, and to divine
> What's meant by every sign.
>   – Ben Jonson.

The Mitre Tavern, a favourite of Boswell and Samuel
Johnson, was destroyed by the Great Fire of London in
1666. When the owners rebuilt it the following year, they
gave recognition to the Society of Musicians, who for
years had held recitals on the premises. Displayed over
the door was the society's emblem: a lyre, with a swan
depicted above it. Local wits quickly came to refer to it
as the Goose and Gridiron.

A few steps from the almshouses near London's Westminster Abbey, where William Caxton established
England's first printing press (1476), there stood two
taverns. One was called Heaven, the other Hell. Heaven
was at one time a private home; Hell graduated to
tavernry from its original use as a debtor's prison. Not
surprisingly, Hell was a bit of a dive. Diarist and civil
servant Samuel Pepys spent many happy hours scoffing
roast birds and ale in Heaven. Nearby there was a prison.
Its name? What else: Purgatory.

Communications problems have always been with us,
and sometimes an alehouse owner achieved oddity in
spite of himself. The publican of an alehouse called the
Seven Stars observed his sign was in need of repair, and
engaged an artist to repaint it. Asked by the artist what
the landlord wanted on the sign, the response was a
preoccupied shrug: "Oh, the same, yet." The artist followed instructions and to this day the house bears the
sign "The Same Yet." The fact that it is still there illustrates that landlords had a livelier sense of humour in
those days than they have now. Try pulling that trick on a
bar owner of today.

The Belle Sauvage Inn is another example of a communication gap between owner and sign painter. The

name is drawn from a French romance in which a beautiful woman is discovered running wild in the forest (a savage). The sign painter, not much of a reader of French romances, depicted a bell and a wild man (again a savage, though with a slightly different connotation in the artist's mind).

Times change and alehouse signs often change with them, publicans being nothing if not sensitive to the ebb and flow of sentiments and beliefs. This was especially so in the time of the Reformation in sixteenth century England. Before then, religious symbols often denoted an inn. But with Henry VIII's accession to the throne of England, and his subsequent break with Rome, signs like the Nuns were quietly changed to the Angels, while the Catherine Wheel became the Cat and Wheel.

There are in England over seven hundred inns or alehouses called the Royal Oak (it has also figured prominently for hundreds of years as a name for ships in the Royal Navy). The name dates back to 1651 when Charles II, fleeing Cromwell's troops after the battle of Worcester, eluded them by hiding in an oak tree. The adventure caught the public imagination and Royal Oak inns sprouted like weeds throughout the country when Charles was eventually restored to the throne.

We will probably never know how the Cock and Bottle originated. At present the sign carries the image of a cock, and beneath it a bottle. Some derivations have been suggested: it could be a corruption of Cock and Battle, in reference to cock-fighting, a bloodthirsty pastime of earlier days. Or the name might allude to the even crueller sport of cock-throwing, in which a bird was tied to a stake and the sportsmen stood back and threw bottles at it. Sweet bunch of chaps they were in the old days. Another understandable, and indeed appropriate, version is the Cork and Bottle; similar signs already exist, showing a cork popping out of a foaming bottle. Yet a further explanation, and one as logical as any advanced, is the word cock as another expression for tap or spigot. As far back as the late fifteenth century the term cock signified a tap or valve to control the flow of liquid. Thus Cock and Bottle could legitimately refer to a bottle and a tap through which ale was drawn from a cask; bottle and barrel – certainly a pertinent choice for the name of an alehouse.

As we have seen, time changes all things, and alehouses are no exception. The Bull and Mouth, an incongruous combination, was originally Boulogne Mouth, named after the French city and its harbour's entrance. With time, however, the English took the *gne* and pronounced it *on*, then *an*; a *d* then seemed a logical addition to form a recognizable word, and *voilà*, the name of the alehouse became Bull and Mouth.

A popular name for an inn, both the genuine article and the pseudo-British pub of North America, has been the Pig and Whistle. One derivation of this name is "peg and wassail," referring to King Edgar's pegging of drinking horns a thousand years ago in an attempt to moderate drinking, and the Saxon pledge *"woes hoeil"* or wassail, "your health."

You wonder, though, at the commercial value of an alehouse sign that bears the curt injunction "Pass By." Another is called, simply, "Q." You could miss it altogether unless raging thirst drove you in desperation to the door.

The alehouse sign had its origin in the illiteracy of the people. No point in writing "The Queen's Head" over the door if no one could read it. Instead, you got some talented fellow to paint the monarch's likeness on a board and hang it outside the alehouse entrance, then locals could direct a stranger: "Turn right at the next alley, old chap, and carry on until you come to the sign of the Queen's Head."

All well and good for the visitor, but not so good for the queen. So appalling were the renderings of the royal profile that Queen Elizabeth I, in a fury of wounded vanity, ordered every one of them burned. Henceforth the artist's talent was first proven; only then was he permitted to pick up his brush and announce to the world the opening of yet another Queen's Head.

The pun creeps slyly into many alehouse signs, the English being great ones for the play on words. Alehouses called the Sun, and there are a number of them, will often offer "The Best Ale Under the Sun." In London in the early nineteenth century there was an establishment called the Brace Tavern, originally owned by two brothers whose name was Partridge. The witty patrons, of course, referred to them as a brace of Partridges, hence the tavern's name.

The American pioneers adopted the old English custom of displaying inn signs, and for the same reason: general illiteracy. While there were talented sign painters in the eastern U.S.A., not many of them went west, judging by the quality of pioneer tavern signs. Chicago's Wolf Tavern displayed an image that could easily have passed for a sheep; a species of vegetation welcomed you to the Green Tree; and you would swear it was a turkey that adorned the sign of the Eagle. Ironically, in order to identify the illustration, you had to be able to read the sign!

In England early alehouse signs were executed by the artisans who painted the coaches of the wealthy. Egos then were as rampant as they are now. Coach owners had their vehicles decorated much as the drivers of today's custom cars will embellish their automobile creations. The owner's coat of arms was a standard design, if he *had* arms; if not, the coach painter would produce something pastoral perhaps, along the lines of the impossibly romantic work done by the leading portrait painters of the day. Indeed, by the 1700s much of the coach painting passed into the hands of these same professional artists, who augmented an often meagre living by illuminating coaches. The situation was not unlike professional novelists of today who make an attractive dollar, and keep eating between novels, by writing sales catalogues, newspaper articles, commemorative brochures, and similar "commercial" projects.

Until the mid-1700s there was even an outlet for "off the rack" alehouse signs. Artists would bring their signs to market – a special sign market existed in London – and a prospective customer would browse, fingering this, sneering at that, bargaining in an effort to bring the price down.

Among the recurring symbols used in inn and alehouse signs is the heraldic lion. Particularly popular is the red lion of Scotland. Also seen frequently in England is, naturally, the gold lion of England. Black lions, blue lions, and white lions abound, and are features in the coats of arms of various noble families. Neighbourhood alehouses and inns took these heraldic symbols from the arms of a prominent local family and incorporated them in their signs. To add confusion, however, simpler minds, unfamiliar with the arcane terminology and imagery of the armorial art, gave a common twist to the terms. The crescent became the "Half Moon"; roundle azure, "Blue Ball"; lion gules, "Red Lion"; boar azure, "Blue Pig"; chequé, "Checkers" or "Lattice," sometimes even "Lettuce."

Strange and incongruous name combinations were often simply the result of a merger of two alehouses, as in the Magpie and Crown. Sometimes the common people took a name that was a mouthful and reduced it to a more manageable form; thus God Encompasses Us, which is a name and a half, became the Goat and Compass.

The incomprehensibility, not to say absurdity, of many English inn signs leads us to believe that their origin might lie not in merger, or misunderstanding, or ignorance, but simply in the blind whim of an idle moment. Over the door of one London alehouse there used to hang a sign which said "The Four Alls," and bore an illustration of four men: a king, a priest, a soldier, and a common man. Under each was an appropriate motto:

king, "I rule all"; priest, "I pray for all"; soldier, "I fight for all"; and under the common man, in bitter resignation, "I pay for all." Well, at least it's understandable; a bit of humour in an alehouse sign. By the early 1800s, however, the sign had been altered to read "The Four Awls." A misunderstanding? Or perhaps a carpenter had purchased the alehouse and, struck by the name's phonetic similarity to one of his tools, had changed it to reflect his former trade. Or was it mere whim; nothing to do one afternoon, so they changed the sign?

Wild times, and localities that are fraught with danger, attract daring individuals, and most of those who are drawn to these dangerously exciting places do not have all their marbles – indeed insanity seems a prerequisite. How many sensible people sought gold in the Klondike? Exactly; comparatively very few. The gold-seekers' oddness was reflected in the names they gave to their drinking places, the dance halls, gambling halls, and saloons. The town of Skagway, gateway to the Yukon, had its share (Skagway, from the Indian *skagua*, "Home of the North Wind"). Oh, there were a number of normal names, of course; the area itself naturally generated names like the Klondike Saloon, the Nugget, the Northern, the Aurora, and the Bonanza. Then there was the Hungry Pup, the Mangy Dog, the Red Onion, the Board of Trade, the Always Open, the Home of Hootch, and the Dainty Toe.

Giving odd names to drinking places was not the private preserve of the Klondike gold-seekers, of course. Farther south, in the U.S.A., saloons were sometimes called "doggeries." England, as noted, also saw some strange names and images. Eastern Europe was no exception. *U Supa*, for example, is a medieval alehouse in Prague. The name gives a bleak cast to an old and venerated drinking place: *U Supa*, the Vulture. I don't know if I'd want to do much drinking under the sign of the vulture. Still, I understand a brand of pale beer has been on draught there for six hundred years, and connoiseurs claim the thick head can be sliced with a knife.

Martial, the Roman wit (Marcus Valerius Martial, c. 38-103 AD), claimed that Rome was simply one vast saloon. Wall-to-wall taverns were not, however, peculiar to the Romans. Commenting on the number of alehouses in

England's cities in the seventeenth century, a contemporary noted: "A whole street is in some places but a continuous alehouse, not a shop to be seen between red lattice and red lattice." (A red lattice was sometimes the symbol of an alehouse, as was the bush. As noted, the illiteracy of the time altered the word and we thus have alehouses named the Lettuce.) Neither Rome nor England did much to change the situation; the wine of one empire matched the beer of the other, with saloons as the common bridge across fifteen centuries.

In the mid-1600s, coach traffic from Dover and much of the south of England stopped at the south shore of the Thames River, at the foot of London Bridge. The narrowness of the bridge (it was only forty feet wide and lined on both sides with houses and shops) prevented the coaches from crossing into the city of London itself, on the north bank. At the south end of the bridge there were twenty-three taverns and inns to slake the thirsts and rest the aching bones of the many travellers (aching bones in spades: there was not much in the way of springs or shock absorbers in seventeenth century coaches. As the old joke says, if you rode over a sixpence you could tell if it was heads or tails).

An interesting sidelight on London Bridge: In the seventeenth century it was still the only bridge across the Thames, and remained so until Westminster Bridge was completed in 1750. London Bridge was supported by nineteen stone arches, an engineering gaffe that produced roaring falls and rapids beneath the bridge. So deadly were these rapids that small boats travelling the river were obliged to disembark their passengers on the west side at Swan Stairs (named after the old Swan Brewery nearby). Passengers then walked to Billingsgate Wharf just east of the bridge, re-embarked in other water craft, and continued their journey.

Instead of sensibly debarking west of London Bridge, walking to the east side and taking another water craft, some river travellers with more bravery than brains elected to "shoot the arches," a gamble that for many was their last. Wagner in *London Inns and Taverns* tells us "shooting the arches ... was ordinarily such a perilous enterprise that the landlord of the Bear Inn derived no small part of his custom from half-drowned passengers whose boats had been swamped or overturned in the process."

The Bear was a well-known medieval London inn. Records show it prospered in the very early 1300s. Its position at the south end of London Bridge provided it with much of the river traffic and coach trade between London and the south and east; it was eventually demolished in 1761 during the widening of the bridge. A contemporary engraving of the area shows the inn amid a hodge-podge of ill-assorted buildings, all clustered at the southern entrance of the bridge. Atop the archway leading onto the bridge is a score of pikes bearing the heads of criminals. A Royalist ballad of the mid-seventeenth century mentions them:

> Farewell Bridge Foot and Bear thereby
> And those bald pates that stand so high.
> We wish it from our very souls
> That other heads were on those poles.

Boswell and Dr Johnson, like most Londoners, accepted the London Bridge transportation hiatus with equanimity. On a trip to Greenwich, downriver from London, Boswell remarks, "We landed at the Old Swan and walked to Billingsgate, where we took oars and moved smoothly along the river." Unconcerned, they changed boats just as you and I would change busses.

Perhaps it's a bit severe to lean accusingly on the early London engineers and call their bridge efforts a gaffe. In 1582 they installed watermills in the bridge, and the hellish noise of these mills, together with the roar of the cataracts beneath the bridge, could be heard all over London. Add to this the dangers and inconvenience caused to river travellers and . . . well, yes, I guess you'd have to call it a gaffe. A seventeenth century engraving shows the bridge choked with buildings, many of them four and five storeys high. Living conditions in these dwellings must have been appalling, if only because of the noise of the river roaring through the arches beneath them.

And now a little bit of exciting info for the kiddies. The old song "London Bridge is falling down" refers to the bridge's delapidated condition. In 1481 one of the houses that crowded the bridge fell through the rotting planks, sank into the raging waters, and drowned five persons. As early as 1289, a century after the bridge had been built, it had been allowed to deteriorate; "the Bridge was so sore decayed for want of reparations, that men were afraid to passe thereon." Even 375 years later nothing had changed: Samuel Pepys remembers returning to the city on an October night in 1664. "Dark when we came to London [south end of London Bridge] . . . through the dark and dirt over the bridge, and my leg fell in a hole broke on the bridge; but the constable standing there to keep people from it [caught me], otherwise I had broke my leg – for which mercy the Lord be praised."

Alehouses and inns sprang up wherever there was heavy traffic. Highgate, now a part of Greater London, was in 1826 a village on the outskirts of the city and a busy confluence of stagecoach lines. As many as eighty coaches rattled through the town every day, bound to and from London and the northern counties. Nineteen inns provided travellers with rest and refreshment.

Proliferation of outlets for drink is not a British phenomenon. Hardly does man put his foot down in a new land than he's brewing something, and moments later sets up an establishment in which to sell it. The Pilgrims had just got off the boat in America when Samuel Cole opened the first tavern in Boston (1634). The year 1773 saw Captain Cook produce New Zealand's first beer. He hove to at the southwest tip of the southern island and waded ashore. His boots were barely dry before he was boiling up a batch of spruce, then adding molasses and yeast. After a couple of days the brew (sometimes called chowder beer) was ready to drink. In New France, you remember, Jean Talon was quick to build a brewery, and made a comfortable profit for the new colony. By 1896, Montreal boasted, if I can use that expression, a greater number of retail liquor outlets than the combined totals of Toronto, Vancouver, Halifax, Quebec City, Hamilton, Ottawa, London, Saint John, Winnipeg, and Calgary. Montreal was a real friendly town.

In nineteenth century America, the tavern was just getting off the ground, comparatively speaking. What with settling the western plains and exchanging views with the Indians, the pioneers had other things to do with their time. In 1830, the west – and in those days that meant anything on the other side of Detroit – was virgin bush. The western extent of the stagecoach line out of Detroit was the settlement of Niles, Michigan. The line was shortly to reach Chicago, but in 1830 Niles was it; Niles was where you got off, for good. Beyond Niles, commercial accommodation for food, drink, or rest was limited. In fact it was as limited as you could get: Zero. If you wanted to eat west of Niles you took it with you or you didn't get it.

The lack of taverns or inns obliged the western traveller to seek an alternative, especially when often the only accommodation he could see was a twenty-foot snowbank in sub-zero weather. Before commercial taverns became more frequent along the frontier roads, the traveller sought accommodation at a settler's cabin. The frontiersman's hospitality has, with time, become a legend; but the legend is not borne out by contemporary writers and diarists: they were there, and often received a welcome that was reluctant at best. The attitude of many settlers was, frankly: You don't want to stay here by choice, and I don't want you here either, but you're here now, so let's make the best of it. Sometimes the traveller was roughly turned away, regardless of his need.

As the number of taverns grew along the roads to the west, so did the "hospitality" of the settler's cabin decrease. To save a buck many money-conscious travellers would pass up the tavern and cadge accommodation at a farmer's home. As more people moved west, a settler found that his hospitality was ruinously expensive. Many frontier homesteads came to take a jaundiced view of the "needy" traveller, resented being made the instrument of his thrift, and simply refused to offer accommodations of any kind.

Paradoxically, in many instances the tavern owner was happy to see these travellers bed down with the local farmers. Settlers migrating to the west were the tavern-keeper's biggest group of customers, and generally the bunch he liked the least. It was simple self-interest: he would never see them again, thus there was no promise of repeat business to justify his attention to their needs; in addition – and this was the tavern owner's basic beef – the penny-pinching swine were foolishly intent on saving their money for the new life out west and spent as little as possible in his tavern.

"Inn", a Saxon word, originally meant simply a room. With time it came to apply to a larger dwelling, often a noble family's mansion. Medieval times – apparently a period of friendly openhandedness – saw these mansions used as rest houses for travellers when the owners were away, a naive exhibition of trust that would be astonishing today.

In those early days, to journey over an appreciable distance usually meant stopping at a monastery. Lunch might be enjoyed at one, supper and a bed at another. Two factors dictated this: the welcome and comfort of the clerical establishments, and the gross inadequacies of the wayside inns. The inns were little more than filthy hovels, and the wise traveller avoided them except under the most stringent necessity; the monastery, however, offered security, superior accommodations, good fare, and conversation that was more interesting and intelligent, not to say more spiritually uplifting.

In seventeenth century England – and little has changed over the years – alehouses catered to a specialized clientele. Literary types frequented one house in order to escape the coarser company of raffish journalists and gazetteers, who had their own tavern. Honest tradesmen avoided, for obvious reasons, the alehouses of cutthroats and highwaymen. If an alehouse was near a stream it almost automatically became an angler's house, happy to take a fisherman's catch, cook it, and serve it to him. Samuel Pepys remembers buying a salmon for eightpence in Fish Street, London, then popping next door to the Sun Tavern, having them cook it for him, and scoffing it on the premises. Attend a funeral and you were sure to find an alehouse, suitably sombre, and conveniently near the edge of the cemetery, that catered to mourners.

Within the larger towns and cities, these alehouses and inns saw competition grow in the form of coffee-houses, the first of which opened in Oxford, England, in 1652, according to Hackwood. The next decade witnessed the introduction of tea. The coffee-house served both, and as the taste for the new beverages grew so did the number of coffee-houses, which, like alehouses, catered to all classes. Though today they have intellectual and literary overtones, the coffee-houses of the seventeenth century were centres of radical politics and dissent, which could still be called intellectual, I suppose; the coffee-house did indeed seem to foster thought and discussion, and was the place you sought if you wanted to read a newspaper or exchange ideas, or simply take a cup of chocolate (another new drink, introduced in 1657) and smoke a pipe of tobacco, though in those days it was not called tobacco smoking but tobacco drinking.

In the 1780s, certain alehouses in England were known as smoke shops or smoking houses. There you would find a room, perhaps twenty feet long by fourteen feet wide with a meagre eight-foot ceiling, occupied by as many as thirty or forty men, each with an ale in his hand and a pipe in his mouth, and all of them puffing away as if they were trying to win a bet. It was the century of snuff, but there were still a lot of pipe smokers around. The waiter followed a standard ritual if someone came to the door and asked for one of the gentlemen in the smoking room.

"Is Ralph in there? I want to speak to him."

"Ralph? Good question. Just a minute." The waiter then passed among the smoke-shrouded patrons. With a pair of bellows he would blow the smoke away from the face of one. "Ah, Charlie. How's tricks?"

"Fine, fine, Phil. Look, do you want to watch those bellows? You're blowing ash all over my pants."

On to the next individual. More wind from the bellows. "Ralph? Oh, George; thought you were Ralph."

Voice from the doorway: "Any action, Phil? Is that Ralph?"

"No, it's George. Sorry, George. Here, let me brush off your pants."

And so it would go, until a violent puff of air from the bellows would blow ash all over someone else's pants, but would reveal Ralph hunched over an ale. "Ralph, someone wants to see you."

"Tell him I'm not here."

In seventeenth and eighteenth century London, drinking clubs enjoyed a vogue that has endured to the present day in one form or another (the local bar, cocktail lounge, or tavern is, after all, primarily a drinking club. Let them try serving lemonade and cookies, and see how long they keep their customers). Even in Greece of the fifth century BC there were clubs dedicated wholely and frankly to drinking. Sparta and Athens, to name just two cities, had drinking clubs of such closely knit fellowship that they became powerful political entities. The English drinking clubs, too, had strong partisan leanings which grew out of the violent political feelings of the period.

There were, for example, Royalist alehouses; but there were many others where the king's name was anathema. You had to select your drinking places with care. In some alehouses if you raised your glass in a toast to the king you might never be seen again. Literally. You'd end up in the river wearing the seventeenth century equivalent of a pair of cement shoes. The Black Dog Tavern, or "The Dog" as it was commonly called, was a Royalist hangout in London at the time of Cromwell's Commonwealth. There you heard quiet talk of Charles II ("when we did use to talk of the king . . . privately." Pepys) and a lot of muttering about the Restoration, and if you openly remarked, that old Cromwell was doing a damn fine job you would be taken home on a stretcher.

Politics apart, the main thrust of the drinking clubs was drinking. One group was called "Facers," a name derived from one of the house's rules: when a club member called it a night and rose to leave, if any ale was left in his glass he had to fling it in his own face. This would have been pretty rough on face and clothing, so the members habitually drank every drop; not too harsh a rule to observe, really, as these were fellows who would spend a shilling on ale before they'd see two farthings go toward food.

Still, in England as in America (and indeed everywhere), alehouses and politics, like meat and potatoes, seemed unavoidable. In nineteenth century America, towns sprang up in the wake of the western migration and the tavern was usually the first dwelling. The sequence was repeated in tiny settlements across the area: a settler would build a log cabin in the wilderness, the cabin would become a stopping-off place for travellers, the settler would decide to make it a paying enterprise and change his cabin into a tavern (or build one nearby), other settlers would build around him, and a small village would be born, and frequently take the name of the original settler, who was now the tavern-keeper. The tavern owner became an upstanding member of the community, and his tavern the focal point of civic activity and the unofficial chamber of commerce. This high profile, and the self-interest that led him to promote the town's commercial advantage, often carried the tavern owner on to political office: mayor of the community, magistrate, even governor of the state. The tavern was the political centre, where deals were made and unmade; the taverner, knowing everyone, and particularly who was who, and who was not, was right in the middle, wheeling and dealing with the best of them.

In the first half of the 1800s, while the American pioneers built their new settlements around the wilderness tavern, London builders extended the boundaries of the city in much the same fashion. A row of houses would go up, but only after a pub was constructed on the corner. The ratio of pubs to houses (families) varied greatly, but to provide the publican with sufficient custom a ratio of 1:160 was considered satisfactory. This meant, on average, a pub every two hundred yards.

In the latter half of the century, the Victorian upper class tended to frown on alehouses. They felt the tavern was low class: cloth caps, unspeakable dialects, and not an Oxford grad in the bunch. The gentleman's club, and the class distinction it fostered, became the vogue. Class distinction was not, however, unique to the club. Within the "low class" pub could be found the public bar, the saloon bar (a bit more expensive), the private bar, boxes which offered even more privacy, the ladies' bar, the snug, all with their own clientele, rigidly structured in the Victorian way. The snug, particularly, held (and still holds) an attraction for many drinkers, an attraction to which the Temperance advocates were unalterably opposed. The snug is a private compartment, accommodating from two to six persons. It's usually dimly lit, which is an element of its snugness (a gasp of outraged propriety from the Temperance folk; who knows what goes on in that dimness, that atmosphere heavy with hops and the wanton smiles of women, and men ... together ... in the dim light ... and the liquor).

The last two decades of the nineteenth century saw the popularity of these public-house compartments reach its zenith. Some London pubs had as many as nine or ten. They were often no more than three or four feet square, enclosed by head-high partitions, and were open to the bar at one end. At the opposite end a door gave access. Some were accessible only from the street and were partially closed at the bar end by an ornate glass or metal screen, open at the bottom just enough to permit drinks to be served, very much like a ticket window in a railway station. The opportunities afforded by such privacy were not lost on the authorities, who expressed a lot of concern; many recommended they be done away with. There were instances of robberies being committed in snugs. But it was difficult to deny the snug's attraction; privacy has its appeal. A man might like to have a drink with a lady, but for reasons of his own might not like to do it in public; businessmen preferred the snug when discussing the private aspects of their affairs. In some instances, due to pressure from the authorities, the snug disappeared, but the snug principle of privacy remained in bar divisions, elaborate eight-foot-high separations of scrolled wood and glass that extended three or four feet out from the bar.

A painting by Crowther, *circa* 1881, shows the interior of a London alehouse; at first glance it looks like a teenagers' malt shop. Opposite the fireplace, booths line the wall and you expect to see bobbysoxers of the late 1940s tucking into banana splits and ordering lemon cokes.

Yet it's difficult to accept Crowther's painting when we see interior photographs of Victorian pubs of the same decade. They gleam with glass and polished wood, highlighted by the newfangled electric light. Though gaslight was the illumination of choice, many public-houses had introduced electric fittings, and these were relatively common in the 1890s.

On the streets outside London pubs, at the close of the nineteenth century, street lighting was in its infancy; in many areas there was no lighting of any kind – other than the gin palace. The gin mill was a glorious beacon in the night. Some had as many as six standard lamps ranged along the pavement in front of the establishment, aug-mented by a further series of lights bracketed to the face of the building. As street lighting became more preva-lent and dimmed the splendour of the gin palace, the drinkeries installed bigger and more elaborate lamps. One light manufacturer produced a hanging lamp of such magnitude that four men could stand upright inside it.

Back inside the pubs, photographs show them alive with the Victorians' passion for detail and decoration; no surface is left unadorned, no adornment escapes further adornment as flourishes and scrollwork mount one upon the other. Beautiful glass windows and ornaments exquisitely etched and engraved, were prominent features of the English pub in the latter half of the nineteenth century. The embossed (etched) glass was treated in much the same way as a printing plate: the background was given a protective coating, then the glass was subjected to a bath of acid which ate away the unprotected, or image, area. The acid-treated glass was then ground, and the finished product presented a clear background and a softly obscure image. When back-lighted, naturally or artificially, the effect was striking.

Enamelling was another method of decoration in which a fine veneer of coloured glass was applied to the clear glass. Sometimes a design or lettering was gilded, using the same embossing procedure: The image (or lettering) was left unprotected and the acid was allowed to burn through the coloured veneer to the clear glass, on which the gilding was then applied. Compared to the beauty achieved by these processes, the ultimate advertising purpose to which they were put seems an anticlimax. "Irish whiskies" and "Fine cigars" appear somehow crass and uninspiring.

The London authorities took a dim view of the pub's passion for embossed glasswork. Glass partitions and screens were covered with curlicues, flourishes, birds, vines, bunches of grapes, and goddesses. Windows onto the street were impenetrable; embellishments went right up the wall (along with the authorities). To check what was going on inside the pub or bar or snug was impossible. The magistrates insisted that glass be adorned no higher than four feet; above that it was to be left clear – a ruling that met with much bitterness from fashion-conscious publicans, and in effect was largely ignored.

In New York, from the earliest days of the Victorian era, there has flourished a saloon named McSorley's. The bar's frontage on East 7th Street has to be the plainest in town, but it's nevertheless a New York monument. Established in 1854, McSorley's serves only ale, porter, and stout. It does not serve anything else – and that included women, until a 1970 legal action by a women's organization changed all that. A decade before the legal contretemps, the Irish novelist and playwright Brendan Behan described McSorley's: no hard liquor, and no women; lots of good ale and a first-rate raw onion sandwich, but no hard stuff and no feminine company. Behan had to leave his wife outside while he had a couple of jars inside the saloon. Grand old place, apparently; unchanged for over a century, which makes it somewhat special in these fast-moving times, where anything that's remained the same for more than twenty minutes is considered an antique.

In the 1890s in Chicago, for example, many saloons simply never closed. All night, all day Sundays and holidays; they were always open for business. The story goes that when a new saloon opened its doors the owner would walk down to the waterfront and toss the key into Lake Michigan.

Bartenders in the saloons were, for the most part, nondrinkers. When a patron offered them a drink they would demur, then add "But I *will* have a small cigar, sir," and select one from the saloon's box, "saving it for later." At the end of their shift the bartenders would return the evening's accumulated cigars to the box and take a credit in cash from the till.

There was an air of illegality about the saloon, even before Prohibition; an atmosphere of something secret, almost shameful, that should not be exposed to the light of day. Swinging doors hid the interior, and windows were blocked by grilles and potted plants. Inside, saloons bore a marked similarity; see one and you've seen them all. A bar ran along one wall, and a brass rail supported the weary drinker. Sawdust covered the floor. Behind the bar a mirror reflected an array of bottled wines and liqueurs that no one ever drank, but they lent a spurious tone to the bar, as if to imply that many of the regular customers took a glass of bordeaux on occasion and engaged in learned discussions of the merits of one vintage over another. Almost mandatory was a reproduction over the bar of a naked woman reclining on a settee. Her figure suited the taste of the times: an exaggerated hourglass. "You could span her waist with your two hands, but she couldn't sit down in a tub."

These were the saloons of the larger cities of the east. But step outside the metropolis, especially if your step took you westward, and you were in another world, tavernwise. No more brass rails, fancy mirrors, or sawdust on the floor ("Floor? What floor?"). The pioneer tavern, or "hotel" as some enthusiastic landlords called it, was often just a log cabin; a single room, as small as twelve by twelve (that's feet, though to the guest it must have seemed like inches). Windows were frequently nonexistent. Doors were doorways; no doors; at best just a blanket draped across the opening. The floor was often Mother Earth. Faced with the tavern's primitive sleeping arrangements many travellers resorted to the Tucson bed. Very simple: you lay on your stomach; your coverlet was your own back.

Privacy was an unheard-of luxury. The Tucson bed may have been pretty basic perhaps, but vastly preferable to the experience of an eastern sophisticate who woke one morning in a midwestern tavern to find that during the night another guest had arrived, found all the beds occupied, and had climbed in with him. Complete stranger, never seen him before. The easterner tried to discourage him by saying the bed had lice. The newcomer shrugged and said, "It's okay, so have I." Hoist by his own petard, the easterner returned back east – scratching.

Far from the glitter of the eastern saloon, the western tavern was unique – entirely *too* unique in the opinion of many travellers. Picture the frontier tavern of the early 1800s: a log cabin, with cracks between the logs through which you could drive a truck; a single room, sometimes without a fireplace, with blankets across windows and doors. Within these four walls the entire life of the tavern was conducted: eating, drinking, even dancing, and – at the same time – sleeping. Enter, and an incredible *mélange* of bodies meets the eye. A travelling preacher sleeps next to a hunter (complete with dogs); swearing, tobacco-chewing teamsters stretch out beside a pregnant woman with a small child; there are a couple of calves in a corner. Not quite the image generated by the flossier drinkeries of New York and London, whose bars were becoming more elaborate, and less discriminatory in clientele.

The flashy gin palace of nineteenth century London, with its higher degree of comfort and service, was responsible for the appearance of more and more women in the Victorian public-house. Few women with any self-respect would have been found within a thousand yards of the early "vulgar" drinking places ("Heavens no, my dear, the people are so ... so *common* ... really not our kind of people at all"), in contrast to their American sisters who, in the democratic tavern of the pioneer west, we have found cheek by jowl – often virtually in bed – with complete strangers.

The British pub, though staggering under the weight of the Victorian taste for finicky embellishment and endless decoration, nevertheless saw some minor changes generated more by convenience and utility than the decorator's nightmarish fancy. The 1890s saw beer-engine handles change from the ornate china of mid century to a plainer variety, sometimes trimmed with brass. (The china handles are now avidly sought by collectors. Will collectors generations hence seek as eagerly the draught beer handles that now carry the brewers' gaudy symbols?) The huge casks of whisky that once towered over the bar were also passing into history as more pubs turned to the stylish and convenient glass spirit urns. These dispensers were similar to the modern apparatus in today's cocktail lounge that serves a meas-ured shot into an upturned glass. The rococo Victorian urns were supported at intervals along the bar by wildly decorated standards. Urns and standards sported a lot of glass, all of it groaning beneath its freight of engraved vines, leaves, stars, diamonds, scrolls, cupids, and tons of other horticultural and mythological trivia.

Nineteenth century London pubs, like drinking places everywhere, tended by their very nature to be similar in layout. This sameness was alleviated occasionally by the taste, imagination, and interests of the owner. The walls of many establishments carried hunting prints, or maps; an ex-pugilist might put up photographs of prizefighters; one pub displayed the owner's collection of 80,000 butterflies; another pub, of a carnival inclination, had a two-headed calf on show; yet another public-house had a bugle, the very one, it claimed, that had sounded the charge of the Light Brigade at Balaclava (1854).

Along the Roman roads of ancient Britain the con-querors established *tavernae*, where a traveller could get a night's lodging, a nosh, and a flagon of wine. These wayside houses were not drinking places, specifically, but rather oases of rest and nourishment. Certainly there was wine, but purely as a facet of rejuvenation; the main purpose was rest and nourishment, for man and horse.

Taverns and inns, being natural gathering places, pro-vided the opportunity for men to discuss commerce; the inn has been a place of business since inns first opened their doors. The first man to order a beer probably did so on behalf of his client, and then proceeded to sell him something. Taverns and inns, around the time of the Restoration (1660), had no dining rooms or bars; guests would have their meals served in a private room, thus the businessman would have his prospective customer all to himself, free from the interruptions so detrimental to his selling pitch.

Down through history, inns have also been convenient for the conduct of legal (and sometimes illegal) affairs. Magistrates held court there. Mary Queen of Scots was imprisoned, briefly, at an inn before being transferred to a series of prisons where she languished for eighteen years until her execution in 1587. Guy Fawkes and his unsavoury associates did much of their plotting in inns (and in vain, as it turned out). In the mid-eighteenth century James Boswell, lawyer and ultimate chronicler of the life of Dr Samuel Johnson, often discussed legal affairs with his clients in a friendly tavern. This was by no means a peculiarity of Boswell; as noted, the tavern as a place of business was a firmly established practice in that time. In England, until the turn of this century, many legal functions – special sessions, inquests, and so on – were carried out in the local alehouse, especially in rural areas. But in 1907, by law, the alehouse was no longer considered a court; henceforth legal matters had to be conducted in England's recognized courts of law.

In the early nineteenth century, London's pubs also provided facilities for social organizations and entertainment. Local clubs, benevolent societies, fraternities, and a vast range of other groups (from the Postman's Federation to the more esoteric Society of Cigar Box Makers and Paperers, and the London Society of Sawyers, Clickers, and Rough Stuff Cutters, whatever that was) all met and conducted their business in the pub. Most establishments had a large room upstairs, available for meetings, musical evenings, or stage productions. Soon these rooms were too small to accommodate those who came to enjoy the singers, dancers, and theatrical performances (and have a couple of pints, too). Larger halls, or saloons, were added to the original pub. In many, people could enjoy a meal (and drink) while they watched the show. One such saloon, part of the Eagle Tavern, first opened its doors in 1831 and boasted accommodations for 10,000 patrons.

The meeting rooms were the seeds which eventually grew into the variety theatres that flourished at the beginning of the twentieth century. The meeting room of the 1800s became the centre of local entertainment, and progressed over the years to music halls that were part of the pub. Everything went well until 1843, when a law was passed requiring the pubs to name their game: either they were music halls (no drinking in the auditorium) or they were pubs (no entertainment in the bar). Many made the break and became fully independent music halls, and over the span of half a century, evolved into the immensely popular variety theatres.

As was the case in England at the time, the American tavern on the road to the west also served various needs. It was an auction room, a government land office, even a pulpit for travelling evangelists, in addition to its more frequent use for local civic promotions and club meetings. Like its English counterpart it served as a courtroom. The circuit judge often stayed at the tavern. His visit was the signal for a holiday, and brought settlers in from the surrounding area to join in activities such as horse-racing, visiting friends, loafing with other loafers on a bench in front of the tavern, or just plain drinking. Drinking was the big activity; so much so that often the noise of the singing, shouting, and general crashing around in the adjoining barroom stopped the legal proceedings, and the judge and his associates had to march sternly and resolutely into the bar – and have a couple of snorts themselves.

The medieval distinction between English tavern, alehouse, and inn was, up to the seventeenth century, quite marked. The inn accommodated the traveller, and the tavern sold food and drink. Cross over that well-defined line and you could find yourself in the magistrate's court. In the mid-1600s, however, the line between the two was beginning to blur, and understandably so; you could hardly expect an inn to adequately care for the traveller's comfort without offering him something to eat or a glass of restoring ale to put the glow of health back in his cheeks.

Taverns were victuallers, and sold food and drink on a more substantial basis than did the alehouse. In the beginning the tavern sold only wine, and the owner was called a vintner. Again, the dividing line between tavern and alehouse was firm and clear. The law did not permit casual drinking in the tavern; you went there for a meal, with which you could drink wine. If all you wanted was a couple of jars (or more, but just drink), you went to the alehouse.

Credit was as much a problem then as it is today. ("How much is the beer, George? Seventy-five pence? Got change for a £500 note? No? Well, how about I pay you next week?") These lines displayed in an English inn typified the standard view held by innkeepers:

> Since man to man is so unjust,
> I cannot tell what man to trust:
> My liquor's good, 'tis no man's sorrow,
> Pay today. I'll trust tomorrow.

In England, during the 1600s, there occurred a short-age of small coins, and businesses which dealt with large amounts of small change suffered. The first half of the century in England saw the bourgeoisie of small shop-keepers expand, and trade – in the sense of daily purchases of a loaf of bread, a chunk of meat, a pot of ale – demanded more of the tiny coins of the realm: halfpennies and farthings (quarter-pennies); remember, at this time you could get perhaps a couple of quarts of ale for a penny. What happened if you just wanted one quart, or a pint?

What happened was the birth, in 1648, of the trader's token. Lack of trust caused the withdrawal of James I's farthings, and the Civil War (Cromwell and his bunch) delayed the issue of genuine small change. The shop-keeper thus had two choices: he could offer credit (not bloody likely) or mint his own change. He wisely chose the latter. During the time they were in use (1648-1672) over three thousand kinds of tokens circulated in the city of London alone, and close to a thousand of these bore the name of a tavern or inn. The tavern tokens, in denominations of halfpenny and farthing, were approximately three-quarters of an inch in diameter, and usually carried on one side the sign and name of the establishment and on the reverse the street in which it was located and the initials of the owner. For example, the Mitre Tavern in Fleet Street:

Obverse: *Will Paget at the* (illustration of a mitre)
Reverse. *Miter in Fleet Street W.E.P.* (that is, Will
Paget)

Apart from serving as a means of exchange, the token,
because it displayed the tavern's name and sign, was also
a mild form of advertising; the sign particularly, as many
potential customers could neither read nor write.

Circulation of the tokens was understandably limited.
The diarist John Evelyn, writing at the time, remarked,
"they were payable through the neighbourhood, though
seldom reaching further than the next street or two." A
shopkeeper would accept tavern tokens only if he recognized the coin, knew the source, and was personally
acquainted with the tavern owner, which naturally
restricted the token's use as a medium of exchange.

The vast array of bottles behind the bars of today's
taverns and restaurants makes it difficult to visualize the
limited choice in the saloons of a century ago, especially
in the pioneer west. We have to bear in mind the primitive conditions that existed in the nineteenth century
western tavern. In the centre of the barroom, set in a box
of sand, was the stove. In winter it provided heat and hot
toddies and water for washing and shaving. The walls of
the room were whitewashed; rough benches and
wooden chairs stood casually about. Slippers hung on
the wall, and guests could wear them instead of their
own mud-covered boots. Along one wall was the bar,
cluttered with the guests' coats and packages; amid all
this was a pile of newspapers, some candles, a tinder box
for cigars and pipes, an inkstand and quill pens perhaps,
for those who might wish to write a note to friends. Any
space left over was used to serve drinks.

In the saloons of the cities you could have a beer (not
by brand name, just "beer," because before the Prohibition era the average saloon was owned by a brewery and
served only one brand of beer). Or you could have a
whisky. Behind the bar were bottles bearing the labels of
popular whiskies (though reports claim they all contained the same whisky). In the early 1800s a gallon of
this whisky cost twenty-five cents (the "take-out" price).
Per glass prices over the bar were, from the time of the

Civil War (1860s) until the 1890s, five cents for a beer and ten cents for a shot of whisky (you can bet your shirt the gallon jug of whisky didn't cost you twenty-five cents in *those* days). Dives charged a nickel for a shot of whisky, but made up the difference by cutting the liquor with water, and maybe adding a touch of cayenne to give the customer the jolt lost in the cutting. The yardstick was: if it didn't leave permanent scars in your throat, and have the top of your head smoking, then it wasn't the real thing. If you ordered a whisky you got a bottle of bourbon, an empty shot glass, and a glass of water as a chaser. You poured your own shot and drank it straight (not to do so was an indication that you were not a real man). If you poured your shot to the very brim of the shot glass you would be asked, icily, if you wanted a towel, implying you were having a bath in the stuff. If you didn't want beer or whisky, the only other thing you could get was a fight, and there was usually someone to oblige you.

In the 1830s beer in London sold for threepence to fourpence a pint. A typical gin palace charged you three to four-and-a-half pence for a quarter-pint (5 oz., 150 mL) of gin; it was usually bought by the glass, or gill (one-eighth of a pint, 75 mL). One gin shop calculated that they served in the ratio of nine gins, nine rums, one brandy, and four ports. Brandy was ninepence or tenpence for a quarter-pint, and port was fivepence.

On the west coast of the U.S.A. during the latter half of the nineteenth century, a shot of whisky cost a little more than it did in the saloons of the east and midwest. In the west a shot cost a "bit," as in two-bits (twenty-five cents); a bit was twelve-and-a-half cents. (The term "bit" originated with the Spanish presence on the west coast of North America. The Spanish peso was divided into eight small silver coins, or bits. The Spanish coin is gone, but the bit is still with us in the terms two-bits, four-bits, and six-bits).

How much a bit was worth depended on the saloon you frequented; some charged you the "long bit," fifteen cents, or the "short bit," ten cents. In most places, however, standard practice was to give you two whiskies for two-bits. You paid your quarter and got two shots. But if you only wanted one, the bar issued you a brass check which could be used for one shot at some future time (a west coast variation on the traders' tokens of England's earlier days). By World War I the bit and the brass check were history, and a shot of whisky cost you a flat fifteen cents; French champagne was $1.75 a pint, which illustrates that the ratio in price of whisky, beer, and champagne hasn't changed that much over the past century.

As if to compensate for the primitive (not to say neo-lithic) conditions in many American taverns and inns of the nineteenth century, the barroom provided a reading "room" for the traveller's use. Often little more than an area next to the bar, it nevertheless carried newspapers from the east, and contributed to the tavern's position as the communications centre of the community and the place to exchange ideas and information. If you wanted to read the newspapers, however, you had to be fast; patrons soon pirated the pages for use in the outhouse.

In the latter part of the nineteenth century American taverns and saloons were more than just social centres where a man could drink and talk with his friends. They were the very hub of political activity, both savoury and otherwise, where politicians bought and sold votes, and aspirants to civic office found their hopes raised or dashed according to the political climate or the whim of the powerful. "The groggery," said the St Louis *Daily Republic* in 1888, "[controls] the city's affairs." New York's Greenwich Village in 1850 had a saloon on almost every corner, which is understandable as the majority of its inhabitants were Irish and German, all fair hands with a cool stein. At election time candidates circulated among the saloons, smashing people on the back, glad-handing anyone who was warm and stood upright, and buying beer for one and all. The passion for politics and affairs of the day, both foreign and domestic, was such that committees from each of the parties tested the country's political waters with a tentative toe by visiting the taverns in an area and listening to the opin-ions expressed there.

Drinking and the political process went hand-in-hand in pioneer America. The tavern was often the polling place in elections, which was a very profitable arrange-ment for the tavern owner, and of course convenient and refreshing for the voters. It seemed quite normal, if not altogether acceptable, that these voting days turned the tavern into a noisy, brawling, drunken place to be avoided, where it was rare indeed that a voter emerged unhurt. A contemporary reported he felt himself lucky to have suffered *only* a broken arm and various bruises while having a quiet drink at the bar on voting day.

The term "caucus," meaning a gathering of politicos for the purpose of electing from among themselves representatives in a constituency (or the engineering of an election, as the cynic might view it), is said to come from the Greek *kaukos* (cup). The etymology is not so surprising, really, when you consider the beer drinking that must have gone on both in and out of caucus; certainly the political hopefuls in the U.S.A. at the turn of the century used any cup, *kaukos*, mug, glass, or flagon to lubricate the flow of votes in every saloon in town.

7

Drinking Vessels

Anglo-Saxons esteemed drinking vessels to a degree that seems exaggerated today. They buried cups with the dead; tankards of various kinds were also bequeathed, with the expressed wish that they be used to toast the memory of the donor; in early woodcuts of kings victorious in battle, the pile of booty always displayed numerous cups, horns, and flagons, implying that drinking vessels were valuable prizes of war.

The ancient Gauls drank from the horns of wild oxen. These primitive cups were often ornamented with gold and silver. But the Gauls were not restricted to the ox horn. They also slaked their thirsts from the skulls of enemies slain in battle; or, to lend a touch of ancestral pomp to their frequent draughts, they used the skulls of their own parents – certainly a worthy filial gesture. From these vessels the poor drank beer or hydromel (mead with herbs for flavour); the rich and powerful drank wine.

Drinking from a skull. Well . . . frankly, as a drinking vessel the skull, even a family one, is revolting, plain and simple. However – no accounting for taste – the idea of drinking from the skull of an ancestor appealed to Lord Byron. Tales of the Gauls holding aloft the ale-filled skulls of their forebears incited the poet's young imagination. He dug around the graves on his family's estate in the hope of unearthing a satisfactory example. He didn't find one. His ancestors had no head for drinking . . .

There is another version of this skull business. J. P. Hughes maintains that the "skull" referred to is actually a word of Scandinavian origin, *scull*, meaning goblet. From this comes scullery, the storage place for goblets and other kitchen utensils, and the surname Scullion, to identify the lout who worked in the scullery (the Oxford

English Dictionary does not agree, but when do we ever get a consensus in matters of etymology?).

Old prints and woodcuts show us the eating and drinking habits of our ancestors. The impression gained is one of gargantuan appetites and thirsts. In some prints the celebrants flourish round-bottomed glasses, indicating that the vessel could not be put down while full, hence the term "tumbler", a word originating in the time of the Saxons, who were great ones for not putting down a full glass. These ancient woodcuts seem the work of untalented children. The characters are stiff, their expressions . . . well, wooden. They exhibit little emotion; the artist appears unable to invest them with any expression other than a cold and Frankensteinesque detachment. Rigid and indifferent they stare out at us. Perhaps they're simply resigned. They may even be more than a little irritated over the instability of the tumblers; even we, as much as we like ale, would rebel at having to hold the glass all evening. Or maybe they're just stunned by the strength of the medieval ale.

While the characters portrayed in these prints were Saxons and other types from the Middle Ages, they were certainly not the first in their capacity for drink or for their inconvenient vessels. The Greeks were pretty fair right- and left-handed drinkers, too, and used a vessel called a rhyton, shaped like a ram's horn. Try putting a ram's horn back on the table while it's still full of ale.

England's George – Prince Regent, and later King George IV – possessed a number of little, and not-so-little, idiosyncrasies. He was a snuff freak, and that is no idle slang expression; "freak" is the only term. In his numerous residences he had special rooms set aside exclusively for the storage of huge quantities of snuff, enough for a dozen lifetimes. Another of his quirks was to break the stems off wine glasses so they could not be put down while they contained any wine, a habit he must have learned from the Saxon ancestors of his subjects, whose round-bottomed tumblers encouraged deep and frequent draughts.

Many of the older drinking vessels were made of leather and coated with pitch on the inside to make them watertight. The black jack, for example, or the bombard. One of the earliest mentions of black jacks occurs in 1383, where a document records the purchase of some "leather pots" for King Richard II. The bombard, a short bulbous cannon with a wide muzzle, gave its name to the enormous leather jacks used to carry ale to the table, where the brew was then decanted into piggins (wooden cups) or smaller black jacks. (The name "bumboat," the small harbour vessel that carried supplies to the larger ships in port, is also derived from bombard.)

The term "black jack" is generic, signifying leather drinking vessels of all sizes, from the handy half-pint mug to the mammoth multi gallon variety that could hide a small boy. Some of the larger ones, the bombards, were of necessity fitted with spigots, which is understandable when you consider the tidal wave that could result from trying to pour a pint from a seven-gallon bombard (provided you could lift it). In almost absurd contrast to the huge bombards, the Chinese artisan Hao Shih-chiu (circa 1600) produced porcelain wine-cups of such breathtaking delicacy that each weighed less than one-forty-eighth of an ounce.

Leather black jacks had an advantage over other containers. When our forefathers felt like a beer they didn't play around with today's effete eight-ounce glass. Two-quart tankards were not out of line. There were pewter flagons which carried two *gallons* and weighed a staggering twenty-three pounds ("Evening, Mr Smith, what'll you have?" "Oh, twenty-three pounds of ale will be fine, George."). There were leather black jacks, however, with a capacity of over seven gallons that weighed a mere seven-and-a-half pounds – an early version of light ale.

Unlike German ceramic steins, the English black jack was generally without a cap or closure. I say "generally" because right away someone is going to show me a jack with a metal cap. These infrequent capped jacks appeared in small villages, tiny communities that could not support an alehouse. A thirsty citizen who wanted a quantity of ale for home consumption might have to go a considerable distance to the nearest outlet. If you have to go to that much trouble you don't want to spill a drop, hence the cap.

Black jacks came in numerous sizes. They ranged from cups of perhaps a half-pint to mighty jacks sixteen to twenty-one inches high (almost half a metre), containing six to twelve quarts (five or ten litres) or more. These, as we have seen, were pitchers; those who sat round the table then poured the beer into pewter cups or other more convenient drinking vessels.

Gispens were small leather mugs of a quarter- to half-pint capacity. In the casual spelling practices of the sixteenth and seventeenth centuries they were also called gyspen, gyspyn, and gespin, which pretty well covers all the bases. The gispen was an insignificant item. It lacked adornment, and no skill or artistry went into its manufacture. Comparatively speaking, there were few gispens in common use; the majority of mugs were of wood. Large varieties, of perhaps a quart or more (a litre, say), were similar to barrels in construction, with wooden staves held together with metal hoops. Unlike today's drinking vessels, small cups and mugs were often little more than shallow bowls (or deep dishes if you prefer), a design that undoubtedly developed as a result of the irritation and spilled ale caused by clumsy medieval tumblers and drinking horns.

Some leather mugs, adorned with small silver bells, were called, appropriately, "gyngle-boyes" (an early journal called them "jingle-boxes"). "It formed a test of sobriety for the person to drink from the vessel without producing a tinkling." Glasses, too, carried ornament, some in questionable taste: one, the "Last Drop Glass," bore an engraving on the inside of the base depicting a hanged man swinging from a scaffold, a grisly reminder that at the bottom of this glass, at least, the "last drop" would always remain.

Another odd, but at least utilitarian, cup was the whistle tankard. Attached to the brim, or sometimes part of the handle, was a whistle which the drinker sounded when he needed a refill. (Could this be the origin of expressions like "wet your whistle" or "if you want something, you can whistle for it"?)

While not constituting a drinking vessel *per se*, the "growler" nevertheless is part of the beer-drinking tradition. The name, according to H. L. Mencken, comes from the Dutch *grauw*, the "great masses of the plain people." The growler was a can or pail used to carry out beer purchased in a saloon for consumption off the premises. Typical Temperance engravings of the late nineteenth century showed a little girl – never a little boy, always a sweet, innocent little girl – picking up a bucket of suds for Daddy. We see her in the doorway of the saloon, surrounded by leering, drunken ruffians, all deeply into the sauce. The artist made a big thing of the harsh lights of the saloon, backlighting the men, their eyes glowing satanically, the little girl's face in full light, radiating purity and innocence. In any event, for the purposes of our discussion, the bucket she carried was a growler.

In King Alfred's day (ninth century) the tun, a barrel containing 200-250 gallons, often took the place of rent: so many tuns of fine ale, perhaps, for the use of certain lands. This suggests a reliance on the brewer's integrity that was absent in later years. In the early sixteenth century Britain prohibited brewers from making their own barrels. The reason appeared in the act promulgated in 1531. "Whereas the ale brewers of England have used, for their own profit, to make their barrels of much less quantity than they ought to be, to the great hurt, prejudice, and damage of the King's people ... " To paraphrase a great American president: You can trust some people sometime, but you can't trust some people *all* the time. And of course, there are some people you can't trust *anytime*.

To attempt to rationalize old English measures is enough to cross your eyes at the best of times. And as eye-crossers, ale and beer measures met the most mind-boggling criteria. There were barrels, tuns, butts, puncheons, casks, hogsheads, firkins, kilderkins, pipes – the list is staggering. In addition, the meaning of each term seemed to fluctuate, casually, at the apparent whim of the moment. A tun was equivalent to two pipes or four hogsheads, and contained (sometimes) 252 gallons. But wait! A pipe was generally 105 gallons; with two pipes to a tun, two times 105 leaves you a bit short of 252 gallons. More confusing still, a hogshead held 100 to 140 gallons, which gave you a certain latitude, though I suppose much depended on whether you were buying or selling. Yet, wait a minute; a butt had two hogsheads of ale sloshing around inside, for a quantity of "usually" 108 gallons, which meant that *one* hogshead was fifty-four gallons – a substantial departure from the happy hundred-gallon hogshead mentioned earlier. Puncheons were the equivalent of two barrels, or seventy-two gallons. A firkin was a quarter of a barrel, one-eighth of a puncheon; or, if you wish, a half-kilderkin. A kilderkin itself carried sixteen to eighteen gallons. Thus a firkin contained eight or nine gallons; a barrel thirty-two to thirty-six gallons, or approximately 144 quarts; or you could take a cask, which held just about anything you cared to name, then multiply by the number of days in the week, subtract your age, and divide by two . . . and you have the best argument in the world for the metric system.

Barrels were fine for carrying large quantities of ale around, but these days they're not that convenient for home consumption. You can't nip over to the beer store for a six-pack of hogsheads, not unless you're an Olympic weightlifter. Bottled beer solved the problem (a further refinement was the beer can, introduced by an enterprising Virginia brewery on 24 January 1935). Legend gives the humanitarian award for the discovery of bottled beer to Alexander Nowell, the dean of St Paul's Cathedral in London. Back in 1563 the noble churchman took a day off to fish one of the local rivers. For his refreshment he carried a handy bottle filled with ale and stoppered to prevent it from spilling. He followed the course of the river, fishing the more likely pools, and absentmindedly left the bottle of ale on the riverbank. A few years passed. One morning he rediscovered the brew by the river. He found that the ale was not only still good, but actually *better*; it had matured in the closed bottle and was foamy and full-bodied; it was "not a bottle but a gun, such was the sound of it when opened."

Storing a bottle of beer on a riverbank, notwithstanding the dean's success, isn't smart. Repeated exposure to the morning sun will have its effect. Good storage methods have been developed over the years. For example: Do you ever find yourself with half a beer – a half you don't feel like drinking? Yeah, I know, maybe once or twice in a lifetime, but seriously: it happens, and you can't throw it away, can you? Yet, if you leave it overnight in the fridge, you'll end up with flat beer. Well, over a century ago a Yankee doctor gave us the answer: Take the bottle, "put in the cork firmly, and turn the cork end downwards in a large tumbler or other vessel nearly filled with water. This prevents communication with the external air." Well, not too many beer bottles carry corks these days, but avoiding contact with the air is a good point to remember. Store your bottled beer upright, not on its side. The reason for vertical storage is simply a matter of exposure to air: resting horizontally, more beer is exposed to the air in the bottle. The fifty-beer-a-week man may find a certain amusement in the term "store," given that his beer hardly has a chance to pick up a modest chill in the refrigerator before it's scoffed, either by him or his equally thirsty friends – and a man with fifty beers in the fridge always has friends.

8

Beer and Food

In the early sixteenth century, before the insidious habit of starting the day with a cup of coffee took hold, a pot of ale was *the* morning drink. A typical breakfast for two – for the upper classes, admittedly – consisted of a loaf of bread, a quart of beer (that's forty ounces, or 1.18 litres) *and* a quart of wine, two pieces of salt fish, and ten herrings. Not bad for openers. The common man and woman also drank their share. Breakfast for the rabble was a loaf of bread, *two* quarts of beer (eighty ounces, 2.36 litres), and three boiled mutton bones. Neither were the children denied; they had a couple of small loaves of bread, a quart of beer, a dish of butter, a piece of salt fish, and a dish of sprats. Then along came supper, and the grown-ups sat down to a loaf of bread, a *gallon* of beer (that's four quarts, 160 ounces, or around four and a half litres), and a quart of wine.

The queen's maids of honour in the time of Henry VIII must have been Amazons, I mean proper *Valkyries*! Don't get on the wrong side of *these* girls. Before they were hardly out of bed of a morning they put away *two gallons of ale*. A very substantial way to start a day. For lunch there was another gallon of ale. For supper yet another. Knowledgeable twentieth century sources claim that the human body requires three pints of fluid daily. I guess the queen's maids of honour were pretty safe. These same modern-day pundits maintain that tales of the gargantuan thirsts of the sixteenth century English are exaggerated. Take the queen's maids of honour: four gallons a day. Great Scott, that's sixteen quarts! Exaggerated? Perhaps. But exaggerated to what extent? Maybe they only drank *half* that much. A mere eight quarts. A little simple mathematics will show that *those* consumption figures, at least, *are* exaggerated. The human body –

and it hasn't changed that much in four hundred years – eliminates around half an ounce of alcohol per hour. Four gallons of ale, even at today's 5 per cent strength, adds up to thirty-two ounces of alcohol. You'd need a sixty-four-hour day to eliminate it all. Those girls must have had livers like sharks'.

These maids of honour were not unique in their Rabelaisian consumption. A gallon of ale (say, thirteen or fourteen of today's bottles) was the normal daily intake for everyone in the sixteenth century. A contemporary observer noted that the English drank no water, except for religious purposes, or perhaps as a penance. The Duke of Northumberland allowed each member of his household a quart of ale per meal; even young lads eight years old got their quart.

In these same Tudor kitchens the caterer provided – what else? – "cates." Cates were the delicacies, as opposed to standard fare such as beer, bread, and sides of beef. Being of a perishable nature, they were the responsibility of one individual, the caterer. You did not, of course, find caterers operating among the rabble. The masses didn't have a problem with perishables. First of all, they could afford neither the caterer nor his delicacies; perishables? the man on the street never gave them a chance to perish. He scoffed them.

The sixteenth century was a thirsty period. With only a gallon of ale for breakfast, and faced with the bleak prospect of having to wait simply *hours* for the afternoon gallon, there was frequently a break around noon for a "nunchion" (from *noon* and *schencken*, to pour). Those oriented toward semantics will want to compare the word *luncheon* (from *lunch*, a large chunk of bread). A bit of confusion naturally arises from the similarity between the two words. Don't let it bother you. If you're having a piece of bread, call it luncheon; if, like many of us business types, you're drinking your lunch, it's nunchion.

In those days ale had a very high profile. Its consumption was monumental, and it was a major item on a very short list of comestibles. Both the upper and lower classes saw little variety on their tables. During the reigns of the three Edwards (I, II, and III, spanning the years 1272-1377) the ordinary Englishman on the street (in those days the agricultural labourer) enjoyed a limited diet: herrings, beer (naturally), rye bread, some peas and beans perhaps. Special occasions saw a piece of cheese appear on the table. A typical Elizabethan breakfast often featured beef or ham – and ale, of course. Those who could afford it drank wine and ale with supper. (Even today some European countries drink ale, liquor, and wine with meals; and at the same time, too, not in any arbitrarily established order.)

At the time of the Tudors and before, the evening meal sometimes consisted of a chunk of bread – a *sop* – drenched in soup, gravy, wine, or similar. Thus from *sop* comes *supper*, the last meal of the day. In the early 1500s the Percy family of Northumberland – whose regimen is as good an example as any of noble habits – left their beds at six in the morning, quaffed their morning draught around seven o'clock – and you can bet it wasn't beer in that wealthy and powerful household dined at ten, and sat down to supper at four o'clock. Sack time was nine o'clock in the evening. Queen Elizabeth I (1558-1603) followed much the same routine: up at six, at seven a couple of fast flagons of ale, dinner at eleven, and then it was off to the theatre to catch the one o'clock show. Supper was around five or six o'clock.

In the 1800s, while much of Europe starved as a result of incessant wars, the British farm labourer still managed to tuck away a breakfast that would put most of us in the emergency ward. A slab of bacon "as big as a man's coat," a couple of gallons of boiled beans, "and a brown loaf the size of a beehive." Also, to wash it all down, a flagon of mead, "sweet and mellow, but strong as brandy."

The ale of those days was strong and inexpensive. A labourer once said that he didn't think much of a beer if it didn't give him three falls for a shilling, which, I suppose, is as good a yardstick as any.

Beer or food, alone or in combination, have always been synonymous with hospitality. Especially beer. What friendly door ever opened without a glass being thrust into your hand? Ancient Britons, naked as jaybirds, gave you a mug of mead to wet your throat while you painted your body in preparation for some wild pagan celebration. Early Egyptians eschewed the European glass or tankard and simply stuck a fresh straw through the scum on their communal tub of beer and invited you to drink your fill. Sydney Smith, with his hospitable tongue in his cheek, reminds us that the South Sea cannibals were never without cold missionary on their sideboard. Even Temperance folk, proving the rule by the exception, would make a point of *not* giving you a drink.

Hospitality has taken some bizarre forms. When Czar Alexander I of Russia visited London after contributing to the defeat of Napoleon (the first time, 1814), his English hosts whisked him off to a brewery – what better symbol of British life? On all sides he saw vats the size of ships, and was suitably impressed to learn that the monetary value of the contents could maintain an army in the field for months. Pushing tradition a bit farther than the Czar might have liked, the brewer served the monarch a steak, fried up as nice as you please on a shovel and accompanied by a pint of the brewery's best.

Steak on a shovel might have been all right for visiting Russian monarchs such as Alexander, but domestic royalty demanded a frill or two. In 1811, for example, at Carlton House, the London home of George, Prince of Wales (later George IV), the Prince Regent gave – some might have said flung – a midsummer fête for some two thousand guests. The main table was graced by the Regent himself and the exiled royal family of France (Napoleon was still doing his *shtik* on the continent); the banquet table extended for two hundred feet beneath the gleaming chandeliers of the mansion's Gothic conservatory. The table creaked under its freight of fish and fowl; out-of-season fruits overflowed from silver bowls. There was champagne for all. Amid this bounty a winding stream could be seen, wending its tinkling way between the dishes for the full length of the table. Guests could glimpse gold and silver fish moving languidly below the water's surface.

Well, if you can't have a peanut butter sandwich and a glass of beer, you just have to make do with what you have.

At the same time – worlds away from George's silverware and sparkling streams, powdered wigs and mincing ways, bright Regency dreams and leisurely days – the American pioneers "dined" in the wayside tavern on the road to the new lands of the west. Tavern dining along the American frontier in the early nineteenth century was an exercise in self-preservation. Definitely *sauve qui peut*. Like Pavlov's dogs the guests were called to the table by a bell, and like a pack of hounds (or a drove of swine as one witness put it) they poured into the dining room, often causing a bottleneck in the doorway where hopeful first-sitting diners struggled, pushing and kicking. Others behind fought to get through. It must have looked like something from the Keystone Kops. To save the women from physical injury they were allowed in before the bell sounded. If you missed the first sitting you might have had to wait a whole three or four minutes for a place at the table; eating was silent and efficient, and the best utensils were a long arm and a sharp elbow. It was every man for himself.

A further wry counterpoint to George IV's convoluted magnificence – and this is not intended in the slightest degree as a knock to the Scots or a commentary on their thrift – was the reception of Charles II in East Fife in 1651, on the occasion of that monarch's coronation in Scotland. A carpet – very nice; excellent material – covered the table. There were some buns "of fine flour," some wheat bread, and nine or ten gallons of strong Scottish ale. They fired off a few cannons when the king left.

Between the extravagant tastes of George IV and the simple frugality of the Scots (many of whom weren't too keen, anyway, about having Charles II as king) lies a kaleidoscopic panorama of food and drink that makes the mind reel. One of the distinguishing features of humankind, as fundamental to the race as the opposed thumb or a sense of humour, is its inability to leave well enough alone. And nowhere is it more exemplified than in matters of eating and drinking. Hand a man a simple preparation and right away he has to *add* something to it. Adding, adding, always adding.

On a cold winter's eve in Olde England, at meal's end, along with a fragment of fine old cheese, our merry forefathers settled down to a pot of strong ale to which they added a spoonful of ginger; the ale was then boiled on the fire. When it was steaming fragrantly they served it in a tankard over a slice of toasted bread. (The addition of pieces of toast to a soup, or a slice of toast to a beer punch, adds the aromatic properties of bread released in the toasting.) In the early 1700s, instead of supper, you might have had a pot of buttered ale: unhopped ale, sugar, cinnamon, and butter, served hot. In the fourteenth century, a less complicated time, a customary bedtime snack was simply a gallon of beer and a quart of wine.

More adding to and playing around with drink went on in Henry VIII's time, too. Court memoirs of the period tell us that "at coronations or banquets it was invariably the custom to dilute the genuine wines, and to cover the harshness and acidity which they possessed by mixing them with honey or with spices." Thus compounded they passed under the generic name of piments (or pigments), because they were originally prepared by the *pigmentarii* (apothecaries), and used in the same manner as the liqueurs of modern times. Flagons of strong ale and mead were also available with which the noble knights toasted the ladies present at the feast.

Henry VIII didn't originate the diluting and adulterating of wine. Among the Romans it was the accepted practice to add salt water to wine to bring out the flavour. If you drank your wine straight, undiluted, they considered you a lush. This Roman view was probably the result of their (often violent) contact with the Gauls. The Gallic boyos didn't fool around with water in the booze. Straight beer and wine – undiluted sauce, that was the ticket. The second century Greek historian Appian claimed the Gauls were, by nature, a bunch of drunks. History backs him up a hundred per cent.

The Canadian Indian, in the old days, didn't mess around with fancy sauces, delicate seasonings, or any of the other elaborate culinary additives of our decadent society. Cook it till it's done, eat it while it's hot, stop when there's no more left. Nice and simple. Here's a sample: Fill big metal pot with beans. Boil. Put beaver tail over fire. When skin loosens, pull it off. Add beaver tail to beans. When ready, eat.

Well, it's nutritious; but even the Indian had to add something.

Still, the adding to and embellishment of recipes for food and drink has, from earliest times, had only one goal: pleasure. Be it taste, sight, or aroma, the paramount aim is the pleasure experienced by the consumer.

"Food for pleasure, not just nourishment," said Nicolas Freeling, noted cook and gastronome, "is best cooked in one's own kitchen, and eaten with the feet under one's own table." While true, this shouldn't limit you to eating at home. Food for pleasure, that's the key. One authority maintained that those who are indifferent to the pleasures of the table are generally gloomy, charmless, and unamiable. Avoid that sad state and strive to enjoy your food and drink wherever you may be.

A particularly enjoyable combination is the hors-d'oeuvre, served with the drink of your choice. Hors-d'oeuvres span the taste and visual spectrum from the simple to the obscenely complex. Simple is best. An example was the delightful hors-d'oeuvre once offered by a Montreal cocktail lounge. Your waiter brought a small Hibachi to your table, the charcoal flickering warmly, and served you a plate of beef cubes which you then grilled yourself while you sipped your drink. It was great for the lounge; every afternoon at cocktail time there was a line-up to get in. But the practice had to be discontinued. The establishment's adjoining restaurant was a wasteland of empty tables. After five or six drinks and a couple of plates of beef cubes, who wanted supper? The Hibachi and beef cubes may have had their origin in the tidbits so successfully provided by a fellow called Cooper, who kept an alehouse in London in the nine-teenth century. Patrons could choose from a selection of beef cubes, chops, and so on, and take their choices to the grill chef and have them cooked to order.

Simplicity is often the secret to the enjoyment and state of well-being we all seek. H. L. Mencken recalled the habits of the night editor of a Baltimore newspaper whose early evenings, at least, were generally examples of well-being, "for there was a good dinner under his belt, with a couple of globes of malt to wash it down, and all of his reporters were transiently sober." Simple pleasures, not the least of which were sober reporters.

Mencken again tells of an elderly gentleman of Balti-more who for years performed prodigies at the supper table at Tommy McPherson's eating-house in that gastro-nomically oriented city. Every evening the old man walked the eight blocks from his hotel to the restaurant – dressed to the nines in tail coat, white waistcoat, and gold-headed cane – sat down, and began. First: three straight whiskies. Then *two* double porterhouse steaks, *two* large plates of peas, *two* plates of French fried potatoes, *two* plates of coleslaw, and uncountable slices of rye bread. Occasionally he called for more potatoes or bread. To help all this on its way, he drank two quarts of burgundy, and ended the meal with three more straight whiskies. He then lighted a cigar and strolled back to his hotel. This ritual was repeated, without deviation, every night, year after year. To prepare himself for his evening meal, he ate a light breakfast, and no lunch at all. He believed beef was the only safe, wholesome, palatable food; he took the vegetables, more or less, to give the steaks a little company on the plate. He considered Maryland whisky "the most healthful appetizer yet discovered by man."

However, simplicity (if simple is the word for the Baltimore gentleman's diet) can be pushed too far. Ogden Reid, the millionaire American newspaper tycoon, preferred the brash company of his newspaper cronies over the titled dinner guests that nourished his wife's social pretensions. Great wealth did not necessarily mean wealthy tastes. In the kitchen of his 84th Street New York mansion languished a chef of international fame, while Reid, blind to the delights of pheasant under glass, champagne, and sole *Marguery*, subsisted for days on the olives from martinis and the free lunch in Jack Bleak's speakeasy, conveniently located next door to Reid's New York *Tribune*.

Toward the end of the Roman domination of Britain (500 AD) the original inhabitants would gather for an *al fresco* supper around three-legged tables set in a forest clearing. Meat and fish, both boiled and broiled, accompanied bread baked in the ashes of the fire. The natives drank quantities of mead and beer from cups of horn or wood, or rough flagons made of brass. As night fell, huge torches illuminated the festivities. The flaming tapers were bundles of rushes, great armfuls twisted together to form torches the size of a man, then soaked in oil and ignited, the flames from which could be seen over vast distances.

It makes a rather homey picture, doesn't it? Bunch of friends, sitting around, scoffing food and drink, maybe a couple of songs in the flickering light from the torches, lots of healthy fresh air, followed by a good night's sleep under the stars.

That was the natives. The Romans were another story. Still, let's give them their due; in Roman times a meal at least started with the veneer of decorum one would expect from the rulers of the world. The Roman dining om was the *triclinium*: guests reclined on couches around three sides of a table, leaving the fourth side free to facilitate the serving of the various dishes. Some claim the *tri*, or three, prefix had a deeper meaning. Each couch sat three people, reflecting the three Graces: Aglaia, Euphrosyne, and Thalia, symbols of all that is joyful, charming, and beautiful. Three couches, or nine people, represented the nine Muses: Calliope (epic poetry), Cleio (history), Erato (love songs), Euterpe (lyric poetry), Melpomene (tragedy), Polyhymnia (song, rhetoric), Thalia (comedy; she was also one of the Graces – they were moonlighting even in those days), Terpsichore (dance), and Urania (astronomy).

The Romans might lounge around in their triclinium; the Greeks, however, in the thirteenth century BC, sat on chairs placed around the walls of the dining room. Between each of the chairs was a small table. Ranged along the walls, the diners must have seemed like attendees at a church social, though most ecclesiatics of today would frown at the Greek's habit of spearing food with his knife and scoffing it with his fingers.

Not leaving well enough alone had its Roman expression in a loud and liquid catalogue of excesses that stretches as far as the eye can see down the corridor of the Roman centuries. Oyster scoffing, for example, is not a recent aberration. The Roman emperor Vitellius (emperor for a very brief period – a few months in 69 AD; hardly time to scoff an oyster, really) could "with beastly voracity exemplify the gluttony which prevailed in the time of the caesars by eating a round thousand of oysters [no more, no less]."

In those days, dining not wisely and entirely too well could be hazardous to your health in ways other than those to be found at the table. Roman roads were superb from Rome to London, but local pathways often left much to be desired. To guard against an adverse end to a pleasant orgy at a friend's house, the Roman guest brought, as part of his retinue, servants called *adversatores*. These boyos would light the lords home along the dark roads, holding high a lantern and pointing out, much as a tour guide might, dangerous stones and other perils unseen by their merry masters.

Ancient times saw the emergence of the "sin-eater." The sin-eater was obviously familiar with basic marketing: look for a need and fill it. When someone passed away, along came the sin-eater who offered to take onto his own shoulders the sins of the dear departed, and send him directly from this unhappy place to Paradise. No stops along the way; no Purgatory. There was, of course, a small charge. A piece of bread, a pot of ale. No big deal. Small enough price to pay to ensure the happy deliverance of the soul in question.

The sin-eater's compensation of a pot of ale and a piece of bread was a common combination. The tie between beer and bread has always been close; the origin of the word bread, as we have seen, is the Saxon *bréowan*, "brew." In the medieval monasteries the brewery was generally next to the bakery. Mmmm, what a grand aroma must have risen from that area of the monastery.

"To earn one's daily bread" was more than just an expression in the medieval English monastery. The numerous factotums (factoti?) serving the establishment received their wages in ale and bread, perhaps with a bit of meat and some fruit. ("Well now, Marcus Pluribus, how long have you been with us? xxv years? My my, *tempus* certainly does *fugit*, doesn't it. Well, I've decided to give you a raise from two to three quarts a day, starting *Januarius primus*.")

Dining habits during the Regency (1811-1820) would have disgusted most present-day diners. A contemporary observer notes that "your plate would contain, say, a slice of turkey, a piece of stuffing, a sausage, pickles, a slice of tongue, cauliflower, and potatoes. According to habit and custom, a judicious and careful selection from this little bazaar of good things was to be made, with an endeavour to place a portion of each in your mouth at the same moment." Even first-year engineering students will know that this is impossible using the standard fork. A corollary of Murphy's Law states that food falls off a fork when it is one inch from the mouth and the diner is wearing his best clothes without napkin. The only answer – a revolting one, and still practiced in some circles – was to mash everything together on the fork with your knife until you had what amounted to a coarse purée forced between the fork's tines.

Regency diners, incredibly, felt that wines like bordeaux – and burgundy for Heaven's sake – were "poor, thin, washy stuff." Instead, they started, at the very sound of the dinner gong, with sherry and port, and didn't put their glasses down till the final belch. A couple of bottles each was not out of line. Understandably, many finished the meal absolutely bombed out of their minds, unable to rise from the table unassisted, which suggests that the scores of footmen at these soirées were not there to serve the numerous courses, but rather to carry the diners to the smoking room where the supper guests would toss back two or three double brandies and complete the work begun by the sherry and port.

Even in tough times there have been those who have found a way to indulge in excess. For many Americans at the turn of this century, the relentless sameness of their days, and the pennies (literally) they gained from their work gave a dull cast to their eyes, minds, and attitudes. But Diamond Jim Brady dazzled, and gave a still-current epithet to the language through the jewels that gave him his name. Brady was a super salesman, a representative for an American railroad supply house when railroads were proliferating like rabbits. His credo was: "If you're going to make money you have to look like money." Brady, with his almost pathological penchant for diamonds, looked like a million. And sold accordingly. His commissions put him into the seven-figure bracket overnight, and he lived up to his image. He once gave a dinner for fifty friends that lasted from four o'clock on a Sunday afternoon until nine o'clock Monday morning (some of the guests had to go to work, which must have been a ludicrous exercise, given the 500 bottles of champagne consumed over the seventeen-hour banquet). The bill came to more than $100,000 – plus tips.

Diamond Jim's financial excesses are the stuff of legend; no less so are his prodigious efforts at the supper table. A nondrinker, he would begin with a gallon of chilled orange juice, followed by sixty or seventy oysters, a saddle of mutton, five or six chops, a roast chicken, a couple of ducks or partridges, and a soufflé containing a dozen eggs. If a dish was particularly nice he might have a second helping. His friends used to place bets on when he would drop dead. Once, after a noteworthy supper, Brady said: "that sole was marvellous. I've had nine helpings and even right now, if you poured some of the sauce over a Turkish towel, I believe I could eat all of it."

Diamond Jim liked attractive scenery, and while demolishing the food, would surround himself with a number of the chorines from Ziegfeld's current Follies.

Someone, he felt, had to be there to drink the champagne.

We have seen the Roman emperor Vitellius lay the pattern for Diamond Jim by consuming a thousand oysters at a sitting, and Brady's sixty-plus shows he was doing his best to live up to the emperor's example. Oysters are not in themselves a symbol of excess, but somehow they always seem to be around when excesses are going on. "In the old days," said Brillat-Savarin, "any banquet of importance began with oysters, and there were always a good number of the guests who did not hesitate to down one gross apiece [that's 144 of the little fellows]." Calculating that a dozen oysters weigh in at around four ounces, a gross totals a substantial *three pounds* (almost one and a half kilos, if you're metrically minded). And this is the antipasto! Then comes the fish, the fowl, the entrée dripping with fragrant juices and sauces, the salads, the cheeses, fruits, pastries – the mind reels.

And yet, who first ate an oyster? Who, driven by what mortal hunger, cast aside his revulsion, closed his eyes, muttered a prayer, and . . . swallowed one? The poet John Gay (1685-1732) agrees:

> The man had sure a palate covered o'er
> With steel or brass, that on that rocky shore
> First op'd the oozy oyster's pearly coat
> And risked the living morsel down his throat.

In the years before World War I, Chesapeake Bay oysters were glorious beasts, the pride of Maryland. "Fat, yellow, eunuchoid monsters at least six inches long," according to H. L. Mencken, who undoubtedly scoffed his share. Visitors to Maryland, faced for the first time in their lives by such an oyster, generally turned white. However, if they were oyster fanciers they tried one and it usually went down without choking them. "An oyster is a very pliant and yielding animal," said Mencken, "and is also well lubricated [and, in the natural course of things, further lubricated by countless steins of beer]. To cut one up would be regarded, in Maryland, as an indecency to be matched only by frying soft crabs in batter . . . soft crabs are always fried (or broiled) in the altogether, with maybe a small jockstrap of bacon added."

Then there is the story of the titan known to history only as "The Irish Oyster-Eater," whose accomplishments in 1839, on the very threshold of death, still astonish us. "The day before he finally took to his bed, from which he never rose, he devoured [240] full-sized Malahides in 19 minutes and 35 seconds, with ease." That's one oyster every five seconds.

Leaving aside the sexual aspects of oysters, they are also very nutritious. They even have medicinal properties, apparently; the famous diarist Samuel Pepys once used oysters to combat seasickness. As a public servant in Britain's Navy Office, he occasionally found himself aboard ship. In early April of 1660, around nine in the morning, he was on board one of the navy's vessels at the mouth of the Thames when a high wind came up and the ship started to pitch and roll. "I began to get dizzy and squeamish," he said. "Before dinner my Lord sent me down to eat some oysters. After dinner, and all afternoon, I walked upon the deck to keep myself from being sick, and at last about five o'clock, went to bed and got a caudle made me [caudle: a dish of thin oatmeal, laced with ale and spices] and did sleep upon it very well." Let's hear a round of applause for the iron-clad stomachs of the Restoration.

When we consider excess in food and drink we tend to think only in terms of gluttony, volume, ultra-sophistication, and lavish display. There is, however, its antithesis, and it's just as valid. Excess lies at both ends of the spectrum: gluttony – and starvation. The term "epicure" suggests exaggerated refinement of culinary taste; some see the term as synonymous with gluttony. Yet the Greek philosopher Epicurus himself (341-270 BC) claimed he lived on bread and water. Bread and water indeed, sneered his enemies. They alleged he fasted only after he had abused his stomach with an overabundance of rich food and wine. His weakness, they laughed, lay in his self-control as well as his philosophy. Yet he wrote to a friend, asking him to send a bit of cheese, that he might put it to one side until he felt like "a sumptuous feast." The Metropolitan Museum in New York has a head of Epicurus, the bearded face grave and unsmiling, as if he were a little disappointed, even secretly hurt, at the meagre supper – bread, water, a small piece of cheese – that has been set before him in the belief that a crumb of cheese was, as he claimed, a banquet in his eyes.

An example of excess, in its grimmer sense as the opposite to opulent dining, occurred in the winter of 1812, as Wellington's ragged army retreated to the hill country of the northern Portuguese border. The men were freezing, drenched by icy rain, racked by disease, without hope, and with little food; in their extremity they ground their few grains of wheat between the rough stones found along their route. "Queer it was, to see and hear an army sitting on the sod, each man with two big stones grinding his dinner."

The winter of 1898-1899 saw sophisticates in Montreal relaxing, warm and comfortable in fragrant restaurants, scoffing with satisfaction steaming birds, fish, and tender beef. Across the continent, struggling over mountain passes in temperatures of fifty below, with raging winds tearing the frozen flesh from their faces, the Klondike gold-seekers dined, if I can use that expression, on beans dropped along the trail by previous stampeders. The beans, unspeakably dirty and frozen to the consistency of bullets, eventually thawed in their stomachs, providing the nourishment the men needed to press on blindly to the golden rivers of the Yukon.

Mencius, or Mang-tze (fourth century), a Chinese philosopher and considered second only to Confucius in the history of Chinese thought, believed that the fundamental nature of men was to be good(!), and that the evils of society were the fault of bad governments, not bad men. Given that kind of odd thinking, Mencius' equally odd taste in food doesn't surprise us all that much. "Fish is what I like," said old Mang-Tze, "so are bear's paws; but if I cannot have both, I will forego the fish and choose the bear's paw." Well, there's no accounting for taste. Though perhaps "taste" is not quite the correct term, because bear's paw must be cooked until it's tasteless. Once you've achieved this, continue simmering after adding pieces of ham, or a touch of sherry, or something along those lines, for flavour. You might think about beer instead of water and sherry.

Strange tastes, stranger food. An ancient Sybarite, tasting with a dubious spoon the Spartan's black broth, that purportedly nourishing bowl whose constituents are unknown, exclaimed, "I am not astonished that you Spartans are so fearless of death on the battlefield, since anyone in his senses would rather die than be compelled to live on such execrable food."

Strange tastes indeed, especially when compared to the uncommon good sense of the Puritans. Their view of what was sensible often clashed with that of the drinking public, but even the Puritans knew the nutritive value of beer. When they settled in the new world at Plymouth they brought beer with them. Fresh vegetables were not always available, and beer took their place in the pilgrims' diet. As their ship progressed along the coast of North America, a passenger's diary recorded the pilgrims' prime concern: "We could not now take time for further search . . . our victuals being much spent, especially our beer." Good thinking, lads. First things first, by George. You can settle a new country anytime, but the lack of beer is serious!

Shrove Tuesday, the threshold of Lenten abstinence, in earlier days often saw a feast of beer pancakes, a delightful nosh celebrated in the children's rhyme:

> The pancakes made of milk and beer
> Are made for no one present here;
> There's one for Peter, two for Paul,
> And three for Him who made us all.

Further to this Lenten dish, an interesting twist to Sunday morning pancakes is a topping of beer and brown sugar. I'll leave the consistency up to you; some like it thick, some like it shloopy.

Milk was quite the thing in seventeenth century London. In many of the city's parks it was the fad to drink a can of milk straight from the cow. Little kiosks dispensed it to passersby. Charles II had a milk bar in St James's Park. On a summer's day you would hear the cry, "A can of milk, ladies, a can of red cow's milk, sir!"

Red milk?

Notwithstanding the milk fad, beer and ale were still the preferred beverages in those days. Even in the barnyard. An English recipe book of 1671 tells us how to fatten poultry: "Let them have . . . strong ale to drink [along with their food]. They will be very drunk and sleep; then eat again." Get bombed, eat, sleep, then get bombed again; sounds like a pretty strenuous regime.

There are those who can spend a satisfying hour over a pot of ale and a good Havana cigar, and in their minds plan menus for themselves. Silently, alone in their delicious world, they visualize the various courses, from antipasto right through to the final fragment of cheese. To sit reading a book next to these people can be a distracting experience, what with the frequent grunts and whinnies of pleasure as they picture a particularly nice dish, or a fleeting flourish of the cigar as they silently instruct the waiter exactly how they wish the dish prepared. After an hour of this they are cross-eyed with hunger.

Eccentric perhaps, but then the history of food and drink is awash with eccentrics. Oddities abound, though often odd only to those unused to local habits. Moose milk, for example, is not an oddity to the people on the east coast of Canada. Feel like a snack? Go ahead, have a sandwich and a smash of moose milk. I'll leave the sandwich to your own taste. Moose milk? Well, we have our friends in the Maritimes to thank for this one – if "thank" is the term I want – at least for the fiddleheads: One part fiddleheads (puréed in your blender), one part clam juice, three parts wine.

There is nothing eccentric in marinating fish in beer before you cook it; it adds to the flavour. Fish-eaters might bear this in mind. Real fish-eaters, like those on Canada's East Coast, probably prefer to drink the beer rather than expend it in a marinade. These are the people, after all, who, during the haying season in Nova Scotia (at least in the early nineteenth century) enjoyed a lunch of bread, curd cheese, and thick strong rum.

Brewis is a Newfoundland delicacy, a fish stew, consisting of, roughly – again the cook's hand controls the originality of the dish – a boiled conglomeration of codfish, hunks of potato, pork fat, and ship's biscuits (the enduring pilot biscuits which "when you bang 'em on the table you break the table.").

The similarity between the Newfoundlander's brewis (pronounced *brooz*) and the north of England farm worker's *brose* catches the attention (if only momentarily), though the construction of the two dishes is quite different. The Englishman's brose was simply raw oatmeal drenched with boiling water, sometimes relieved by the addition of a lump of butter. The ploughman's lifespan was understandably a short one.

Leaving Newfoundland and pressing on farther north, we stumble over "Pounded Dry Fish Pudding." Yes indeed, there's no accounting for taste. Take half a dozen dried, smoked whitefish. Pound them, add sugar to your particular taste, a bit of grease, then add cranberries! The Inuit used the fish in this recipe to feed their dogs. At times, when forage was hard to come by in winter, the same fish provided feed for cows. Recipes like these make you appreciate the sight of Asterix, the Gaul of cartoon fame, chomping away at something as straightforward as an entire roast boar and drinking foaming beakers of *cervoise*.

In the *Accounts of the Lord Treasurer of Scotland*, from the fifteenth century, appears the entry: "for [1000 gallons] of cider and beer, nine pounds [sterling]; for 12 barrels of ale for the King's ships, 14 shillings and fourpence; for ale that the King's horse drank, ninepence." You can lead a horse to water . . .

Hey, hold on a minute. Let's just think about that for a moment. That's a lot of ale for one horse. Your handy pocket calculator will tell you that fourteen shillings and fourpence for twelve barrels of ale means around twenty pints for a penny. If the horse drank ninepenceworth . . . holy mackerel! One hundred and eighty pints of ale! Those fifteenth century horses didn't fool around.

Then again, it may be that the term "horse" signified a mounted troop of cavalry; troopers have never refused a pint, ever. But perhaps – and I feel this is closer to the truth, human nature being what it is – this was an early instance of padding the king's bills. If you can't rip off the nobility, who can you rip off?

In October of 1274, Richard de Insula, bishop of Durham, journeyed from London to his home county in the north, and along the way stopped for the night at the Angel Inn in Blyth (now a North Sea port). A "light" nosh before retiring consisted of:

Pane
   (bread) .... 10 shillings
Cerevisia et vino
   (beer and wine).................. 33 shillings 5 pence
Prebenda feno
   (hay for horses) .... 18 shillings 9 pence

Admittedly, the usual bunch of retainers accompanied him, but still, thirty-three shillings for ale and wine! At perhaps a penny or two for a quart of ale in those days, and even two or three times that for wine, that's still a lot of quarts. Bishops, like everyone else in those thirsty times, had a firm hand when it came to emptying tankards.

Business being business, prices varied just as they do today. In the time of King Edgar of England (tenth century) the beer drinker could get three or four gallons for a penny. As always prices were a reflection of costs. In the thirteenth and fourteenth centuries the cost of beer related to the cost of grain. In 1266 when barley was one shilling and eightpence a quarter (eight bushels, or 3.5 cubic metres), brewers sold two quarts of beer for a penny. A half-century later, in 1302, three shillings and fourpence was the cost of a quarter of barley, and beer was three to four pennies per gallon, or about double the price. Later in the fourteenth century – a good period for beer drinkers – a penny bought four quarts of ale. In fifteenth century England the price of ale, fixed by law, was one-forty-eighth of the cost of eight bushels of malt: If those eight bushels were selling for two shillings, a quart of ale cost the consumer a halfpenny.

Beer was considered such a necessity of life that it was natural the unethical brewer would try to take advantage of what was already a very good thing by refusing to brew, thus holding the thirsty public to ransom in order to jack up the price. The city of London took a very dim view of this. A law of 1533 stated that if "any of the said brewers, of their forward and perverse minds, shall at any time hereafter suddenly forbear and abstain from brewing, whereby the king's subjects should be destitute or unprovided of drink . . . " then they got the axe, in spades; no fooling around. The penalty was outright confiscation of the brewery. One day the brewer would be laughing; the next he'd be sitting in the street, an ex-brewer. Try pulling that on the millionaire multinational brewers of today.

Twentieth century beer drinkers are sadly aware that the halfpenny quart of ale is nothing more than a pleasant memory of medieval times; to the masochist the nineteenth century, too, carries reminders of good times long gone. Hey, remember Flannery's? Flannery's saloon in New York's Greenwich Village, *circa* 1880, offered beer in glasses "as large as parlour aquariums." Price: a cool five cents.

In London in the 1890s a pint of beer cost you twopence in a pub's public bar, fourpence in its saloon bar. Gin, on which in Hogarth's time (eighteenth century) you could get "dead drunk for twopence," cost twelve times as much in 1890: two shillings, but you got a *pint* of it.

Mention the word "saloon" and most people will visualize brass rails, sawdust on the floor, moustachioed bartenders, foaming beakers of beer, maybe a snatch of ragtime piano – and a free lunch. Now, let's be realistic: "free" lunch? The saloon was a business just like any other, and no business stays in business by giving things away free. The saloon permitted you to sample the free lunch *only* if you were generating some action at the bar. Somewhat the same situation existed in England. In Samuel Pepys' day the working man could bring his piece of meat or fish to the pub and have it cooked and served to him – on condition that he buy a pint of ale. If he didn't buy a beer he would certainly have been requested to leave. In the American saloon they didn't play around with "requested to leave." The bouncer grabbed the seat of your pants, the back of your collar, and you didn't touch the ground till you landed in the street. (That's probably the *real* reason for the swinging doors: the bouncer didn't have a free hand to open an ordinary door, thus swinging doors were not for ease of entry, but rather ease of ejection.)

So much for the "free" aspect of the free lunch. How about the "lunch" part? The sardelle, a tiny fish, was a mainstay. It was marinated in brine and very salty, and (a key point) less expensive than the sardine, whose oil inhibited the action of alcohol, and neither the saloon nor the customer wanted that. There were dry sausages such as cervelat and bologna, dill pickles, maybe some green onions. Often a large pot of baked beans occupied the centre of the table, flanked by a glass of dirty water containing a number of forks used by the customers to sample the beans. All this came with lots of rye bread. The amount and selection of food could vary from one saloon to another, but the accent was unfailingly on saltiness and cheapness, and its availability based unequivocally on the purchase of whisky and beer.

Thus we see that the idealized picture of the saloon's free lunch as a delectable montage of food, yours for the taking, is without foundation in fact. The actual free lunch in the average saloon was limited, of dubious quality, and almost without exception highly salted to generate thirst. Its very last purpose was to provide nourishment. Only the most expensive establishments offered anything that would today be considered a satisfactory buffet. Bouncers discouraged the freeloader; in the poorer saloons the bartender himself vaulted the bar, suitable club in hand, and did his own discouraging.

In 1902 if you had a dollar in your pocket you could buy a dozen quarts of premium Canadian ale. Eighty-five years later when, for many of us, if a dollar was dynamite we couldn't blow the fuzz off a bee's back, those same twelve quarts set you back about twenty dollars. When you consider the buying power of the 1902 dollar was the equivalent of approximately ten dollars in today's currency, you realize intuitively that you are getting shafted for close to ten bucks, and we all know where *that* goes, don't we? (The price of a beer in Canada in 1984 – and have things changed? – was split three ways: one-third to the brewer, one-third to the retailer, and one-third to the tax man.) Britons, to cite only one example, are familiar with the same story. They annually spend about $18 billion on beer, give or take a billion or two, of which 39 per cent is taxes (1985).

Cost and prices of food and drink tend to find their equitable levels if left to normal day-to-day market influences; drastic fluctuations are due to violent natural and social upheavals like wars, plagues, crop failures, and famine. One such period was the Klondike gold rush of 1897-1898. During the first winter in the Yukon the gold miners faced unspeakable privation, where food and drink had no cost at all: Food was beyond price because, quite simply, there was none. In 1897 in Dawson City – the settlement that sprang up at the confluence of the Yukon and Klondike Rivers – an omelet was unheard of, if for no other reason than the need, really, of more than one egg. One egg, if you could get one, cost one dollar. The price alone would make the omelet a rarity: at a buck apiece for eggs you'd hesitate to break one.

The following spring (1898), the first man to reach Dawson City with eggs – he had 200 dozen – was welcomed as if he were the Messiah. Within an hour he sold the lot for $3,600. A buck and a half an egg; compare that at your local supermarket. Remember, in those turn-of-the-century days, down south in civilization, you could buy an entire meal for four-bits. As a comparison, a dollar and a half is like paying $15-$20 an egg today. Again, down south, a nickel bought two *baskets* of tomatoes; in Dawson City they were $5 *a pound*. Mencken tells us that during the same expensive period in the Yukon, reporters in faraway Baltimore were allowed fifty cents for supper money. "Across the street from City Hall," he said, "there was a saloon in which a dinner consisting of a T-bone steak, a dab of fried potatoes, a slice of rye bread and a cup of coffee could be had for a quarter, and most of the reporters patronized it, and so made a profit of the other quarter."

Dawson City saw life change abruptly with the arrival of supplies in 1898. The golden Klondike capital became known as the "San Francisco of the North." To paraphrase the song, everything was up-to-date in Dawson City; they went about as far as they could go. When dining, gentlemen wore tailcoats; string orchestras played opera as the men and their ladies sampled *pâté de foie gras* and sipped imported French wines and champagnes. In Belinda Mulroney's Fairview Hotel, breakfast could set you back a cool sixty bucks if you had champagne. And, of course, you had champagne, *n'est-ce pas*? Down south, in so-called civilization, the average fellow was happy to get $35 a week. How would you like to pay, today, the equivalent of two weeks' salary for breakfast?

Yet, for miners coming to the Klondike goldfields in that year, conditions appeared deceptively normal when they arrived in the coastal town of Skagway, a favourite point of debarkation three hundred miles south of Dawson City. Elmer White, a Skagway newspaperman, reported that prices were reasonable in the rough, makeshift restaurants of the Skagway of 1898. "A square meal at a bare boards place could be had for twenty-five cents; bare boards and paper napkins were rated at thirty to thirty-five cents, while tablecloth and real napkin places ran from forty to fifty cents." There *were* some exceptions: at Skagway's Pack Train Saloon a shot of liquor cost two-bits, two and a half times the price down south.

But in the North the kings of the Klondike and their friends didn't waste time with loose change like quarters and four-bit pieces. In the settlement of Circle City, situated on the Yukon River some hundred miles west of the Yukon/Alaska border, the smallest coin in circulation was the silver dollar.

There is the story of the tough times following a severe snowstorm that struck a small mining town in Idaho at the turn of the century. The town had seven saloons and when the settlement was cut off from the outside world there was but a single four-bit piece in circulation. (It's difficult to accept such a bizarre state of affairs, but that's the way the story goes.) Until spring this fifty cents made the rounds from one saloon to the next. For those whose minds are entertained by such things, it's impossible not to marvel at the financial juggling that must have gone on to give the Yankee miners their beer (and food) and at the same time keep that four-bit piece moving along the mercantile channels so that nobody starved – or worse, went dry.

The Idaho miners must have felt that times couldn't get much tougher. They were wrong. Times could, and did. The miners at least *had* the beer; it was there in the saloons. All they had to do was get their hands on that four-bit piece for a few minutes.

But the grey skies of privation that troubled the small mining town were nothing compared to the angry storm that was building just over the horizon; the brooding clouds of Temperance and Prohibition were moving ponderously across the land. For generations the bitter advocates of Temperance had agitated first for reform, then total abstinence. And abstinence meant you, too, buddy; drop that glass and sing hallelujah! But now, as the world stumbled into the first decades of the twentieth century, the Great Darkness was no longer just a threat. It was here and now.

9

Temperance

The principal measure taken by those who wish to curb drinking has almost invariably been to close the liquor outlets in the mistaken belief that, denied the recognized source of drink, people will stop drinking. As the philosophers say, those who will not learn from the errors of history are bound to repeat them, and they have repeated them with soporific regularity down through the centuries. A Chinese record, written thousands of years ago, says: "Spirits are what men will not do without. To prohibit them and secure total abstinence from them is beyond the power even of sages," a view apparently generated by the intemperance of that time in China, of all classes, whose excesses threatened the very existence of the country.

Edgar, the Saxon king of England, like many before and after, sought to control his subjects' drinking. He restricted towns to a single alehouse at the instigation of St Dunstan, the archbishop of Canterbury. In addition – and this was a mistake – he decreed that the country's drinking horns be fitted with pegs, eight pegs to a cup, and that those who drank more than one peg's depth at a draught be subject to stiff penalties. (This really wasn't such a painful restriction; each peg permitted a solid half-pint.) Far from being scared off their beer by Edgar's law, drinkers found this a delightful new game. Around the alehouse table the drinking horn passed, sloshing gaily from one to another, each merry friend downing a peg's worth of ale. Drink less than a peg, or more, and you had to pay up; win some, lose some, it was great sport. For Edgar and St Dunstan it was back to the drawing board.

In thirteenth century England the king levied a tax, or "scot," on ale consumption; every time you picked up a glass it cost you. But ale drinkers, since the first cave dweller, have figured out ways around these taxes, and thirteenth century drinkers were just as sharp as anyone before or since. The Common Law of the time did not apply in virgin forests, so enterprising foresters established "scot-free" alehouses deep in the country's wooded areas where drinkers could refresh themselves and save a dollar or two. The tax man turned to the Church for help in curbing this practice. In 1256 the bishop of Salisbury decreed that scot-free ale drinking was forbidden, and instructed his priests, under pain of horrible punishment in the Hereafter, to see to it that their parishioners obeyed the injunction. It didn't work too well, though. The problem was, the priests did all *their* drinking in the scot-free alehouses.

One of the most pointless exercises in medieval England was the enactment of laws to restrict the number of alehouses. In the time of Edward III (1327-1377) the law permitted only three taverns in the city of London. In 1553, Edward VI ordered that the maximum number of taverns trading in London be fixed at forty, and that all must be licensed. However, the law did not apply to inns, nor to the selling of beer and ale at fairs. As there were inns at every crossroad, and fairs every day of the week, the law was senseless. Lawmakers have always been great ones for enacting laws, then making exceptions that effectively nullified the very law they'd just finished enacting.

Though they were the prime targets, alehouses were not the only establishments to feel the weight of the law's disapproval. In 1675 the English government suppressed the coffee-houses. This is surprising by today's standards, but three hundred years ago coffee was not considered the innocuous morning beverage it is now. As in so many instances, it was not the inherent evil of the drink itself, but rather the company it kept: political radicals, anarchists, hotheads – not our kind of people, according to government spokesmen, who had enough problems. The coffee-houses – where never a beer was seen – were the focal point of dissent, and thus suffered the government's wrath.

The eighteenth and nineteenth centuries in England saw such staggering abuses of spirits (gin, primarily) that the authorities enacted a law to promote the sale of beer and ale. Intended, naively, as a measure to curb the gin traffic, the Beer Act of 1830 allowed virtually any person to sell beer, but nothing else; no gin, or any other spirit. No licence was necessary, no controls were applied; as long as you sold only beer, and paid an insignificant excise fee, you were in business. For a few weeks after the introduction of the law the city of Liverpool, for example, witnessed the opening of fifty beer shops a day. Within ninety days tens of thousands of persons had paid their fee and were selling beer with both hands – often from dim and odious cellars that were far from what the authorities had in mind. They were plain and unsophisticated outlets whose only purpose was to sling beer to the thirsty, and bore none of the social attributes of the regular public-house. In 1830 the country supported 24,000 beer shops. Within five years the number jumped to 46,000. These beer shops were *in addition* to the public-houses, or pubs, which alone numbered 56,000. Thus, for a population at that time of 15 million, there were over 100,000 outlets for drink. Twenty years later the figure was in excess of 123,000, roughly one beer outlet for every 120 persons. Instead of getting better, things got worse.

Faced with this dramatic increase in drink outlets, the authorities panicked and encouraged the beer sellers to sell spirits (like gin, for example, the very spirit they were trying to suppress!) because retailers of spirits came under stiffer licensing restrictions. The magistrates felt that in this way they would have greater control over the beer sellers, which was a dream that turned into a nightmare. Retailers of spirits, to fight the attractions of the beer-only retailers (who could now sell spirits, remember), built bigger and better drinking places which drew crowds of thirsty customers and contributed to a marked increase in sales of – you guessed it – gin.

In the way of laws everywhere, reform legislation took some strange twists. As puritanism became stronger in the early seventeenth century, the laws prohibiting drunkenness became more pervasive. Before, it had been acceptable to sit knocking back the ale with a merry hand; now it cost you money in the form of stiff fines, plus a few hours in the stocks, enduring puritan jibes. Informers were encouraged; one witness was enough to send a man to the stocks; one drunk in a group could thus save his own skin and send his erstwhile pals into those same overworked stocks. (Heaven help him the next day, though; six hours in the stocks under a hot sun, with a hangover, gives a guy a long memory and a short temper.) Town officials informed on their very neighbours; travellers, even, were not exempt: Pass through the town with a couple of jars in you, and into the stocks you go. Yet, throughout all this vicious repression, at fairs and festivals a man could get drunk with impunity; beer was sold from unlicensed makeshift booths at every fair in the country. Just don't stagger back home through the town, that's all, otherwise it was straight into the stocks.

There was a movement a century later that sought to replace the demon gin with the demon rum, and thus wean the drinking public from the spirit that was destroying the country. The justification for rum was that it would also benefit England's colonies in the West Indies. Pretty fuzzy thinking, really. The idea was to push the sale of a mixture of two parts water to one part rum – two-water-grog the sailors called it – but the proposal died on the drawing board. Just as well; gin drinkers wouldn't have liked that bit about two parts water.

The term "grog" first came into use in 1740 as a nickname for the British admiral Vernon, and derived from the fabric of his cloak, grogram, a coarse stiff wool. Vernon's dubious claim to fame came when he put a stop to the issue of straight navy rum on board His Majesty's ships and began adding water to it. Not a popular move. From "grog" comes "groggy," originally meaning simply drunk, but now used to describe any condition marked by confusion and lack of coordination.

Ever since people began drinking, others have tried to stop them. One notable exception to this rule was the experience of the North American Indian, who at first was *encouraged* by the early traders to drink liquor.

In Captain Cook's time the Indians of the Canadian Northwest had yet to be introduced to alcohol. In 1778, when he arrived in Nootka Sound, he offered the Indians a glass of liquor but it was refused as "unnatural and disgusting." Yet, in common with some of us, they quickly acquired not only a taste for it, but a driving passion. A Spanish botanist, Mozino, visiting the same Nootka Sound a mere fourteen years later noted that "they have become fond enough of wine, whiskey, and beer, to all of which they give themselves to excess when someone provides it . . . the thought does not seem to have occurred to them to procure these liquors through the medium of commerce."

The first record of liquor's entry into the diet of the Canadian West Coast Indian occurs in 1790. An officer of a Spanish ship entertained an Indian friend in July of that year and served him "wine and biscuit of which he was very fond." In 1792 the Spaniard Galiano said of Maquinna, one of the West Coast Indian chiefs: "[He] drank wine with pleasure and in order that his mind might not be fogged left others to determine the amount which he should drink of that which he called 'Spanish water'."

In 1793 when Captain George Vancouver anchored off the northern tip of the Queen Charlotte Islands, he entertained various Haida chiefs with bread and molasses, a nosh that always went over big. The Haida in return offered him a glass of "superior quality" whale oil. Fighting back waves of nausea, Captain Vancouver refused, but to offset this offence to the Haida's sense of propriety, countered with a round of grog, "a large glass of rum, a luxury to which they seemed by no means strangers."

From the latter part of the 1700s to the turn of the century the Canadian West Coast Indians and the traders themselves saw liquor, beer, and wine only as adjuncts to social and commercial intercourse. A couple of drams put the natives in a more receptive mood to barter. But after 1800, competition for the Indians' sea-otter skins grew fierce, intoxicating liquor became a major part of the barter, and the lucrative – and disastrous – trade developed.

It was not until the Indians had become hopelessly involved with the white man's sauce that the first dedicated Temperance movements gained a foothold in eastern North America. Unfortunately for the Indian, the Temperance people had their hands full out east, and decades passed before the Indian's tragedy caught their attention.

Beer seems a magnet that draws criticism. It was ever thus. Intoxication among the settlers of New England caused the enactment, in 1637, of a law banning home brewing; henceforth only "common brewers" were allowed to brew (common brewers: brewers who, as brewing methods became more involved and costly, grouped together to serve their customers). As so often happens – nobody thinking ahead – the "common brewers" and their facilities were not able to meet the demand, and people turned to spirits, the penultimate step in the historic cycle: man gets bombed on beer; prohibit brewing; man gets bombed on gin; re-introduce beer; man goes back to getting bombed on beer. The law-makers never learn.

In 1621 England's John Taylor wrote: "Your inns and alehouses are brooks and rivers and their clients are small rills and springs, who all pay their tributes to the boundless ocean of the brewhouse. For, all the world knows, that if men and women did drink no more than sufficed nature; if any reason were used in drinking, what would become of the brewer then? Every drunkard is a post-beam which holds up the brew-house." Taylor, a Thames River boatman, was called "The Water Poet." Judging by the volumes of poetry and prose he produced on the subject of beer, the sobriquet "Water Poet" is ironic: he obviously never touched the stuff.

Taking a lighter view, a London wit enunciated the seven levels in the progress of drunkenness: Perky, Irritable, Mellow, Pugnacious, Affectionate, Tearful, and Collapse. A doctor, however, perhaps influenced by Temperance doctrines, reduced these seven stages to five, in the cold and humourless way that doctors have. Each stage progressed grimly and inexorably toward the ultimate collapse: Animation, Gaiety or Sadness, Incoherence, Coma, Death.

But in eighteenth century England, ale was far from being the major evil. In 1736 England enacted a number of stringent laws against the gin epidemic. Sales of less than two gallons required a licence at a cost of £50; a tax of £1 was levied on every gallon; distillers and retailers, too, paid additional taxes, all of which increased the price to the consumer. Selling gin without a licence incurred a fine of £100. Despite the fine 12,000 individuals were charged over the next two years, and the consumption of gin doubled.

In the mid-1700s, an English bishop mourned the growth of robbery and murder in the land. "Accursed spiritous liquors which, to the shame of our government, are so easily to be had, and in such quantities drunk, have changed the nature of our people, and will . . . destroy the very race." He was almost right. Gin-scoffing had reached such a horrendous level by 1743 that England's parliament enacted more exacting licensing laws: Only inns and alehouses would be permitted to sell gin. Previously you could get a shot of dubious gin in almost any shop in town – drapers, fishmongers, livery stables, some even dispensed it from wheelbarrows in the streets. One ingenious individual hung the figure of a tom cat outside his place of business. Thirsty passersby had but to drop a coin in a slot and a slug of gin gurgled out of a pipe concealed in the cat's paw. The contrivance made a fortune for its operator, an itinerant con man named Bradsheet, and is surely the first instance of a coin-operated drink machine.

Over the short span of less than a quarter of a century – 1689 to 1711 – a series of English laws illustrated that the politicians simply weren't paying attention. Bearing in mind that England was having serious gin problems around this time, just check these enactments: In 1689 beer suffered a 50 per cent increase in tax, and one year later a law went through allowing anyone to distil and sell spirits. (Remember, there's a gin problem, okay? The solution? Fight the gin problem by allowing *anyone to distil and sell gin* . . .) Naturally, the production of cheap gin and its consumption just went out of sight. In 1692 they bumped up the tax on beer again to such a degree that beer consumption in London, for example, dropped a staggering 25 per cent. Two years later further restrictions on the retailing of beer came into effect, and in 1697, for the first time, the authorities introduced a duty on malt, the very basis of beer. In 1711 the first tax on hops was introduced, and, for good measure, yet another hike in the malt tax (but this was eventually repealed – a century and a half later). All this while the country was being destroyed by gin.

A medical professor of Leyden, Holland, named Franciscus Sylvius (1614-1672), developed gin originally as an inexpensive diuretic. And indeed it was and still is, though perhaps not so cheap anymore. Unfortunately, its very cheapness, at a time when taxes on ale were mounting, lent it universal appeal, and with the spread of its popularity came the social problems that drove England to the brink of self-destruction, and not incidentally drove the puritans up the wall – again.

Gin and beer both start the same way. A mash of barley malt is fermented to make beer. The beer is then distilled; to the resulting spirits juniper berries and other botanicals are added, and then the product is distilled a second time, producing gin. The name gin comes originally from the French word for juniper: *genièvre*. The Dutch called it *genever*. The English soldiers who introduced it into England shortened the word to gin.

The damp, miserable campaigns in the Netherlands during the Thirty Years War (1618-1648) gave us the term "Dutch courage." Denied their habitual strong ale throughout the course of the struggle, the English soldiers, like soldiers everywhere, drank whatever they could get. In Holland what they could get was *eau de genièvre*, Professor Sylvius's "medicine." Good for what ails you. *Very* good. What ailed the soldiers, over and above the cold and the damp discomfort, was a fear of getting killed. Their officers saw, however, that even the most faint-hearted became a fighting machine after a couple of smashes of *eau de genièvre*. Thus "Dutch courage" entered the language as an expression of artificial bravery and aggressiveness induced by drinking.

But, gin or beer, it made little difference to the Temperance people. They denounced the one as easily and as vociferously as the other. But gin had the higher profile in that brutal period of England's history, and much of the puritans' rhetoric was directed toward

> Gin, cursed fiend, with fury fraught,
>   Makes human race a prey;
> It enters by a deadly draught
>   And steals our life away.
> – Townley.

Undoubtedly Englishmen ate and drank to excess as far back as their Celtic days when they ran around naked and scoffed mead, but the period that brings these excesses most forcibly to mind is the four hundred year span of the fifteenth to the nineteenth centuries; beer-drinking, pipe-smoking, snuff-taking, gin-drinking, even plain ordinary gluttony - all were practised to the absolute limit of human endurance, and often beyond. Early Temperance advocates looked about them in dismay and everywhere saw the Devil's work.

During the reign of Edward IV of England (fifteenth century), George Neville became the archbishop of York. In those days when the slightest excuse was cause for a feast, the occasion of the enthronement of an archbishop generated gluttony of Homeric proportions, and was no less intemperate for having a clerical flavour. To celebrate the event a bit of a nosh was prepared: 104 oxen, 6 wild bulls, 1,000 sheep, 304 calves, 304 swine, 400 swans, 2,000 geese, 1,000 capons, 2,000 pigs, thousands of small birds, 4,000 cold venison pastries, 500 stags, 608 pike, 12 porpoises, and so on, *ad nauseam*. A lot of solid material there, which they washed down with 300 tuns of ale (75,000 gallons, or 280,000 litres, give or take a glass or two) and 100 tuns of wine. Belch.

One of the best arguments in favour of a simple pot of good ale was the Babylonian excess practised by those who favoured hard liquor. Modest beer punches were as nothing before the monumental efforts of, for example, the commander-in-chief of the English navy at the end of the sixteenth century. As an offering to his ships' companies (6,000 men in all), he had the basin of a huge marble fountain filled with (are you ready for it?) 80 casks of brandy, 9 casks of water, 25,000 limes, 80 pints of lemon juice, 1,300 pounds of sugar, 5 pounds of nutmeg, 300 biscuits, and a giant cask of Malaga wine. One of the ships' lads paddled across this man-made lake in a small boat, dispensing cups to the merrymakers. Every fifteen minutes or so, the lad was replaced by another, the first boy being led away, staggering from the fumes that rose from the miniature sea of alcohol. Assuming even a modest content to the casks listed, the fragrant marble basin contained at least 9,000 gallons of potent punch, or six quarts (five and a half litres) for every sailor present – less what the young lads inhaled.

Excessive consumption and the places in which it was practised went hand-in-grisly-hand as far as the Temperance people were concerned. They fought the spread of drinking places with an unrelenting bitterness. And, give them their due, they had a lot to fight: In their garden of rectitude, alehouses sprouted like rank weeds. In the latter half of the sixteenth century in England there were almost twenty thousand alehouses, inns, and other outlets for ale. This worked out to one establishment for every 187 persons.

King James I didn't help matters when in 1618 he gave Sir Giles Mompesson the exclusive right to license English inns (on the cosy understanding that Sir Giles could keep half the fee for himself). Granting such a monopoly to his friend, while the government was striving to circumscribe the traffic in liquor, was an infamous act that drove the puritans crazy, especially when the avaricious Sir Giles set about licensing any place that had more than two walls. Within four years he had issued almost 13,000 licences, in a country of less than five million people (one inn or drink outlet for every 350 people; ironically, an improvement over the previous century, in spite of Sir Giles's efforts). In addition, alehouses doing business without a licence were subject to a fine of 21 shillings, a sizeable sum in those days. The alternative to a cash settlement, in the event your cash flow was a bit tight, was whipping. Most of the offenders, because of their impoverished state, ended up at the whipping post. This suggests the condition of the alehouses they operated: Often they were iniquitous rat-holes in which any person of discernment wouldn't have been caught dead.

The puritans were livid. They felt an alehouse-to-population ratio of 1 : 350 was appalling. But time changes all things (unfortunately for the puritans) and a century later, in 1739, William Maitland reported that the city of London supported 16,000 outlets for drink (at that time there were around 95,000 houses in London). This meant there was one drinking establishment for every *forty-seven* people in the city. Across the sea in Dublin the ratio must have been the same in order to support the *seventy* breweries that existed in that city in the same year.

The English scholar Sir John Hawkins (1719-1789) recalled that in the space near the Royal Exchange and Threadneedle Street (cheek by jowl in the middle of London) there were more than twenty taverns. One was named the Crown, and it was a normal morning that saw the proprietor broach a 120-gallon barrel of Malaga wine and serve over 3,800 four-ounce drinks – an average of roughly a glass every four seconds. Even for one of the thirstier periods in history, that's a lot of liquor. Of course, many (if not all) of the patrons were ambidextrous and could knock off a brace of glasses with both hands, frequently at the same time. The Crown Tavern burned in the Great Fire of London, in September 1666, but was quickly rebuilt; if you can unload 3,800 drinks in a morning you don't waste time slapping together a new tavern. The establishment continued to prosper for another hundred years.

London didn't hold a monopoly on alehouses. In the early 1800s in the town of Nottingham there was one alehouse for every eighty people. A street in Plymouth – quite a short street, actually; there were only twenty-seven buildings along its entire length – had thirteen licensed alehouses; every second building was an outlet for drink. It would have been perfectly acceptable if the buildings had been thirty-storey office complexes, but this was 1897; not too many skyscrapers around in those days.

Perhaps as a result of the spirited (if I can use that expression) competition for the drinker's dollar 123,000 liquor outlets in 1850 – English publicans sometimes added a little dividend to their wares. One example: to a barrel (say, thirty-six gallons) of porter add twelve gallons of liquor (gin, for example), four pounds of coarse sugar, and one pound of salt. Maybe add a little vitriol (*vitriol?!*). You now have a vitriolic barrel of porter that is 25 per cent *gin*. This is an example that amply illustrates the reason for the number of purity of ale laws that were enacted down through the centuries.

Our latter-day concept of Temperance had its birth in Hesse in 1600, on Christmas Day as it turns out (probably as a result of a particularly heavy party on Christmas Eve). A group of "redeemed" drinkers formed an organization called The Order of Temperance, and its rules would not have offended the most seasoned drunk. The members pledged to drink not more than twice a day, and on those occasions not more than *seven glasses of liquor at a time*. Hardly stringent, by any yardstick; indeed many of today's drinkers would find it difficult to *meet* the Order's maximums, let alone exceed them.

Hessian capers aside, the serious business of Temperance crystallized in the eastern U.S.A. at the beginning of the 1800s, its driving force the sometimes stern ethics of Protestantism: honest toil, self-control, thrift, and sound moral attitudes. "Woe unto them that rise up early in the morning that they may follow strong drink." (Isaiah 5:11) To give equal time to the followers of strong drink, we should remember Proverbs 31:7: "Let him drink, and forget his poverty, and remember his misery no more." However, "The Devil," as Shakespeare tells us, "can cite Scripture for his purpose." (*The Merchant of Venice*, I, iii). Regardless of the source of the words, the Temperance advocate, in righteous wrath, heard everywhere the Devil's evil voice. Even Socrates would not have escaped their frowns of disapproval. "Wine does . . . 'moisten the soul' and lull our griefs to sleep," said the Greek, "but I suspect that men's bodies fare like those of plants . . . When God gives the plants water in floods to drink they cannot stand up straight . . . ; but when they drink only as much as they enjoy they grow up straight and tall." Sounds reasonable, but to Temperance folk any word that did not knock liquor was the word of the Devil.

The Temperance movement was born to fight this devil and the destructive social conditions created by the immoderate use of alcohol. Six thousand local branches of the movement were flourishing in the U.S.A. by 1833. In England, the Temperance Society was formed in 1862; Scotland and Ireland had an active movement; and in 1874 the Women's Christian Temperance Union was founded in Cleveland, Ohio, and soon became worldwide.

Few Temperance societies have been as violently zealous as the one formed in New Zealand in 1835. They fought the demon rum like mad things, with rifle fire, tarring and feathering, ship searches and barrel-smashing, until the very sea was flavoured with liquor. Yet, within half a century, there were eighty-nine breweries in New Zealand.

The enlightened Dutch Temperance League, formed in the mid-1800s to combat the abuses of Holland gin, rejected the fiery intolerance of their counterparts in other countries and gained their ends through common sense. They promoted the brewing of sound beer, and fought to have all beer taxes removed (an action enthusiastically supported by the breweries and consumers alike). They avoided violent or coercive measures, depending successfully on the temperate use of beer.

Wrote an observer in 1886: "At fairs, exhibitions, and public festivals they established drinking halls, where only beer was sold. A few years ago, at the Colonial Exhibition of Amsterdam, the beer halls conducted by the Temperance societies did the most thriving business."

To a movement whose aim was the betterment of mankind – and indeed it did alleviate much suffering through its selfless dedication and effort – the reaction *against* Temperance must have seemed inexplicable and perverse. The answer undoubtedly lies in the Oxford English Dictionary and its definition of the verb "temper": "To reduce to the desirable condition, free from excess in either direction." The Temperance movement may have begun as an effort to moderate man's drinking habits, but it quickly degenerated into the very intemperance it fought.

The narrow views of the puritans did little to help the cause. "A good Victorian," said Will Durant, "[was] uncertain of his theology, but strong in his moral faith." "Good Victorians" would probably have considered the historian's remark an unqualified compliment, and perhaps they would have been right, although Durant was never above taking a light dig at the foibles of mankind. He probably had a chuckle at some of the puritan efforts to save us from Satan's clutches. When translating the Psalms, for example, the puritans frowned at "my chalice inebriateth me" and changed it to the more sober "my cup runneth over." And while I hesitate to give them an inch, they deserve their due: try saying "inebriateth" after six beers. The puritans, of course, would stamp their feet and scream that you shouldn't be drinking six beers while reading the Psalms.

Thomas Hobbes (1588-1679), the English philosopher, was the ideal adherent to sensible temperance. He claimed that he had not been drunk more than a hundred times in his life, an infuriating expression of temperance by puritan standards, but at the time, 1670, akin to being a teetotaler. While Hobbes's view seems moderate to some of us – bombed once a year doesn't sound unreasonable – to the advocates of Temperance it was completely unacceptable. George Bernard Shaw, however, obviously agreed with Hobbes's relaxed opinions on temperance. "I'm only a beer teetotaler," he said, "not a champagne teetotaler."

The origin of the term "teetotal" is supposed to have come from the society formed in 1832 that pledged itself to total abstinence from intoxicants. Some of the more moderate members of the society tried to explain that temperance did not mean *total* abstinence, but one of the fire-and-brimstone members adamantly declared that "total" was the only way to go. To accent his stand he repeated the initial letter of the word: "Nothing but tee-tee-total would do."

This immoderate stand generated more resistance to the Temperance cause than any other. Many considered Temperance a direct and vicious assault on the English-man's personal liberty. Said a nineteenth century doctor: "If every man is to forego his freedom of action because many make a licentious use of it, I know not what is the value of any freedom." A bishop claimed he "would rather see England free than England sober."

It was the Temperance advocate's unceasing clamour for total abstinence that in the nineteenth century prompted Nova Scotia's premier Joseph Howe to make the analogy between women and the prohibition of alcohol. A woman's love, he felt, was God's greatest gift to man. "Yet, when even love is indulged in to excess, when reason is overpowered, when passion hurries on to folly – how numerous the victims, how blasting the effects! Yet who would deny to man the companionship which alone makes existence tolerable?" Are we, he asked, to lock up all the women because some men make fools of themselves?

Half a century after Joseph Howe, Ontario embarked on its brief experiment in Prohibition and drew similar broadsides from the defenders of personal freedom. H.A.C. Machin, Tory MPP for Kenora, Ontario, and one of the most relentless adversaries of Prohibition, in the spring of 1919 pointed with bitter scorn at the government's faithless theft of the people's liberty. "The human passions are the same whether they concern strong drink, lust of women, greed of gold, love of power, or the simple sport of chasing sinners . . . Today the great sins of this world, this country and this province are intolerance and selfishness."

But the total abstinence zealot wasn't listening. Ontario's Prohibition years bred believers whose unyielding intensity was without equal before or since. Long after the fight against liquor had been lost (as far as the prohibitionists were concerned) E.C. Drury, premier of the province during that repressive period, said, "Fifty years ago I believed that total prohibition was the only solution to the liquor problem. Nothing that has happened since has caused me to change my belief . . . I stand where I have always stood, and I think my position is sound." This unbending rectitude was characteristic of Temperance thinking then and since.

In the late 1800s many among the moderate faction felt that if the minds of the Temperance people were guided more by history than the blind, fanatical zeal that inflamed them, they would realize that the standards of morality and moderation were far higher in the nineteenth century than they were in times past, and even the most cursory glance at the records of those earlier years shows this is true.

The followers of Temperance, though, weren't having any of that "guided by history" and "nineteenth century morality" garbage; they'd been there and had seen what alcohol did to countless homes.

At the close of the nineteenth century in Canada the fires of prohibitionist sentiment were raging, fuelled by the throbbing rhetoric of throngs of temperate Christians – though their Christianity and, indeed, their temperate qualities were open to serious discussion, as shown in part by the heart-tugging songs written especially to whip up support:

> Ye people of Canada listen,
>> I've something I want you to hear.
> There's trouble in store for our nation,
>> Because of the whisky and beer.
>
> It hinders our moral advancement.
>> It menaces every home.
> It fills every soul with its ragings,
>> Who drinks of the poisonous foam.

followed by the tub-thumping exhortation

> Then, down with the traffic
>> In whisky and beer,
> That drives from the home
>> Every comfort and cheer.

And much more along the same intemperate lines. Actual temperance, defined as "moderation; the avoidance of excess," was the farthest thing from their minds. Zero, that was their aim; not a drop. Today, of course, there is little need for a strong Temperance movement. A mere glance at the recent price increases on whisky and beer is enough to make teetotalers of us all.

Sundays in Toronto in 1919 left a lot to be desired if you were looking for some action, unless, of course, you were a prohibitionist. If you were fighting the liquor interests you could apparently disregard many of the puritanical laws then in effect. If, for example, you had been in Toronto one Sunday in September 1919 you could have joined the crowd at the Toronto Arena and shouted yourself hoarse with the rest of the ten thousand screaming anti-booze militants and listened to the famous evangelist Billy Sunday denounce the demon rum. (But weren't rallies and similar activities prohibited on the Lord's day? There was even an outfit called the Lord's Day Alliance to watch out for that sort of thing. Ah, I see; the Lord's Day Alliance was at the Billy Sunday rally.) All well and good, I suppose, but a candidate in the provincial election muttered in disgust: "If some of the labour men in this city got up on a platform and used language like Billy Sunday used they would be called Bolshevists." Meanwhile, back at the corner store, on this same Sunday afternoon, it was against the law for a little kid to buy an ice cream cone. Yes indeed, as Gerald Hallowell wrote, "Toronto the Good" was a curious place.

Sadly, Ontario was not alone in its observance of the Lord's day. In 1904, in Winnipeg, there was no end of Presbyterian brouhaha when someone was naive enough to suggest that perhaps a concert of religious music might be uplifting on a Sunday afternoon. On Sunday, nothing; ab-so-lute-ly *nothing*. Lock yourself in an empty room and read your Bible. But don't turn the pages with too much enthusiasm, otherwise they might think you're having a good time, and then you'd be in trouble.

In Ontario, *circa* 1919 (and before, and after, too), the Lord's Day Alliance guarded the Sabbath. The only thing you could do on Sunday was breathe. You couldn't even go out and buy a cigar. And don't play any of those sneaky tricks like buying it on Saturday and *smoking* it on Sunday. But we can't knock Ontario alone; the crackdown on simple pleasures was a North American phenomenon. Across the border in Michigan legislators went so far as to try to ban the wearing of high-heeled shoes. Ontario agreed and suggested a ban on cosmetics, too; "drug store complexions" was the term used.

Lofty morals seemed to be a sign of the time as well as the place. To match Toronto's fight against Sunday ice cream cones for the kids, turn-of-the-century Regina took a firm stand against young boys who played marbles for keeps. My, my, must have been some pretty tough kids in Regina in those days: hard-eyed, ruthless, ready to take their place next to Al Capone. Today, with the horrors of a couple of world wars under our belts, it's a bit difficult to comprehend our ancestors' moral outrage over ice cream and marbles; most of us would find our hearts longing for those comparatively innocent and uncomplicated days when the worst crime on the books was drinking a glass of beer on a Sunday afternoon.

Cause and effect. We've seen the effect: A militant Temperance movement that, at least in the nineteenth and early twentieth centuries, was anything but temperate, epitomized by axe-swinging, saloon-smashing weirdos like Carrie Nation, an American Temperance leader in the 1880s, who believed she had been told by God to destroy the saloon, and for whom the term "not playing with a full deck" must have been coined; she couldn't have dealt a hand of blackjack.

The cause of such immoderate behaviour must have been equally as immoderate, and history shows us it was. Excess was the name of the game. The Greeks and the Romans all drank prodigious quantities of alcohol. The Anglo-Saxons almost bathed in the stuff, and pictured their gods as perpetually drunk. In ancient India both priests and people drank excessively; their gods, too, seemed able to function only when drunk. The prayers of the faithful frequently invited the gods to join them in drunkenness. "[The] conception of the gods," says one Sanskrit record, "was but a reflection of the character of the people themselves." Around 1100 BC the *Shoo-king*, a Chinese history of the period, put Heaven itself on the side of the drinkers. "Strong drink," it claimed unequivocally, "is intended to be used in entertaining guests:

such employment of it is what Heaven has prescribed." Bounce *that* off the next Temperance type you meet at a cocktail party.

Yet none of these societies gave birth to the powerful Temperance movement that grew in response to the horrors of the eighteenth and nineteenth centuries, when England faced, in the opinion of many, literal self-destruction through the mindless consumption of alcohol. Paradoxically, during this same period, the British Empire rose to greatness, and we can't help but wonder: how? In the early 1700s to be permanently drunk was *de rigueur* for much of the working class; Durant tells us that even in the sixteenth century England accepted drunkenness as man's normal condition. England's leaders rarely saw a sober moment; the commercial class, too, was not one to refuse a glass; nor were literary or artistic figures pillars of sobriety. Yet, together, they were creating one of history's great social and economic structures, illustrating, despite Temperance claims to the contrary, that abstinence and greatness do not necessarily go hand in hand; great things can, indeed, be accomplished by a bunch of drunks.

The sixteenth and seventeenth centuries in Germany, too, were a period of excessive eating and drinking – excesses in all areas – yet also one of great art and of tremendous activity in science and commerce, a paradox that seems to have occurred repeatedly in other countries and other times.

"Everybody drank [in eighteenth century England]," said social historian Frederick Hackwood, "and nobody drank moderately . . . No [man] ever thought of leaving the table sober." This was a vice not restricted to the lower classes; the nobility did its share. The nobles drank wine in addition to gin and beer, "and every man among them liked to boast himself a two-bottle man." Hackwood also tells us that in early nineteenth century London "it was not an unknown incident for an intoxicated member of Parliament to attempt to address the house, when he was scarcely able to utter a word." A politician scarcely able to utter a word? Sounds like a great idea.

The ascendancy of gin over beer and ale during (but not only) the eighteenth century in England appalled the authorities. "Not only the vicious and immoral give in to this practice," said a justice's report in 1736, "but also those who are in other respects sober and regular; not only one person here and there in a family, but whole families, shamefully and constantly indulge themselves in this pernicious practice."

The fact that the authorities themselves were responsible for the "pernicious practice" seems to have been conveniently forgotten by the writer of the report. The distilling of gin from the surplus corn crops, the government's encouragement of gin's distribution, sale, and consumption, plus gin's low price and the prohibitive taxes applied to beer and ale – all government initiatives – paved the path to nationwide drunkenness.

Perhaps the only person largely untouched by the passion for gin was the farmer. Crops and cattle couldn't wait upon the bonecrushing hangovers the urban dweller suffered. The farmer went about his daily tasks, pleasantly awash in the strong healthy ale he brewed himself, and was exempt from the "pernicious practices" of the evil cities.

England was not alone in this consuming thirst. In the birthplace of the modern Temperance movement, the North Americans held up their end. Turn-of-the-century American newspaper reporters had a reputation (well earned, according to H.L. Mencken, who was there) for heavy, unbiased, ambidextrous drinking. Mencken himself, while a good man at right- and left-handed beer drinking, nevertheless maintained he never wrote anything with so much as a glass of beer in his system. In this, on the early twentieth century newspaper, he was alone. "Between 1899 and 1904," he said, "south of the Mason & Dixon Line [the boundary between Pennsylvania and Maryland, regarded, before the Civil War, as separating the North from the South] there was only one reporter who did not drink at all, and he was considered insane. In New York . . . there was not even one." Mencken remembered his first Christmas on the *Baltimore Herald*; the entire staff was full of what they called handset whisky, a volcanic brew sold in the saloon next door and believed to be made by the proprietor himself. Half the linotype machines in the newspaper's composing room broke down and four or five pressmen were injured, delaying the city edition by an hour. "Nobody cared," Mencken recalled, "for the head of the whole establishment, the revered managing editor, was locked up in his office with a case of bourbon." Had they known,

Temperance folk would have undoubtedly cancelled their subscriptions to the newspaper.

The same followers of Temperance would have fulminated against the educational methods of Eleazer Wheelock, founder of Dartmouth College, New Hampshire. He was remembered lightly in a nineteenth century college song:

> O, Eleazer Wheelock was a very pious man;
> He went into the wilderness to teach the Indian . . .
> Eleazer was the faculty, and the whole curriculum
> Was five hundred gallons of New England rum.
> — Richard Hovey.

Others, more orthodox in their piety than Wheelock, pushed west to bring the Word to the settlers. They found the tavern had preceded them. Early midwestern taverns often served as meeting halls for these travelling preachers. Ironically, the evangelists found themselves crying out against the evils of drink and laying a large knock on saloons in general while they were standing in the tavern itself, knee-deep in suds, and having to shout over the raucous merrymaking that was going on around the bar. You have to wonder which one felt the paradox more keenly, the preacher who was obliged to enlist the Devil to do the Lord's work, or the tavern owner who found himself clasping an adder to his bosom. Meanwhile, in England the preachers' brethren were getting their revenge. In the late 1800s two of London's most infamous public-house/dance halls were purchased by a missionary group, and turned from the primrose path of dalliance to righteousness and nobler works, much to the chagrin of local swingers.

Back on the East Coast of Canada, Eleazer Wheelock's rum was also a favourite drink among the Maritimers. The account books from 1808 of one Nova Scotia general store show they purchased rum with an almost religious dedication, though few customers exhibited the realistic approach to religion as did the one who ordered a New Testament, a deck of cards, and three quarts of rum.

The eighteenth century in England has been referred to as the Age of Snuff, and there certainly was enough of it consumed. Ninety per cent of tobacco was taken in this form; virtually everyone, man, woman, and child, was a snuff-taker. The Queen herself was called "snuffy Charlotte" (though not to her face). A poet of the period noted the habit and its foppish idiosyncracies:

> To such a height with some is fashion grown
> They feed their very nostrils with a spoon.

The reference is to the special snuff spoons used by fashionable young men to transport the snuff to their noses. But it's difficult to imagine how they found the time or the opportunity to "feed their noses" when their noses were almost constantly inside a glass. In 1730, in the city of London alone, there were more than seven thousand gin shops that sold only spirits – no ale. The authorities noted with alarm that nowhere in the city was there an area "wherein the number of alehouses, brandy and geneva [gin] shops do not daily increase." In one part of the city, Westminster, they claimed that one house in every four was a gin shop. (Temperance hearts would have been warmed to learn that some two centuries later, in 1959, the last brewery in Westminster closed its doors.) In the ten-year period ending in 1742 gin consumption in England went from 11 million gallons to 20 million (40 to 75 million litres), illustrating the need for restrictive legislation, and the inadequacy of existing regulations.

A century later, in 1839 the Temperance movement celebrated a minor triumph when a law was passed that obliged the alehouses of London to close for twelve hours – Saturday midnight to noon on Sunday, the period of greatest drunkenness. The law did little to reduce consumption, however. In December 1829, a decade before the law was passed, an enterprising London reporter watched one dram shop and saw an average of 360 people enter every hour; forty years later the country still supported a flourishing host of 118,000 alehouses, all doing a brisk business – but not over the early hours of a Sunday morn.

From Saxon times to the present day a torrent of laws has controlled the brewing, sale, and consumption of beer. It seems to have been an innate driving force in all who gained power; kings, princes, politicians – every one of them, their first day in office, fired off a beer law. Some were pointless (if you checked you'd probably find *most* were pointless), some were downright ridiculous; some lasted a day, others endured for generations like festering thorns. In 1914, in an effort to improve the health of the population – excessive consumption of alcohol was seen as the culprit – England enacted the first law that established formal opening and closing times for the nation's alehouses. London's public-houses, in the 1890s, were open from five o'clock in the morning until after midnight during the week, and from one to three in the afternoon and six to eleven in the evening on Sundays. The new hours varied from one locality to another, but were more or less late morning to early afternoon, followed by a brief closing period, then open for four or five hours in the evening.

The belief behind the new laws was the same old one that had been around for centuries: cut down on the availability of liquor and, ergo, people will drink less. It was repeatedly proven wrong, yet held with such child-like faith that it makes you weep. Ostensibly the law was to last only until the end of the First World War (1918). However, to administer the new law a substantial bureaucracy developed, and we all know bureaucracies: They tend to be self-perpetuating, with an instinct for self-preservation second to none. Thus the odd opening and closing hours were still in effect seventy years later, without having achieved any really notable decrease in consumption.

In 1988, England finally saw the laws changed, allowing pubs to waive the afternoon closing and conduct business continuously from eleven in the morning to eleven at night. In addition, a promotional campaign has been mounted to encourage the consumption of *non-alcoholic* beverages in pubs. Hmm . . . yes, well, great idea, but it's been tried before, back in 1874, and students of history will remember what happened.

In 1874 the People's Café Company was founded. This was yet another move by the powers of Temperance in their fight against the demon drink. The People's Café Company was followed shortly by the Coffee Tavern Company Ltd, and in the next year by the Coffee Public-house Association. The naive thrust of these groups was to offer an alternative to the alehouse and gin palace, and their efforts were certainly well-organized and impressive. The coffee palace offered a broad range of non-alcoholic beverages, food, milk, lemonade, along with sticky portions of reform, religion, and rip-roaring social evenings, and became the meeting place of such exciting groups as the Original Grand and United Order of the Total Abstinent Sons of the Phoenix. It's not clear what these lads did, besides abstain.

The Temperance drinks served in the coffee palaces masqueraded as real sauce – sheep in wolves' clothing, as a contemporary wit called them – and bore names like Cox's Anti-Burton. The brewers of Burton didn't lose much sleep, even when Cox's brew won the first prize offered by a branch of the Church of England's Temperance Society.

Many of the coffee palaces were former alehouses, refurbished and given a more salubrious image by their new Temperance owners. There was always more than a little satisfaction in Temperance ranks when a liquor outlet was reformed and directed into the service of a higher intent. But this righteous satisfaction did not blind them to the advantages of the erstwhile drinkery's bold lights and luxurious fittings; these were retained to attract the drunk and change his sordid habits through healthy drink, upright company, and overall nobility of purpose. And this, a common denominator of all Temperance enterprises, was what doomed the coffee palace: the relentless, unheeding passion to change, to improve, to uplift, whether you liked it or not. A coffee palace? Good idea. Nourishing food and drink? Splendid; definitely good thinking. And if they had left it at that they might have seen a gradual and qualified success; their sensible example might have led a new generation into more temperate ways. But in tandem with their bright but Utopian aims there plodded, like a bleak shadow, the brittle drive to press others into the Temperance mould. Like blinkered missionaries they strove singlemindedly to sell their views to their fellow man. But their fellow man wasn't buying, and the coffee palace failed. By the 1890s many had quietly become alehouses again.

In the wake of the coffee-palace fiasco came another brief and equally disastrous venture, the "improved" public-house. The element of improvement consisted in serving, and indeed promoting, non-alcoholic drinks while also providing standard booze. There were, over the short span of their life, around a dozen such establishments in England, and all were about as successful as the invention of the lead balloon. As usual, a raft of good intentions supported by a rickety structure of juvenile expectations collapsed beneath the weight of good old-fashioned human nature. By the turn of the century Victorian England had not only reverted to the liquor-oriented pub, but pubs themselves were on the increase. For the Temperance folk it was, once more, *sic transit gloria*, Temperance-wise.

Nineteenth century towns in the American Midwest were reminiscent of London in the same period, when alehouses were multiplying at an alarming rate and you could hardly take a step in any direction without bumping into one. In 1808, a small settlement in Ohio numbered a dozen cabins, of which four were taverns. You have to wonder how eight cabins could support four taverns. Another small burg called Lancaster boasted eleven stores and nine taverns. Around 1821, near Pittsburgh, the town of Steubenville was an active (and thirsty) little community of twenty-seven shops, two banks, and sixteen taverns.

On the Canadian Prairies the tavern and the saloon were not the only outlets the Temperance people had to worry about. Thirty years before Prohibition seized hold of Canada, Winnipeg's clergymen in the 1880s were already frowning on the city's grocery stores. Many saw them as a greater evil than the saloons. Within the decade 1872-1882 Winnipeg's population leaped from 1400-odd to 16,000. To serve this throng there were sixty-four groceries selling, among the eatables, whisky by the bottle. A twenty-six-ouncer could be purchased in the store and consumed on the spot while relaxing among the biscuits, barrels, and bolts of gingham. The jar cost around one dollar. In the saloon the contents of the same bottle, served at twenty-five cents a shot, would run $3.25.

Out on the West Coast, 1925 saw the opening of the Crystal Gardens in Victoria. It boasted the largest indoor swimming pool in North America and became a popular spot to spend an evening dancing around the mezzanine dance floor that surrounded the pool on three sides. The dancers moved between scores of potted plants; lights flickered up from the pool, and the stars shone down through the glass roof – it was excruciatingly romantic. But here, too, the patrons felt the heavy hand of Temperance. There were no bars or taverns in the city; drinking was still "sinful" and had to be hidden, and that meant the Crystal Gardens, too. Beneath each table were slots, conveniently the precise width of a mickey of rye, into which, ostensibly, the ladies were to put their purses. Yes, well, it usually became a question of priorities. Purse or mickey? Exactly; the ladies carried their purses, and the table slot was always used for what everyone knew it was originally intended.

Liquor breeds some funny fixations in the minds of those who are against it. In Victoria, before Prohibition, the law said you had to stand at the bar. None of that sybaritic lounging around in sinfully comfortable chairs, by George. There seemed something darkly Satanic about the combination of liquor and comfort, a whiff of brimstone in the contours of a well-upholstered chair.

But after Prohibition, wherever local option permitted beer parlours, the law said you had to sit down. Standing sinner or seated saint, you had to have a program to know the rules of the game.

In the latter half of the nineteenth century Temperance advocates in England saw a welcome decline in liquor consumption and the number of brewers and beer outlets. In 1855 an ostensibly modest change in the closing hours of pubs – allowing them to remain open for an extra hour and a half in the afternoon and a further hour at night – brought about a startling *reduction* in the consumption of liquor: down four million gallons within a year. In 1870 there was one alehouse for every 182 persons in England (103,000 outlets), and over 133,000 licensed brewers. Toward the end of the century in London the authorities moved to reduce the number of public-houses, yet, strangely, they seemed to accept the enlargement of the pubs that remained. It seems a pointless scenario, though certainly typical of bureaucratic thinking.

"Well, George, we've done it. Where once there were ten pubs there is now only one. Ninety per cent closures. Not bad, I say."

"Damn fine, sir; extraordinary. They've done an outstanding job remodelling the one that remains, too. Much more attractive. Quite impressive, really, with that bar eight hundred yards long and a seating capacity of sixty-five thousand."

By 1900 the alehouse count was down to one for every 318 persons. The number of brewers, too, had dropped drastically to less than ten thousand.

Across the sea in North America the Temperance movement was flexing its muscles, but only in the urban areas where the evils were concentrated; among the frozen hills of Canada's North it was business as usual and the stern hand of moderation was unknown. In the 1860s, when the town of Barkerville in British Columbia was the gold capital of the world, the saloons constituted the social centres of the community, pushing across the bar a sophisticated assortment of refreshment ranging from beer to French champagne. Revelry ruled. A noisy poker game could be found next to a relatively quiet game of cribbage – but all fully lubricated by large glasses of ale.

The area's 10,000 population was served by three breweries. Surprising; surely any *single* self-respecting brewery could serve 10,000 people. Still, when you consider that every one of the Barkerville bunch probably drank with both hands, maybe three breweries isn't out of line.

Thirty-odd years later and a few miles farther north, there existed for a brief and riotous six months the small town of White Pass City, four miles south of White Pass, the perilous gap in the mountains that led to the Yukon and the goldfields of the Klondike. White Pass City: "Its name was the only decent thing about it." The settlement consisted of sixteen buildings and seventeen saloons. Colourful characters operated the saloons: there was Ham Grease Jimmy, Three Star Molly, Gum Boot Kitty, and Kate the Greaser. Six months after the town's establishment, the railway from Skagway on the coast to the summit of White Pass was completed, bypassing White Pass City, and to the relief of many the town ceased to exist. Elmer White, a Skagway newspaperman, called it "the toughest, rawest, most Godless town ever known."

Farther north, in 1896, Circle City, "The Paris of Alaska," supported twenty-eight saloons. Its population was 1,200. That's around forty-three drinkers per saloon, which amply illustrates the attraction booze held for the sons of Circle City, and explains why the gold production that year was only a little over a million dollars. In early 1898, Skagway, Alaska, boasted over seventy outlets for drink. "Nearly every building that was not a gambling house and saloon was a dancehall," said Elmer White. The saloons sold everything, "whether it was Budweiser at five cents a scoop or Mumms at $10 a quart."

Temperance people may look at present-day excesses and mutter "*plus ça change, plus ça reste la mème* (the more things change, the more they stay the same)." Huge volumes of ale still move through the timeless cycle. An example that warms the beer drinker's heart, but puts the Temperance fellow in a bad mood for the rest of the day, is the *Hirschgarten*, a Munich beer garden that seats seven thousand thirsty patrons and serves as many as eighteen thousand litres of beer in a single evening (that's about one litre per second). During the Netherlands' Carnival, a three-day pre-Lenten celebration, forty thousand glasses of beer may be served by even a small bar. Depending on the bar's working day, that could mean around one glass of beer every four seconds for three straight days.

Among the enemies of Temperance the greatest, and certainly most active, were the Temperance folk themselves. Intelligent people had to ask: Are these weirdos real?

> Habitual teetotalers – there should be asylums for such people. But they would probably relapse into teetotalism as soon as they came out.
>
> – Samuel Butler.

At one time they circulated the story that the principles of spontaneous combustion would cause heavy drinkers to burst into flames, much as oil-soaked rags might do when left in a basement. Woe unto you if you have a drunk lying around in your basement. What happens is this: The alcohol is exuded through the wicked pores, the body's heat (born of the fires of Hell right here on earth) warms the satanic alcohol to ignition point, and – whoosh! (hallelujah!) – the sinful drunk goes up in a sheet of flame!

Yes, well, they did tend to get carried away on the subject of alcohol. A pamphlet issued in London in the year 1665, at the time of the Plague, claimed that drinking strong beer increased your chances of contracting the pestilence. Also named as prime culprits were a howling cat and a dish of French beans.

There were a number of good people in the Temperance movement, individuals who were struck with horror at the sordid, bestial conditions that excessive drinking had spawned, and who strove to improve those conditions through sensible reform. Some were good. But many of their brothers and sisters were simply unreal. The Temperance folk's conviction that we were all heading for Hell was so determined, so deeply rooted, that you felt if you *did* stop drinking they would be disappointed; you would rob them of their goal, and another cause of damnation would have to be found. The English playwright and lyricist A. P. Herbert had a word for it:

> Well, if it isn't gin
> Was meant to do us in,
> The chances are it's lemonade or dates.

England's Reverend James Townley, eighteenth century "lyricist" of many of the snappier songs sung by the Temperance contingent, had, in a moment of weakness, a few good words to say for beer.

> Beer! happy produce of our isle,
>   Can sinewy strength impart,
> And wearied with fatigue and toil,
>   Can cheer each manly heart.

What can we say, except "Hear! Hear!" Certainly grand sentiment with which every thinking person must agree. Still – not wishing to be a nit-picker you understand – but still, "wearied with fatigue"? Yes, fatigue sure does weary you; in fact it is probably the direct cause of weariness. But beer is wearied? Well, that's what he says; I mean, when you dispense with the paren-

175

thetical "happy produce" and the bit about "sinewy strength," you have "Beer, wearied with fatigue, cheers the heart." Come on, Townley, you're not paying attention.

The same poet (if I may be forgiven the term) matched Hogarth in his fulminations against the demon gin:

> Damn'd cup that on the vitals preys,
>   That liquid fire contains,
> Which madness to the heart conveys,
>   And rolls it through the veins.

Not quite Alexander Pope perhaps, but great stuff for the Temperance folk, who sang it with fervour in mid-eighteenth century England.

The puritans – whose motto was "God Encompass Us," and who were little more than early Temperance types – frowned on just about everything. You name it, they disapproved of it. Drink, food, merrymaking – all the same, thumbs down, knock it off. Just the suspicion of a smile, indicating that you might be enjoying something, and they wrote you off as beyond redemption.

> All plums the prophet's sons deny,
>   And spice broths are too hot;
> Treason's in a December pie
>   And death within the pot!

How embarrassing it must have been for the seventeenth century puritans to learn that their very chief, Oliver Cromwell, no less, was a brewer.

Regardless of your attitude toward Temperance, either the brittle concept itself, or its irritable followers, you must give them an E for Effort. They just never gave up. In mid-twentieth century England – within living memory – they fought to prevent the serving of food in the alehouse because it would "draw more victims into the drinking area."

The playing of games in the alehouse – darts, dominoes, whatever – also drew frowns, and for the same reason: more raging drunks crowding into "the drinking area." One publican wanted to set up a small garden next to his premises, where his patrons could enjoy a beer, or tea, or whatever, on a warm summer evening. No dice, said the Temperance people. Why? You guessed it: It would "draw more victims into the drinking area," and abandoned licentiousness would undoubtedly result.

"Fanaticism," said George Santayana, "consists in redoubling your efforts when you have forgotten your aim." Right on, George. Temperance seemed blindly, senselessly, unalterably opposed to the public-house, regardless of its merits. You felt they would immediately cry out against virtue itself if the Devil expressed his approval of it.

In a speech to the British House of Commons in 1936, Sir Alan Herbert, the Honourable Member of Parliament for Oxford University and a defender of the alehouse's place in the fabric of a civilized society, maintained that the pub was a valuable social institution.

"It is a centre to which people can go for political sanity and, for temperance purposes, it is the instrument of control. It is a place where people who do not own rich houses, who have no billiard rooms or gardens of their own, are able to go for social intercourse, to discuss the troubles of life and the news of the day." To fight the enrichment of these social aspects of the alehouse, he claimed, was to foster the very evil they sought to avoid. Those who oppose improvement "do a great deal of harm ... because they think that improvement will bring more people to the public-house ... what they call the drinking area ... and so they themselves perpetuate the system of the public-house being merely a drinking place and nothing else. For this ... I say that the Temperance party [is] responsible for much of the drunkenness that exists."

A nineteenth century doctor named Moxon saw what he felt was the irony in the Temperance movement. "I believe that to a large extent teetotalism lays firmest hold on those who are least likely ever to become drunkards, and are most likely to want at times the medicinal use of alcohol – sensitive, good-natured people, of weak constitution."

Sophocles maintained that a moderate diet should consist of bread, meat, vegetables, and beer. The Temperance advocates of his day didn't listen to him, and they haven't listened since. Their attitude to beer in the diet was unequivocally the same as to beer in the alehouse; and alehouses, as we have seen, were rejected out of hand by the Temperance movement. However, on the subject of alehouses there *were* voices in the wilderness.

"Before we object to the public-houses," said the poet Leigh Hunt (1784-1859), "and above all to their Saturday night recreations, we must alter the systems that make them a necessary comfort to the poor and laborious."

Hackwood's view of the English public-house of three-quarters of a century ago, and the often unrealistic laws governing it, is to a large extent still true of today's establishment. "In this country the labouring man seeking recreation in a house of public entertainment – less happy than his *confrère* on the continent – is debarred participation in a cheap and simple game, such as dominoes, and is restricted severely to the only pleasure permitted him – that of imbibing drink."

The movement for reform, coloured deeply by strident Temperance types, would have closed every beer outlet in England if it had had its way in 1904. Lord Balfour, in an address to Parliament, told them quite frankly they would never close England's public-houses, and questioned the wisdom of *trying* to.

"What, then, should you aim at?" he asked. "Surely at this ideal: that the public-house should be kept respectable, should be kept by respectable persons, and should be kept is such a manner as will make those who frequent it obey the law and conform to the dictates of morality; a difficult state to attain but one which never seems to occur to certain classes of temperance reformer." Their one desire, he claimed, seemed to be to render the tenure of the publican insecure. "How," he asked, "can you expect the trade, which you deliberately intend to make insecure, to be filled by men of character?"

William Gladstone, England's prime minister during Victoria's reign, rejected the hypocrisy the reformers demanded of him: "How can I, who drink good wine and bitter beer every day of my life, coolly stand up and advise hard-working fellow-creatures to take the pledge?"

John Bickerdyke, a contemporary of Gladstone's and a firm defender of ale, observed: "It is a fact that the best work has always been done by moderate drinkers. The physical condition of rigid abstainers has frequently been commented upon; and without wishing to say anything unkind, or uncharitable, about men who are doubtless honest and conscientious, though in our view misguided, we cannot but suggest the question: Is the appearance of the average abstainer . . . a good advertisement for the opinions he advocates? Does his appearance seem to indicate a physical or intellectual superiority? . . . Each of these questions must be answered with an emphatic negative."

In a Toronto newspaper in 1921, an anonymous reader expressed this view: "[Prohibitionists] class everybody who disagrees with them as selfish persons . . . [The prohibitionists are] women and men who have little first-hand knowledge of the actualities of life." But perhaps the most revealing aspect of his letter was that he wished to remain anonymous so that he and his family "could continue to attend Divine Worship without molestation from over-zealous prohibitionists." Stephen Leacock, writing in 1919, took a harsher view: "The real prohibitionist . . . [is] animated by the evil spirit and desire to tyrannize and compel – to force the souls of other men to compliance with the narrow rigor of their own."

Looking back over the turbulent history of Temperance reform, Norman Longmate wrote in 1968: "The temperance movement today has in fact little in common with its past. Its progressive love of humanity has degenerated into reactionary opposition to 'softness,' its old comradeship has withered into fraternal distrust, its desire to improve the quality of life has congealed into a joyless puritanism."

Yet it was this "joyless puritanism" that saw the hundreds of years of clamourous political pressure bear fruit in the early days of this century. In 1919 the "Noble Experiment" was introduced into the United States and made law.

The Prohibition era had begun.

10

Prohibition

Like all great social changes, the drive for reform in this century, which culminated in the tragedy of Prohibition, did not happen over a single season. In the U.S.A. it began well before the First World War. The 1914 vote in Congress on the Prohibition amendment went 197 in favour to 190 against. Though the Prohibition element did not achieve the majority necessary to pass the enactment, the results were an indication of the country's views. Fully two out of three of those in favour came from cities of less than 10,000 people, while of the 190 against, more than half were from cities of more than 25,000. Clearly, Prohibition was the American village against the American city. Readers of history will not be surprised. The conflict is an old one. It existed as far back as fifth century Greece; there, too, the farmer sought good prices for the fruit of his land and lower prices for the products of industry, while the city dweller fought for higher profits from his manufactured goods and lower prices for the farmer's food. Each considered the other either a pirate or a parasite.

In America the farmer was looked upon as the mainstay of the entire country. As settlers pushed farther west, the entrepreneurial impetus, and the sense of adventure and excitement that drove the newcomers to carve their life from the raw land, came face to face with the grim realities of life on the frontier. The millstones of Nature's simple harshness ground the settler down to the same simple level, producing a straightforward people, honest and uncomplicated, and bred a similar simple faith. Further, it bred a corresponding distrust of other older, more sophisticated religions, those filled with pomp and ceremony – *foreign* religions, the ones imported by the millions of immigrants who flooded the

eastern cities at the turn of the century. This rural prejudice, this small-town thinking, was to form the basis of
the thrust toward total prohibition before, during, and
after the First World War.

The focal point of the Prohibition, or Dry, movement's
activities was the saloon. Freedom for all mankind, true
liberty, trumpeted the Anti-Saloon League, could only
be achieved when man was freed from the chains of
liquor. The democratic concept of freedom of choice
was the people's right, they cried, but man was not free
to choose when sodden with drink, so drink had to go. By
extension, drink meant saloons. Dry areas outside the
cities claimed the proximity of the cities' saloons under-
mined their dry status. This was a particularly thorny
question, and met the same resistance in Canada as it did
in the U.S.A. Any movement toward "local option" laws
was fought bitterly by prohibitionists everywhere. Local
option allowed individual cities, towns, and municipali-
ties to decide their own status: Wet or Dry. Naturally,
prohibitionists went up the wall at the thought of liquor
outlets flourishing on the other side of the boundary of
their own dry area. They claimed, and with considerable
justification, that any dry municipality that found itself
cheek by jowl with a wet municipality became a wet
municipality whether it liked it or not.

In Western Canada, Victoria was a case in point. Canada endured Prohibition, too, and with its repeal there
came, in many areas, the local option question. Victoria
rejected it and remained dry (no liquor by the glass). But
immediately to the west the area known as Esquimalt
voted to permit "beer parlours," and like lemmings
thirsty Victorians poured across the Point Ellice and
Johnson Street bridges to enjoy Esquimalt's beer. This
was fine with Victoria, until the beer drinkers came back
into the city around midnight, filling the streets with
loud cars, the streetcars with loud drunks, and the night
with loud cries; thus Esquimalt made the money while
Victoria reaped the intemperate result.

Beer parlours in Esquimalt or saloons in New York,
they were the same insidious animal as far as the prohibitionists were concerned. For the redemption of man,
cried the Americans, the saloons must be abolished.
Cynics scoffed at all the purple rhetoric about Liberty,
Truth, Freedom, and Redemption, and sneered that the
churches and saloons were simply competitors in the

182

same business: the business of offering consolation to the masses.

And business was, indeed, the name of the game. The moral aspects of Prohibition did not concern the businessman. The poor wages and the industrial hells of the factories turned the labourer to liquor as an escape from a world of endless and sordid toil, with the consequent drop in his ability to produce. The businessman thought only of efficiency and production. "We are not interested in the moral side of the matter," said one industrialist. "It is purely a question of dollars and cents." Closing the saloon meant not only an improvement in production levels, but also – and this profoundly pleased the businessman – the workers' spending power would be increased without a raise in wages, and their improved health would raise levels of production and production quality. What the Drys and the businessmen seemed unable to understand was: How were workers to entertain themselves in the evening? Suggestions that they play whist in the church hall, or read a good book, simply illustrated once more that non-drinkers will never understand drinkers.

In the years before Prohibition in the States the lure of attractive profits drew syndicates into the brewing trade. Shareholders demanded their dividends, so the brewer had to sell more and more beer. Competition increased. Breweries opened new saloons wherever there appeared the opportunity to make an extra dollar. Saloons sprang up on every corner; proprietors with little or no experience were installed to administer the new outlets. Their only precept was profit. They provided back rooms for those who wanted to gamble, and took a kickback from the players. Profit was the guiding principle, and how it was gained didn't matter; the new proprietor, under pressure from his brewery – which owned everything, including the proprietor – had to produce a certain profit every day. The saloon began to serve anybody: drunks, young lads, even children.

In England there were, ostensibly, laws that protected the very young. In the nineteenth century, children under sixteen could not be sold a drink of liquor in a bar; under thirteen they could not get a beer. So if you were fourteen and liked gin you were out of luck, but you could drink beer all night. Funny laws. Yet, if you were old enough to walk, you could pop into an alehouse and buy as much booze as you liked for consumption off the premises, which effectively nullified the aforementioned laws.

As in most business enterprises, if the liquor seller narrowed his view sufficiently he could justify just about anything. The English gin palace was no exception, and in the case of children, adopted the pragmatic policies that maximized profits. Girouard cites Henry Vizetelly's claim that the first gin palace (early 1830s) was an outfit called Thompson & Fearon, a deceptively innocuous London gin shop near Holborn Hill and Field Lane. An 1860 drawing shows it as a rather plain little shop, looking for all the world as if butter wouldn't melt in its mouth, while *we* know that inside there was a blaze of gaslight, unfolding before our eyes "a vision of splendour" in which crowds of thirsty patrons were putting a large dent in the gin casks. One such gin palace, in an early effort at customer service, even had one counter for the grownups and another lower one for the children. Smart merchandising is not a new science.

In the manner of their English brothers a generation before, the American saloons assumed a democratic posture. "Their money [the children's and the drunks'] is just as good as anyone else's; it's their own affair." These were the convenient, elastic ethics that governed the saloon's operations; it never closed so long as someone was prepared to buy a drink. The less ruthless saloonkeeper found himself losing out to the competition. Many shrugged and accepted the new rules.

Observers found little difference in the Canadian West. There was always a dollar to be made from drinks and drunks. In St Boniface, Manitoba, as late as 1928, a livery stable made a nice income picking up the drunks that passed out in the city's alleys (or main streets). Summoned by a constable, the stable's wagon would be dispatched, pick up the body, and deliver it to the slammer. A buck apiece was the charge. The city did all right, too: the drunk was subjected to a ten-dollar fine when he sobered up, which netted the city a nine-dollar profit.

"From a social point of view," wrote James Gray, "the frontier west would compare unfavourably with Dickens' London . . . When there was no work, people went hungry . . . children could be put to work at any age." The streets, crowded with reeling drunks, often gave the appearance of one of the unhappier Hogarth prints.

These were the conditions that drew supporters to the banner of the Anti-Saloon League and spelled the end of the saloon. But hardly had the saloon door been padlocked than, like a hydra, illicit outlets sprang up on every corner and at the end of every alley. Blind pigs, or speakeasies, flourished.

Many of us, at one time or another, have patronized a blind pig. The origin of the term illustrates the inventiveness of sellers of drink in a Temperance climate. At the turn of the century in the U.S.A. there were many localities that prohibited the sale of liquor, but there was, technically speaking, no law that said you couldn't give liquor away free. On that premise a thoughtful individual set up a tent one day and placed on display a blind pig. He then invited the public to have a look at the animal. Ten cents a look was what he charged. As a dividend he gave his customers a "free" drink. How long he remained in business is not known, but the animal lives on in clandestine drinking establishments everywhere.

North American Temperance societies had been growing in power for three-quarters of a century; in 1834 they listed a million members. With the advent of the 1914-1918 war the Dry faction in the U.S.A. turned patriotic. In 1915 they pointed accusingly at the liquor tax, which accounted for over 60 per cent of government revenue. The government, they claimed, had a direct financial interest in the perpetuation of the liquor trade. Banish liquor, cried the Drys, and improve the quality and quantity of war production. The grain consumed in the distilling of liquor, they said, would be better used if turned into bread for our troops. Close the saloons so America will be pure for our brave soldier boys when they return. One politician, however, remarked scornfully that the government would have a tough job prohibiting liquor when the Sears Roebuck sales catalogue conveniently offered a home distilling kit for less than five bucks.

Across the border in Canada, liquor restrictions were already in effect. Back in 1875, what was later to be known as Toronto the Good supported almost three hundred taverns. With a population at that time of 70,000, this worked out to 233 thirsty customers per tavern. This friendly state of affairs was soon to pass. The year before, the WCTU (Women's Christian Temperance Union) established its first chapter in Ontario and was pressing firmly for prohibition. Their efforts were rewarded in 1878 when the federal government passed the Canada Temperance Act (embodying the usual tiresome injunctions: no liquor to be sold, other than for medicinal, sacramental, or industrial purposes, except for brewers and distillers who may sell wholesale quantities – ten gallons or more – to licensed druggists or other authorized persons). A pall settled over the land.

The Ontario Temperance Act, passed in 1916, closed bars, clubs, and liquor outlets for the duration of the First World War. Prohibition, hiding behind the euphemism "temperance," reigned more or less supreme. As with all such unnatural measures from the beginning of time, it was about as effective as prohibiting breathing. Police spent a good part of their working day seizing liquor. There seemed to be oceans of it, sloshing across the province like a fragrant sea. The Ontario Provincial Police Annual Report for 1919 gives a fair idea of the traffic. During the year, the OPP seized a total of 2 barrels,

85 gallons, 1436 bottles, and 62 flasks of whisky. In addition, they captured 5 gallons plus 304 bottles of gin, 108 bottles of brandy, 4 gallons of alcohol, 239 half-gallons of high wines (flavoured alcohol), and 2 bottles of beer.

Two bottles of beer?!

Okay fellas, come on: What happened to the rest of the beer?

Back in the U.S.A., the singlemindedness of the Drys helped to create an efficient organization, and they quickly became politically powerful. The Dry forces (the Anti-Saloon League, for example) maintained a file on all members of Congress who had been elected with Dry support, and kept a record of the direction in which they voted on all measures that promoted the cause of Prohibition. The politicians were made aware of the file's existence and its ability to destroy them in their home states. One senator called it as tyrannical a system as was ever known in the history of government.

The organized Drys had a lot of things going for them, not the least of which was the *lack* of organization of the anti-Prohibition, or Wet, faction. In addition, the open attempts of the rich liquor industry to control Congress played into the hands of the Drys, and they profited by it in their propaganda.

For more than half a century before Prohibition the Drys had been organizing themselves to fight the demon rum. The Wets, though, had formed no coherent front for self-protection. They seemed to feel "it couldn't happen to us." And it probably wouldn't have happened if the Temperance groups had continued to battle the nebulous enemy: liquor in general. But with the advent of the Anti-Saloon League the enemy took form and the saloon became the embodiment of all the evils the Dry faction fought. The saloons, as if to prove their alignment with Satan, continued to fight the competition that came from a turbulent host of other saloons by evading the law in order to make a fast buck, the very fuel that fed the fires of the Anti-Saloon League and ultimately destroyed the saloon.

Up to the end of the nineteenth century, saloons were content to serve the customer who came in and ordered a drink. But as competition increased so did ethics decline. The saloon, instead of passively providing, began actively enticing, and competed against a man's wife and children for his pay packet. The saloon served young children; a man who was hardly able to stand was allowed to continue drinking as long as he could put his money on the bar. "A man should be free to drink what he likes, when he likes" was the self-righteous view of the saloon.

Weakly, and ineffectively, the Wets cried out against the Prohibition steamroller set in motion by the militant Drys. "An instrument of despotism," they cried; the last resource of fanatics who attempt to compel where they are unable to lead. They claimed it would not be in the individual states' best interests to extend federal power through national Prohibition. They rejected the regulation of all human conduct by laws, laws, laws. "If men wanted liquor," they stated bluntly, "they would get it." Oliver Goldsmith, centuries before, voiced the same view on laws. "Nothing can be more certain than that numerous written laws are a sign of a degenerate community, and are frequently not the consequences of vicious morals in a state, but the causes."

In the 1920s, when the country lay in the grip of Prohibition, a frustrated U.S. marshal complained: "The more laws we have," he said, "the easier it is for the bootlegger to escape. We need simple laws like the Commandments, and then enforce them." The marshal's lament was a sad echo of the Annual Report for 1887 wherein the commissioner of the North-West Mounted Police bemoaned the difficulties in enforcing the liquor laws across the Prairies (still at that time known as the North-West Territories). "The law should be cleared of the technicalities that have enabled so many to escape punishment." He then added a solution advanced repeatedly, but unheard in the hue and cry for total prohibition – "The importation and manufacture of a good lager beer, under stringent regulations, would greatly assist the satisfactory settlement of this question."

It was ever thus; history's lessons again and again ignored. England experienced the same legal briar patch a half-century before. As an example – one among many – Britain's abortive Sale Of Beer Act of 1885 stipulated that to get a drink on Sunday you had to be a *bona fide* traveller. The "*bona fide* traveller" quickly became the funniest act in the country, and got funnier as the years went by. People naturally asked, what, exactly, constituted a *bona fide* traveller? Defining the law became an exasperating exercise, so in 1872 the law was clarified: You had to travel three miles to be a *"bona fide* traveller." Overnight, railway stock skyrocketed, because entire villages climbed aboard the trains on Sunday and went a short three or four miles to the next village, drank it dry, and returned home. Great Sunday outing. In 1893 a further amendment was introduced: If all you were after was a drink, then you were not considered by law to be a *bona fide* traveller. Can't you just picture it?

Traveller: "I'll have a Scotch and soda, please."

Barman scowls at traveller. "So it's just a drink you're after, is it?"

"Certainly not," says traveller.

"Ah, well that's all right, then. Scotch and soda, was it?"

The lunacy of the whole thing makes you a bit dizzy. Let's go over it again slowly: If you sought refreshment, the law forbade you to have it; if you did *not* want a drink, then you could have one.

As near as a generation ago there was a Scottish law, similar to the English one, that prohibited Sunday drinking unless you were a traveller. The Scots' definition of "traveller" was a non resident who came from at least four or five miles away. James Cameron, a Scottish newspaperman, recalled that two small villages about five miles apart experienced a complete exchange of population every Sunday, each thirsty "traveller" covering the mandatory five miles to the neighbouring village. The same Scot remembered returning from the Korean War to his home town in Scotland. It was a Sunday. He was dying for a beer. With sinking heart he tried to explain to the barman that he had just travelled over 10,000 bloody miles! Nothing doing; he was in his home town, thus according to the law he was not a non-resident.

On the threshold of Prohibition in the U.S.A., the Wet faction struggled against the big Dry machine. They deplored the breach of personal freedom threatened by the Drys' attempt to legislate the morals of the people. They called for a test period before Prohibition became law. Like shrill Cassandras they saw the difficulties of enforcement on a national scale, and the huge opportunities for profit offered the criminal element. In vain.

Prohibition in the U.S.A. became a fact on 16 January 1920 and almost immediately corruption became a way of life. Bribery and theft were everywhere. Conspiracies, forgery, the falsification of records were daily occurrences. Perjury ruled the courts, extortion was around every corner. Prosecutions could easily be avoided – for a price.

While the Americans went all out in their efforts at total prohibition, and suffered the consequences in widespread contempt for the law, Canadians were more circumspect and tended to at least *try* to look at both sides of the question. Canada's Prohibition didn't last as long, nor was it as violent, nor indeed was it as restrictive. Canadian prohibition beer had a higher alcohol content than that permitted in the U.S.A., domestically produced wines were exempt and freely available, and manufacturing booze remained legal for licensed distillers.

On the West Coast of Canada the full weight of Prohibition was short-lived. In Victoria the 109 liquor outlets (hotels and saloons) were closed from 1917 to 1921; shortly thereafter the British Columbia government shrewdly got into the liquor business and opened its own liquor stores, and hard-core Prohibition disappeared.

But that was Canada. South of the border the Americans were busily instituting laws to stop the flow of beer and whisky. The Eighteenth Amendment to the Constitution prohibited the manufacture, sale, or transport of liquor. The passage of the Volstead Act ostensibly enforced the Amendment and prevented the illegal trade in alcohol. Neither document ever really worked. The border between Canada and the U.S.A. became the widest one-way street in the world. In one area alone, Detroit, the smuggling of liquor generated graft to the amount of two million dollars a week.

> Four and twenty Yankees,
>   Feeling mighty dry,
> Took a trip to Canada
>   And bought a case of rye.
> When the case was opened
>   The Yanks began to sing,

"To hell with the President!
God save the King!"

At sea, large supply ships lay offshore, outside American territorial waters, and unloaded liquor into the rum-runners' smaller faster boats. These high-speed craft then made the often perilous journey ashore to some lonely spot where the bootleggers transferred the liquor to their trucks. Trucking was frequently as dangerous as the water route. Hijacking became a profession like any other – engineering for example, or dentistry – and often there seemed to be more hijackers than primary distributors. There were hijackers that hijacked hijackers; even your own *confrères* couldn't be trusted, regardless of the method of transport. Along the Canadian border, transporting illicit liquor by train car, under a load of coal for example, could invite the loss of the liquid cargo, and not from the obvious source; the authorities might never learn of its existence. The trouble came from local bootleggers on the lookout for some fast, easy, and free product for their operations. If the fellow who was putting the coal on top of the booze didn't keep his eyes open, he could be loading coal at one end of the car while the bootleggers were unloading his liquor out the other, thus leaving the transporter of illegal liquor with a load of perfectly legal coal.

On the Canadian side of the border everything the American rum-runners did was legal. They passed through Canadian Customs and secured visitors' permits. Their Canadian suppliers or exporters provided them with the necessary documentation to show they were, in all legitimacy, transporting the goods on behalf of the exporter to the U.S.A., just in case they bumped into the Canadian cops, who would naturally question the movement of all that booze. This was on the Canadian side. On the American side of the border it was another story. Waiting for them was Customs, if they were crazy enough to pass through a recognized border crossing point. Also there were their Yankee "competitors" waiting to hijack them the minute they stepped across the border. Some of the hijackers couldn't wait, and occasionally ambushed them on the Canadian side, with the usual crashing of cars and wild gunfire that roused the local cop from his bed to watch from his bedroom window. (Not too many rural constables would voluntarily step from their homes into a hail of bullets, with an admonishing "Here you chaps, not so much noise.")

The lucrative border traffic in liquor between Windsor and Detroit (a mere mile away across the river) gave birth to some interesting scams. While the export of liquor from Canada to the U.S.A. ran into trouble at the border, it was perfectly within the law to export to, say, Cuba or other Caribbean ports, which produced this ludicrous scenario: A tiny boat – barely able to navigate a small lake, let alone the Atlantic – appears in Windsor with an export licence and fifty cases of liquor consigned to Cuba, then shoves off into the night, only to reappear a couple of hours later with another licence, more booze, and the same Caribbean destination.

Detroit and "Cuba" were not the only destinations open to the entrepreneurs of Windsor (a Toronto newspaper remarked that one of Windsor's major industries was bootlegging). Ontario, too, was dry in the early years of Prohibition in the U.S.A. The same rowboat that was ostensibly bound for Cuba with its freight of booze (the water inches from the gunwales, the slightest wave soaking the oarsman and getting his export licence all wet) could just as easily row out into the river as night fell, then, in the darkness, turn and come right back into Ontario again, and deliver its cargo at some prearranged inlet where a truck waited to supply the eager thirsts of Canadians from Toronto to Winnipeg. (A word on the so-called export licences: The licences were perfectly legitimate, but required proof of delivery to avoid problems with the Canadian government. For the "exporter," procuring the official Cuban receipt of the liquor was simplicity itself. The licence was sent to Cuba where an official – for a modest consideration – covered the thing with florid stamps and a barrel of Latin-looking signatures, and sent it back to the Canadian "exporter," who in turn submitted it to the government, and everyone was happy.)

Controlling the rum-runners in the Windsor/Detroit area was bad enough, but nothing compared with the problems facing the Mounties along the 1,500-odd miles of prairie border that spanned the frontier from Manitoba to Alberta. They simply didn't make enough cars in those days to allow the lawmen to patrol even the main roads and border crossings. The back roads rarely felt the Mounties' scrutiny and became a part of the happy one-way street for smugglers serving the northern states.

A further difficulty in liquor law enforcement in the West – indeed law enforcement in general; thugs were knocking off banks and burgling homes, too, during Prohibition – was the ratio of provincial police to land area: approximately one cop per 1,000 square miles. Weeks could go by and you'd never *see* a cop.

Back east the same conditions existed in Quebec, and many of the province's small border towns did their share to keep the Americans happy. An Ottawa newspaper reported, derisively, that while every single inhabitant of Granby, Quebec, could be made blind drunk on about a hundred bottles of whisky, the town's liquor sales were more than six thousand bottles a day.

The "booze for export" caper was common across Canada. The locals in Victoria circumvented British Columbia's prohibitive liquor laws by simply ordering from the "export" houses in Alberta, which, like those in just about every other province in the country, were brewing and distilling like mad for other dry provinces, creating a hilarious alcoholic merry-go-round that had the zealots of Prohibition frothing with fury and frustration. Ontario encountered the same exasperating situation. During the entire time the province struggled with the problems of Prohibition, the major difficulty continued to be the twenty-nine breweries and six distilleries within its borders, all licensed by the federal government to manufacture and export liquor. Export came under federal jurisdiction and the feds seemed uninterested in the difficulties and embarrassment these firms caused the province. That the foreign (or domestic) destination of the exported booze might prohibit the entry of the liquor was a matter of indifference to the Canadian Customs; smugglers thus found Canada the sweetest place this side of Heaven, virtually a rum-runner's warehouse.

At the time Prohibition became law south of the border there were over 177,000 saloons in operation across the U.S.A. As these closed, new sources of liquor were born. Within six months of the passing of the Volstead Act, physicians in the city of Chicago issued over half a

million prescriptions for "medicinal" whisky. Throughout Prohibition, doctors' prescriptions for medicinal
liquor in the United States amounted to over a million
gallons a year.

Canadians, too, sought their understanding physician
and pharmacist when a drop of good stuff was indicated,
as we see in the year 1919 when the Ontario provincial
election brought to power an improbable outfit called
the United Farmers of Ontario. The result caught everyone by surprise, including the UFO, who didn't even have
a leader. Staunchly prohibitionist, they soon had their
hands full of the same problems their predecessors (and
successors) suffered, namely the paradox of a province
that came out strongly against drink, but nevertheless
did an awful lot of drinking. The medical profession, as
noted, had the legal right to issue prescriptions for
medicinal liquor. In 1920, 588,000 "prescriptions" were
written for medicinal liquor. Four years later it was still
business as usual, only the prescriptions totalled
800,000. A member of the Ontario government pointed
out that on 23 December alone liquor prescriptions
were written amounting to $55,000. He added, wryly,
that the "epidemic" appeared to subside by 26 December when the figure dropped to $11,000. Though a mat-
ter of grave concern to the prohibitionists, to the rest of
us it simply indicates that it was a fairly normal Christmas and Boxing Day, where only one guy in five
managed to make it out of bed for a hair of the dog.

The scandalous use of prescriptions to get "medicinal" booze prompted one member of the Ontario legislature to state that as much as 90 per cent of prescription
liquor had no medical purpose whatsoever. Indeed, he
claimed, many doctors completely disregarded the law.
One doctor was reported to have issued over two
thousand such "scrips" in a single month, and pocketed
two or three bucks each for them. Not bad; $4,000 to
$6,000 a month, when most men were happy to take
home a monthly paycheque of $60. In the twelve-month
period ending October 1923, Ontario government
dispensaries sold $4.8 million in medicinal alcohol. A
boldly anti-prohibitionist Toronto magazine snorted
scornfully that four million dollars in booze a year
wasn't too bad for a "dry" province. The whole system
was described by many as a ghastly joke. A member of
the Ontario legislature pointed to the laughable irony of

a "dry" government that was flogging more booze than any other bootlegger in the province.

Even so, a historical precedent of sorts did exist. In 1882 in the ostensibly dry Northwest Territories, liquor could be obtained from druggists upon presentation of a doctor's prescription, much like the Ontario setup of 1920. Regina's first drugstore even advertised beer and liquor (for medicinal purposes, of course), a merchandising ploy that would have horrified the Presbyterians of Toronto. (What would the Torontonians have thought of one enterprising western druggist who maintained a washtub full of beer on ice for his customers' pleasure?)

Nevertheless, writing all those prescriptions must have been an exhausting chore, and Alberta doctors, undoubtedly hearing the call of the golf course, would provide the pharmacist with a supply of signed, blank prescription forms. The druggist simply filled them in when a thirsty "patient" popped in off the street. By the end of 1921 the Alberta government had taken steps to curtail this practice. Doctors were limited to 100 medicinal alcohol prescriptions per month. At $2 per scrip, this must have been tough on the doc: only $200 a month – three times the average man's wages – for nothing.

It's reassuring, though, to learn that of the abuses of doctor-dispensed alcohol the doctors of Ontario were themselves the most vocal. Ontario Attorney-General W. F. Nickle claimed that many doctors had asked him, "Cannot something be done to lift from our shoulders the iniquity of being the bartenders for the province?"

In Ontario, while the Licence Board monitored doctors' liquor "prescriptions," the Board of Health cast a jaundiced eye on patent medicines, many of which were little more than flavoured alcohol, and all of which were selling like mad. The Board of Health's concern was not illusory. We have seen the pharmacists making a handsome dollar filling prescriptions for "medicinal" liquor. But their retail efforts extended beyond mere whisky. Ranged along their shelves were scores of patent medicines that also helped the prescription-less customer beat the Prohibition Blues. Among them a pick-me-up called Hostelters Bitters weighed in at 46 per cent alcohol, stronger than the whisky you can buy today. Innocent-sounding Lydia Pinkham's Compound wasn't all that innocent: five times stronger than beer. The manufacturers made a fortune. The prohibitionists were not amused.

Forty years earlier, the prime minister of Canada, Sir John A. Macdonald himself, once commented adversely on the uses of some patent medicines. On the subject of alleged internal misconduct within the North-West Mounted Police, he remarked, "there has been a great use of that most noxious drink, Perry Davis' Pain Killer. It contains a great quantity of alcohol, and . . . has been used largely under the pretence of being medicinal, but, really, as a stimulant."

The Mounties in those early days were a very rough bunch who would drink just about anything, as Sir John found out. A necessary law-enforcement agency, admittedly, but nevertheless a very tough lot. They had little time for the violence and unbridled lawlessness that characterized the settlement of the western plains south of the border. During the building of the Canadian Pacific Railway and the immigration that followed it across the Prairies, relative peace and tranquillity were maintained by the North-West Mounted Police. They were a hard group of men who took a dim view of gun-carrying settlers (or even gun-carrying transients). There were always problems, but, again ironically, the basic nature of the early Mounties – lots of intramural gambling, fighting, and good old-fashioned hard drinking – frequently made them part of the problem rather than the solution.

Another beef of Sir John A. Macdonald was the tendency of the British well-born family to unload its drunks and other embarrassing sons on the North-West Mounted Police as an alternative to Australia or the South Pacific islands. "We found great pressure brought," Sir John remarked in 1881, "to send up gentlemen's sons – educated men of broken habits – and the [NWMP] was to some extent made to serve the purpose of an inebriate asylum . . . there is still a good deal of drinking."

If, for one reason or another, you couldn't drop into your neighbourhood pharmacy, there was always the moonshine fraternity to help you through the dry spell. The criminal element took over the small moonshiner and organized the moonshine industry. Acting as distributor, they made arrangements with small operators – the home "alky cookers," distilling in their kitchens – and supplied them with the basic materials at fifty cents a gallon. The resulting moonshine was bought back by the distributor at two dollars a gallon. The speakeasy bought the 'shine from the distributor at six dollars a gallon and retailed it at a forty-dollar profit per gallon for the "speak's" owner.

Though moonshine contributed little to the overall flow of liquor across the Canadian West, it was still illegal, and whenever they learned of a clandestine still the federal authorities moved "quickly" to destroy it. Sounds easy, but the key phrase is "whenever they learned." Conflicting spheres of jurisdiction slowed the process almost to a standstill. When the local cop discovered the illegal operation he had first to tell his chief. The chief called the attorney-general. The A. G. got through to Customs and Excise. They would okay a search warrant ("*Search*?!" mutters the local cop. "Who needs to search? Dammit all, I'm sitting here having a drink with them!"). Only after receiving the warrant could the Mounties raid the still. Still? What still? By then the moonshiners were in the next province.

These conflicting jurisdictions were the bane of Western liquor law enforcement. The Mounted Police were responsible for one area of the law, the provincial police for another, special liquor inspectors for yet another, and none were allowed to step into another's territory. Clandestine stills, for example, were the exclusive concern of the Dominion Excise Service, and until the excise man appeared on the scene a liquor inspector could only stand and watch as an illegal still merrily distilled illegally.

Pharmacies and moonshiners were two of the public's suppliers; there were other sources, too. An estimated 20 million gallons of whisky disappeared from bonded U.S. government warehouses during the thirteen-year period of Prohibition. Nobody knows where it went. Go ahead, take a guess.

The things that we can, after all, do without (but don't intend to) have always been immensely profitable for the seller. Liquor, gambling, big cars, jewellery, fancy food all carry price tags that render huge profits. And as soon as you make the goods illegal the profits go out of sight. George Ade, an American newspaperman during the latter years of Prohibition, calculated that you could produce a quart of good reliable whisky for about five cents. He estimated that an "honest" speakeasy could sell it, drink by drink, for fifteen dollars. Profit: about 30,000 per cent, spread over the distribution chain. Even a bottle of genuine beer could be put in your hand for two cents, cost. When it retailed for fifty cents the profit was around 2,500 per cent.

On the Prairies the Law sometimes became part of the bootleggers' profit picture, albeit unintentionally. When the authorities raided a hotel and seized a barrel of real (and thus illegal) beer, the natural question would be: What do we do with it? Drinking it was an ethically unacceptable answer. They could, of course, pour it down the drain, and often did, but many chose a more lucrative route: The authorities, seeing a source of revenue, sold the barrel to a legal beer exporter who willingly paid four dollars for it. The exporter then flogged it to a distributor for seventeen dollars. Within as little as forty-eight hours after seizure the distributor had sold the same barrel of beer back to the same hotel again for twenty-five dollars – where, perhaps, a liquor inspector was waiting to seize the illegal beer and . . .

Enforcement of American Prohibition laws was weak and made more difficult by the high turnover in staff among the enforcement agents: Two out of three left the service during the Prohibition era. Of those that left, one in twelve was fired for actions prejudicial to law enforcement. Yet even the pitifully inadequate force of law officers that remained, in spite of legal confusion and ambiguity, produced results. Over the years the number of cases of liquor law infractions that piled up in the courts grew to alarming proportions. In 1932, the year before Repeal, there were over seventy thousand.

During Prohibition beer was still legally brewed in the U.S.A., but its permitted alcohol level of 0.5 per cent made it less inebriating than sauerkraut. You had to drink around twelve bottles of the stuff to get the same kick that one bottle used to give you; an impossible situation that turned many beer drinkers to bathtub gin, or home brew: Close to seven hundred million gallons of home brew were produced every year.

In 1925 Howard Ferguson's Ontario government came up with an answer to the "palatable" beer question, in the hope of pleasing both sides of the Wet/Dry fence: 2.5 per cent beer (4.4 per cent proof). Fergie presented it as a Prohibition drink. "Non-intoxicating," claimed Ferg. Immediately labelled "Fergie's Foam," it did indeed seem to be non-intoxicating. A $100 prize was offered (by a brewery, according to one source) to anyone who could get drunk on it. In court, a Toronto man, arrested for drunkenness, admitted drinking nine quarts of Fergie's Foam but also confessed that he'd had a shot of something more substantial at the beginning. The prize was never claimed.

There was ample opportunity for shrewd brewers to sidetrack huge quantities of the real thing to the thirsty populace, which they did. Many brewers removed the alcohol according to law, then passed it over to the retailer who spiked the beer back to its former alcohol content. Law-abiding brewers sneered bitterly. Produce the near-beer that the law demanded and you lost your shirt because nobody drank it. Brew the real thing and sell it illegally, and you made a fortune. Lawbreakers won, honest men lost: the story of Prohibition in five words.

"Prohibition," said Al Capone, "has made nothing but trouble – for all of us."

Rough estimates put Capone's revenue from illicit beer sales alone at $60 million to $100 million a year. Other gangland bosses enjoyed the same enormous incomes from their bootlegging operations, much of it the result of the "hands across the border" relationship between the Canadian and American underworld. In 1926 you could buy a bottle of Canadian whisky in Windsor for $2.50. Across the river in Detroit the same bottle cost $10. Beer in Detroit carried a mammoth price tag: $3.50 a case. Though Temperance in Canada was in full vigour in 1920, a Montreal brewery still managed to produce and sell during that year over five million gallons of beer, to the "Temperance" standard of 4.4 per cent alcohol.

Along the East Coast business was brisk. From South America to Newfoundland the rum-runners were working overtime. During Prohibition the price of rum in the French islands of St-Pierre-Miquelon – the source of much of the bootleg liquor appearing on the east coast of North America – was 40 cents a gallon. The rum was then resold by the bootlegger in Canada and the U.S.A. for $4 a gallon, representing a profit of 900 per cent to cover operating expenses. A dozen quart bottles of branded liquor cost $7 in St-Pierre. Everyone on the island sold liquor; bottles blossomed in the windows of houses much as pots of flowers bloomed in the homes of the mainland. The island soon became the busiest warehouse on the East Coast. "During all this time," wrote exporter Harry Bronfman, "many buyers came to Montreal who bought liquor for shipment to St-Pierre. This became a large business which we called export business." In one twelve-month period enough liquor was exported to the island to supply each and every inhabitant – from the oldest gaffer to the tiniest child – with almost six quarts a day for the entire year.

The liquor of choice in the Prohibition years was spirits rather than beer, at least from the rum-runner's view, and for obvious reasons: They both took up the same shipping space, but the profit from a dozen bottles of rum was much greater than that gained from a dozen bottles of beer. Yet figures reported in a Halifax newspaper of 1931 indicate that the public's desire for beer was by no means eclipsed by rum and whisky. The first eight months of the year saw the RCMP seize over twenty thousand gallons of spirits, and a surprising eighteen thousand gallons of beer. The quality of that beer was debatable, though; some of it must have been ghastly stuff, made from potatoes and selling for ten cents a quart, and so lumpy it was like eating potatoes with your beer.

Beer-drinking rum-runners isn't an image that leaps readily to mind, but when a ship carried thousands of bottles of rum, frequently in a heavy sea, the incidence of breakage was high and the suffocating miasma of spilled liquor was, to many crewmen, nauseating. The last thing you would want would be a slug of rum. Many rum-running vessels carried beer on ice – large wooden cases containing a gross, 144 nice cold bottles – for the crew's refreshment, kindly supplied as a gift by the liquor wholesalers.

Reference by Temperance types to "the demon rum" simply showed that they really didn't know anything about the liquor situation; they were just against it. Up to the onset of Prohibition, rum held an insignificant place in American drinking habits. Gin, too, got very little play. Whisky was the drink of choice, and in most saloons the only drink. During the Prohibition years, of course, people would drink anything, and shiploads of rum and gin found their way to American shores and developed the taste for rum- and gin-based cocktails that continues to be the vogue today. Until the twenties, gin was considered by serious drinkers as merely a remedy for kidney trouble (indeed, this was the use for which gin was originally intended, as a diuretic), and rum as a cure for colds and throat problems.

Over the span of the Prohibition years, most of the illegal liquor traffic in the Maritimes was rum. Attendees at amateur hockey games in the Maritimes, in the early 1930s, might sometimes have seen the players protect themselves from the cold with a nip or two from an ale bottle – called a "bully" – of bootleg rum. The cork-stoppered bottle seemed a standard measure. A thirsty father might send his young boy to the bootlegger for a couple of bullys of rum.

From Demerara came eighty-gallon puncheons of rum which would be cut on board ship: one gallon of water to two gallons of rum. Burnt sugar would be added to maintain colour. The rum was then generally transferred to five-gallon casks for delivery ashore to the rum-runner's fleet of trucks, thence distributed across the eastern seaboard and as far west as Chicago. At first, Demerara rum was shipped in twelve-gallon kegs, but this was soon changed. In the eyes of the rum-running shipowner the five-gallon keg became the size of choice because it was easier to move around. Not incidentally, it was also *faster* to move, too – over the side, when necessary.

Working for the rum-runners was immensely profitable. Crewmen of the ships that carried the illegal liquor to American destinations earned $250 a month – four or five times the ordinary wage-earner's salary (if the ordinary wage-earner was lucky enough to have a job). Successful delivery of a shipload of rum earned the crewman a bonus of $100. The same attractive financial spread was seen out west. A seaman employed by the Canadian Pacific Steamships earned perhaps $65 a month. But if you worked for the rum-runners operating out of Victoria you, too, like your eastern counterparts, could make as much as $250. And everyone got into the act. A Victoria policeman's son was a known rum-runner. Many of the smugglers operated from coves that were scant minutes from downtown Victoria, and their vessels ranged as far south as San Francisco.

Operating out of Nassau in the Bahamas during the Prohibition era, Captain William McCoy built a reputation for integrity and reliability. He could be trusted never to cut the liquor he smuggled to the American mainland and he always came through; never lost a cargo. His customers held him in the highest regard. When you got a case of Scotch from the Captain, you were assured it was genuine – "the real McCoy." It was McCoy who in 1921 – within a year of Prohibition's inception – introduced a new concept into the old game of rum-running. Why bring your heavy-laden vessel close in to shore to meet the bootlegger's small boats? Dangerous. Often difficult to manoeuvre to avoid the customs men. McCoy, instead, stood offshore, outside the territorial three-mile limit, and sold his liquor to all comers. Soon hundreds of similar vessels, his brothers in rum-running, were ranged alongside and gave birth to "Rum Row," the latest merchandising idea: a seagoing supermarket where you could get any kind of liquor you wanted. On his first trip out McCoy paid for his ship twice over, and for years thereafter regularly cleared $100,000 a voyage, in the days when for the city dweller a mere couple of hundred dollars a month was a princely salary.

Yankee Prohibition gave rise to some poisonous substitutes for good liquor. The writer and critic Edmund Wilson (1895-1972) once told a friend, "your gin ate circles [in my table], and when you spilled some on a page of the *Daily News*, the pictures and print came off on the tabletop like a decalcomania." Some enterprising Maritime bootleggers produced home-made beer which they sold along with the better brands of whisky and rum. The beer sold for ten cents a quart; many felt it would have been expensive at half the price.

One of the ironies of the Prohibition period in the U.S.A. was the increase in sales of carbonated water and soft drinks. The New York representative of a Canadian ginger ale and soda water company made a fortune during the Dry decade. When confronted by a dram of one of the poisons that passed for liquor in those sad days, most people automatically looked for something with which to dilute it, to weaken its sulphuric potency, and not incidentally to make it more palatable. Many establishments, ostensibly adhering to the law by serving soft drinks, would bring you a bottle of ginger ale, for example, at a price that would turn your hair white, and with the soft drink you would also get a "free" shot of . . . well, I guess you could call it liquor. It all depended on the establishments you frequented. Some would slip you Canadian rye, still warm from a recent hijacking. Others would offer you, from a bottle bearing a spurious Canadian label, something fresh from an illegal still in the Adirondack Mountains, made from just about anything you care to name.

Prohibition introduced the cocktail shaker to American drinkers. Before that, the saloons offered you a beer or a whisky. But as the saloons closed, only to re-open as speakeasies, the quality of the illicit liquor deteriorated to such a degree that to be drinkable a host of flavourings were added, a suitable container was filled with ice, and the "cocktail" was shaken furiously until everything was frozen so the drinker would be unable to taste the ghastly stuff that masqueraded as liquor.

As we have seen, the 1920s and early 1930s saw a lot of illegal liquor flowing up and down both coasts of North America and the authorities seized it wherever they found it. "Found it" is, of course, the key phrase. Hiding illicit hooch became an imaginative art. One ingenious method was to fill a toilet's cistern with liquor. In the event of a raid it needed but a simple flick of the chain and the booze was flushed away. *Voilà*, no liquor, no evidence. A faucet on the underside of the flush tank allowed the bootlegger, in the normal run of business, to draw off a dram for his customers.

During the period of Prohibition on the Prairies it was perfectly legal for the hotels to serve the 2 per cent "Temperance" beer. Not too many takers, of course, though there was rarely any need for the beer drinker to suffer what was to him virtually coloured water, because most hotel barrooms installed a simple system that pleased everyone – except the authorities. A modest alteration to the plumbing that brought the beer up to the bar allowed the bartender, with the flick of a tap, to draw good strong ale for his regulars, or, if a liquor inspector dropped in, to switch to the legal stuff.

The musically inclined bootlegger might ship his liquor in a grand piano. You would observe this truck, loaded with three or four grand pianos, tooling along a country road. Not much twanging coming from the pianos; they had all been gutted. Instead of wires and hammers, each piano held a dozen cases of booze. You can bet nobody laughed when the customs men sat down to play.

Bootleggers occasionally indulged their spirit of inno-cent merriment, especially when a new enforcement officer was assigned to their area. Anonymous tips would be passed along to the officer, alerting him to a shipment of illegal liquor hidden in a train car of flour or coal or other really messy and inconvenient material. The new man became understandably very cynical very quickly after emerging empty-handed from his third train car of coal, covered in dust, one or two fragments of coal dropping off his shoulder onto the ground, his thoughts as black as the rest of him.

While there were informers who kept the authorities aware of illegal liquor operations, the information was often of little use to the lawmen. Making a surprise raid on a country hotel was almost impossible. The liquor inspector would ordinarily travel by train, and he could take all the precautions – sneaking aboard the train in the dead of night, wearing a fake beard and dark glasses – but within moments the telegraph operators would flash the word down the line, and when the inspector burst in like Superman from the sky he would find the hotel's regulars sitting quietly, haloes round their heads, sip-ping legal beer, with not a drop of good stuff in sight and the hotel owner getting pretty shirty about police persecution.

In urban areas speakeasies flourished, and everyone who aspired to even a modest social status had his own bootlegger (the term "bootlegger" had its origin in the high boots worn by those gentlemen of the Prohibition era. The tops of the boots hid custom-made compart-ments where they concealed liquor). The bootlegging trade had a romantic image, but it was still a terminally dangerous occupation. Window stickers on the cars of the 1920s – "Don't shoot, I'm not a bootlegger" – showed the readiness of both bootlegger and enforcement officer to exchange gun fire.

The contempt for liquor laws was virtually universal, and sometimes generated situations that were reminiscent of Mack Sennett's Keystone Kops. In court, during a bootlegger's trial, a member of the jury accidentally dropped a mickey he'd been carrying in his pocket. No legal action was taken against him. The same jury, with insulting self-righteousness, found the bootlegger guilty. In another bootlegging case the jury itself was put on trial for drinking the evidence.

Anomalies in Temperance laws often generated scorn. In Ontario if you were caught with a bottle of liquor in your possession you could be fined $200. However, if you managed to drink it, you were fined $10 for being "under the influence of alcohol." As one newspaper put it: "The $200 fine for the bottle *on* you can scarcely be matched up with the $10 fine for the bottle *in* you." As always, the laws seemed to fall most heavily on the ordinary man, yet were not stringent enough to restrict the bootlegger. Even the Americans, deep in their own experiment in Prohibition, found time to mock Ontario's hypocrisy: "Ontario, the paragon of Prohibitionists, continued to manufacture liquor and export it. During 1922-1923, nearly $400,000 worth of Ontario beer was exported to Quebec . . . "

The year before (July 1921), Ontario had banned the importation of beer and liquor into the province, and ordered that any alcoholic beverages moving into, through, or out of the province were subject to seizure. This was stepping on the federal government's toes, and a test case in Windsor ruled that exports of beer and liquor were lawful, and by extension the obviously necessary movement of such exports was equally lawful. Gnashing its teeth in frustration, Ontario then said: Very well, if the brewers and distillers insist on moving beer and liquor through Ontario, we are going to slap a $15,000 a year tax on them. The opposition parties laughed heartily; one member of the legislature remarked, between guffaws, that it was more than a little absurd to lay a tax on something you'd already stated was illegal. In January 1923 the courts ruled that in banning the use of highways for liquor export Ontario was infringing upon federal jurisdiction. The ban was lifted and the lucrative business of moving beer and liquor into the U.S.A. continued much as before.

Surprisingly, if we are to judge by the fines levied on the Prairies around 1912, sex came a poor second to booze on the puritans' list of sins. The girls must have been outraged. Peddle yourself and it cost you five bucks if you were caught; but if you were nicked flogging a bottle of whisky the fine was a cool fifty dollars. But the government offered a form of relief to the bootlegger. The Dominion Income Tax Office in Hamilton, in a move that almost legitimized the illicit liquor traffic, ruled that the fines a bootlegger incurred in the conduct of his operations could be claimed, for tax purposes, as a "business expense."

Prohibition was father to the bootlegger, stout friend of dry souls. Your friendly neighbourhood bootlegger – and indeed he was often your neighbour – made gin, made beer, made wine, and made a bundle.

> Mother makes brandy from cherries;
> Pop distils whiskey and gin;
> Sister sells wine
> From the grapes on our vine –
> Good grief how the money rolls in!

As bad as the situation was, it was not made any better by Fate, who gave the American people Warren Harding and Calvin Coolidge, a couple of presidents, back to back, whose idea of political action was: Don't do anything and you'll never make a mistake. Both spent a good part of their term in office sitting on the fence, not wanting to offend anyone. "If you don't say anything," said Coolidge, "you won't be called on to repeat it." The president who followed the Bobbsey Twins was a seasoned waffler, too. When a new bridge was built in New York in 1932, the Press suggested the structure be called the Hoover Bridge because it was wet below, dry above, and straddled the river.

As the dry decade progressed, powerful forces for change began to challenge Dry supremacy. City newspapers reached out into the country and broke down the isolation in which rural prejudice and bigotry flourished. Communications improved. Automobiles, radio, and movies contributed to national homogenization. People were more mobile, there was a radio in every home, and movies painted rich and exciting pictures of city life. Instead of a sink of evil, the city became the fascinating centre of all delights. Most people began to feel that Prohibition was discriminatory, that it robbed them arbitrarily of personal freedom, and drinking became a symbol of that freedom.

As we have seen, Canada's dry period didn't last as long as the American version (to the immense profit of Canadian liquor suppliers). When Prohibition in Ontario passed into history in 1927, the beer began to flow again and the first government-controlled liquor store opened in June, but Ontarians still seemed a trifle uneasy with liquor. The difficulty with which Prohibition had been achieved was matched by the diffidence alcoholic "freedom" met in the new liquor outlets. People entered the liquor store like thieves in the night, with many a glance over the shoulder. Some continued to justify their purchases as being medicinally motivated ("Actually, I don't drink, but I've got this sore throat, and my grandfather always used to say that Scotch and hot water with a squeeze of lemon . . . ").

When the U.S.A. eventually cut itself free of Prohibition it didn't play around; it severed the Prohibition knot as abruptly and unequivocally as it had tied it thirteen years before; within an hour of Repeal high times prevailed. Ontario, though, being Ontario, approached Repeal warily (in many instances with misgiving) and slowly untied the knot with hesitant fingers. Many restrictions still remained, restrictions which now would seem darkest denial, but which in the eyes of the prohibitionists of the day appeared to open the door to Satan himself.

But in 1927 Prohibition was still in force in the States, though rapidly losing its appeal. The impossible task of enforcing the liquor laws, the open disregard for Prohibition, the mounting wealth and power of the mob bosses, all served to foster a bitter antagonism toward the Drys. During the heyday of Prohibition in the U.S.A. it was estimated that over $4.4 billion a year was spent on bootleg liquor. New York alone enthusiastically supported 32,000 speakeasies. The "Noble Experiment" was anything but noble. (The "Noble Experiment" was a paraphrase of Herbert Hoover's remark that Prohibition was "a great social and economic experiment, noble in motive and far-reaching in purpose.")

The embarrassment of the anti-liquor faction became the encouragement of the Wets. The pro-liquor Wets sought weapons with which to defeat the staggering Dry league, and ironically found them in the Drys' own arsenal – the same weapons the Drys themselves had used a decade earlier. The Wets attempted to influence the government. "Political manipulation!" cried the Drys in horror. The Wets buried the nation's newspapers and magazines under tons of press releases and subtly worded editorial material. "Underhanded propaganda!" the Drys shrieked, undoubtedly with a shock of recognition as their old tactics came back to haunt them.

A 1931 report on the National Prohibition Act and its application found that measures used to enforce the law were meeting with increased resistance. Comparing the Prohibition Act with narcotics laws, the report saw no difficulty in administering the drug laws, even though profits were huge and evading detection relatively easy. The reason, said the report, was that "the laws against [drugs] are supported everywhere by a general and determined public sentiment." A sentiment, in short, that was lacking in the support of the liquor law.

As the Depression deepened and the bleak years stretched ahead of the hopeless and the jobless, thoughts of Prohibition were the farthest thing from people's minds. "What does Prohibition amount to," asked Will Rogers, "if your children are not eating?"

By the early 1930s the Wets were in the ascendancy. Yet the Drys, even as they faced defeat, refused to give an inch. A contemporary saw both sides, Prohibition and anti-Prohibition, as so blindly aggressive that they must conquer or die. In the twilight of their cause the Drys might have been able to salvage something if they had been prepared to compromise, but this was not in the nature of the beast. They wanted all or nothing. In the end, it was nothing.

Prohibition came to an end on 5 December 1933, just short of fourteen years after it began. To many prohibitionists, even those inclined to small-t temperance, Repeal must have seemed a return to business as usual, with all its negative connotations. Andrew Sinclair, in his book *Prohibition: The Era of Excess*, saw the old tale retold. "The drink trade was returned to the hands of private interests, which once again sought to influence state legislatures and Congress, thus beginning again the sad cycle of liquor and politics and corruption."

11

Real Ale versus Light Beer

Sinclair's "sad cycle" is the story of beer in two words. Beer has been beset by myriads of problems throughout recorded history. We've seen many of them in these pages: the vicious repression of Prohibition and its sordid aftermath; the shining ideals of Temperance tarnished by the very Temperance folk themselves; and deviants who, down through the centuries, have persisted in taking good ale and adulterating it with the most curious additives imaginable. We've seen laws by the barrel, rolling ponderously across every country in the world, laws at once laughable and sad and ultimately ineffective. Everywhere faithless brewers have tried to increase profits through devious schemes, businessmen have constantly sought to prey on the beer drinker, and relentlessly the tax man's scythe has levelled us all. Yet the knock has always gone out against beer itself. Beer? Why beer? What has *beer* done? Surely it must be obvious that the problems lie not with beer, but with man.

Many will say that the root of any beer problem is man's thirst for change. More than once we have shown that man simply cannot leave well enough alone, he has to change it, add to it, take away from it. A recent example, still flourishing even now (or still festering, depending on your views), is the swing to light ale, from the 1 per cent "light" (which hardly seems worth the trouble) to the 0.5 per cent beverages that are little more than robust Shirley Temples. Like any fads, these initiatives come and go. Only in recent days has this abortive movement to *reduce* the strength of ale gained any support. And support from whom? From those who really don't drink ale; social drinkers who, for the most part, would be just as happy with a glass of mineral water. How many light ale drinkers do you see drinking twelve pints at a sitting? You could count them on one finger. Yet the breweries are falling over themselves to serve this group, the very group which offers them the least support.

For those who appreciate sound healthy ale, the introduction of light ale to the Canadian market is nothing short of blasphemy. And to drive these people even farther up the wall, there are the virtually non-alcoholic beers. An office-party supply house in Toronto even offers, along with the paper tablecloths, cardboard plates, and funny hats and favours, cases of 0.5 per cent "ale." Some office party that would be. Not a chance in a carload of making a spectacle of yourself in front of the boss. You'd get more alcohol taking a deep breath outside a brewery, or talking face to face with a wino.

Canadians saw the introduction of light beers in 1978, and incredibly they've never looked back. In 1983 they held 10 per cent of the Canadian market; by 1988 they had a firm grip on fully 20 per cent – and the figure is growing.

In 1978 the Canadian beer market stood at $1.6 billion. By 1983 it had grown to $5 billion. In 1987, sales were $7.6 billion annually, from the production of 2.3 billion litres (88 litres per capita). In 1983 the American beer market was an estimated $22 billion. Figures from the U.S. Beer Institute in Washington, D. C., in 1987 raised that estimate to $44 billion. This is a surprising statistic; generally, comparisons between the U.S.A. and Canada are based on a ten to one ratio, given that the population of the U.S.A. is approximately ten times that of Canada. Thus a market of $44 billion in the States would suggest a Canadian market of, say, $4.4 billion, yet here we are, like a bunch of drunken sailors, scoffing beer worth a cool $7.5 billion.

Back in 1985, 95 per cent of Canada's $7.5 billion market was split between Labatt (39 per cent), Molson (31 per cent), and Carling O'Keefe (25 per cent). Three years later, in 1988, the Big Three still controlled 95 per cent of the market, but the percentages had altered slightly: Labatt now claimed 42 per cent. Carling O'Keefe registered 22 per cent, which left Molson still at approximately 31 per cent. Industry observers see Molson's share growing, but to what extent is difficult to determine: Every brewery will tell you they're doing great (as those percentages of a $7.5 billion market will certainly attest! Even Carling's third-place position will sure keep the wolf from the door). The remaining 5 per cent of the market is scattered among the imports and the brewers of "real" ale.

In January 1989, Molson and Carling merged; the Big Three became the Big Two, and Molson Breweries (the merger's new name) has regained top spot with 53 per cent of the Canadian beer market.

The disappointing growth of Canadian beer sales has led the major breweries to seek profits in areas other than beer. In 1983 Labatt gained more than half of its revenue from non-beer enterprises. In the same year 30 per cent of Molson's profits came from non-beer operations. By 1985 Molson's non-beer revenues rose to 43 per cent; 1988 saw Labatt's 50 per cent climb to 57 per cent. Clearly, beer sales, in Canada at least, are not doing what the accountants feel they should be doing; times are tough.

Remember the good old days a decade ago when a case of twenty-four domestic beers cost you all of $7? Today that same case will set you back over $22. As we have pointed out earlier, many maintain that home brew is the only way to go. Aside from the one-time cost of equipment, which can run as low as $40, a batch of home-brewed ale should cost no more than one-quarter of the price of domestic beers. England's home-brew market in 1985 was $120 million, and many British distributors are now selling their equipment, materials, and self-contained beer kits in Canada. In 1985 in Canada home brewing was, technically speaking, illegal. However, if you wanted to brew at home, you could get a free licence to do so from the Director of Excise. Typical bureaucratic self-contradiction: It's against the law, but if you insist on home brewing we'll let you do it for nothing. The licence was probably justified as a means of keeping track of home-brewing enterprises, but I wonder: How many licences have been applied for? Tell you what, I'll give you a dollar for every home brewer who's licensed – provided you give me a nickel for every home brewer who isn't. In anticipation of your cheque, I will be spending the winter on the Riviera.

Modern methods have simplified home brewing. Equipment and materials are now available at very reasonable cost – forty bucks will put you in business – and it's become child's play to produce a sound ale in no time at all.

Perhaps you're a trifle dubious about those nineteenth century beer recipes, festooned as they are with archaic terms and ingredients, and dealing with vast quantities that would keep you in beer for a decade. Something more contemporary? Also something that would fit in your cupboard, rather than occupy your entire backyard and all your spare time? Experts are inclined to shrug when asked for a simple, easy-to-produce recipe that takes five minutes start to finish. "You want a beer in five minutes, go to the beer store." Every home brewer can give you a hundred recipes, and none of them takes five minutes.

Martin Sewell, a Toronto supplier of home-brew materials and equipment, offers this method of producing a standard English ale.

To make twenty litres:

To 15 quarts (14 L) of water add 11 lbs (5 kg) Pale malt, 1 lb (450 g) Crystal malt, 1 lb (450 g) Munich malt, and one teaspoon Irish moss (carageenan; to clarify the brew). Heat at 124° F (51° C) for 45 minutes. Raise heat to 158° F (70° C) for a further 45 minutes. Drain off the fluid into another container. The next operation is called sparging: the residual malt is placed in a special vessel whose bottom is perforated. Water at 170° F (76° C) is splashed over the malt and allowed to drain through the vessel's holes. This second batch of fluid is added to the first until you have 25-30 litres total. You now add 1/2 oz (14 g) of Galena hops and boil for 40 minutes. Then add a further 1/2 oz (14 g) of hops and boil for 20 minutes. Add a final 1/4 oz (7 g) of hops and boil for 15 minutes. Reduce heat to 75° F (24° C) then add one tablespoon (1/2 oz, 14 g) of yeast (yeast is also available in pre-measured packages). Leave for 3-5 days (ambient conditions will affect fermentation time). Draw off the fluid into another container and leave for 12-14 days. Bottle.

In home brewing it's critical that equipment and vessels be scrupulously clean; contamination of any kind could result in a brew you wouldn't give to your worst enemy. A successful brew tends to be smoother, with a pronounced hoppy flavour; there is little head, and the brew itself is inclined to be cloudy, but enthusiasts maintain it contains more proteins.

So there you have one of many thousands of beer recipes, and it should be stressed that each and every one is as sensitive as a jealous heart: The subtlest change to any of the components can give you a more than subtly different brew. Have a talk with your local home-brew supply house before you start. As in any other enterprise, it pays to listen to people who have done it all before. Remember that the condition of the water you use, the very air around you with its freight of bacteria, a slightly different strain of malt, of yeast, of hops, different cooking times, different temperatures, all play a vital role in the production of your beer.

But it's real. The genuine article, and all the better for having been made with your own tender hand; a brew of which our forefathers would have been proud. Real flavour, real goodness – real *ale*.

Real ale: fact or fad? A passing fashion, like sack dresses and Mohawk haircuts, or a profound change in national taste? Canada's big breweries aren't losing too much sleep at the moment; when you have, collectively, around 95 per cent of the Canadian beer market in your hand you know no one is going to take it away from you over the weekend. Still, the so-called mini-breweries appear to sprout like mushrooms; every week sees yet another mention of them in the public press, complete with photographs of smiling entrepreneurs, brandishing bottles with curious labels, telling us how they went from zero to $10 million in four and a half minutes.

The first such enterprise in Canada was the Troller Pub in Horseshoe Bay, BC, begun in 1982. They produced a brew called Bay Ale and sold it in their own pub, and of every five beers they pushed across the bar, two of them were their own brew. Forty per cent; not bad. Were they merely satisfying a local taste? Perhaps. Are we to assume, then, that the scores of other mini-breweries are also simply satisfying local tastes?

Upper Canada Brewing, an Ontario-based "micro" brewery, sells across Ontario and has recently entered the European market. Upper Canada's overseas efforts began in September 1987, when they established distributorships in Holland, West Germany, Belgium, and Luxembourg. At the same time they took their first tentative steps into the vast American market. On the drawing board are plans to set up distribution in Japan, Italy, and Austria. Upper Canada Brewing began in August 1985, and by 1988 their sales were in excess of $7 million. Altogether, that's a lot of "local" taste. Let's just clarify the terms "micro" and "mini" breweries. The Liquor Control Board of Ontario (LCBO), for example, does not recognize "micro" or "mini" with regard to breweries. They are simply popular expressions, and have no significance so far as the LCBO is concerned. "They [the so-called micro- or mini-breweries] get the same licence as is given to Labatt or Molson."

The Troller Pub in Horseshoe Bay was what is called a "brew-pub," signifying a pub that brews for sale in its own establishment; the "cottage" or "micro" brewery produces beer for sale in and beyond its own area. Some manufacturing firms, seeing the micro- or mini-brewery as more than just a passing aberration, are marketing complete mini-brewing plants for as little as $100,000. There are, in 1988, approximately a hundred and fifty such in-house brewing systems in operation in Canada and the U.S.A.

Canada's mini-breweries observe the ancient Bavarian purity of beer laws that were established in the early sixteenth century: Nothing shall enter into good beer but malt, hops, water, and yeast. Ironically, in 1985, a number of West German breweries were charged with adding preservatives to their beer, in contravention of the Bavarian purity of beer laws. One outfit was even fined 45,000 marks ($33,000 Canadian). The breweries' justification was that they were losing a competitive edge to other EEC countries who *did* permit additives. The move to preservatives was the worst possible timing: Other European breweries were clamouring for permission to sell their beers in German pubs, but the West Germans self-righteously rejected the idea, and cited their purity of beer laws – while many of these same

German breweries were busily spiking their beer with preservatives to more effectively compete in other markets.

Real ale is looked upon as something new. Yet our ancestors drank "real" ale as a matter of course. In those early days if you wanted something lighter than ale you drank water – though the number of water drinkers in Olde England could be counted on one hand. Recently, those traditional tastes for good, sound, foursquare ale – the real thing, no added chemicals or preservatives – have surfaced again in international organizations devoted to the re-birth of "real" ale.

The Campaign for Real Ale Canada (CAMRAC) began in Ottawa in 1981, an offshoot of the British CAMRA, an English group who started in the early 1970s to press for a return to unadulterated, additive-free ale. When the British organization was first launched, perhaps one pub in twelve was serving a "real" ale, as defined by CAMRA (malt, water, hops, and yeast – and nothing else). Within a decade the situation was virtually reversed, with only one pub in twelve *not* serving real ale.

The U.S.A. is witnessing somewhat the same subtle, yet real, shift in beer tastes. According to CAMRAC, there are in Seattle over seventy brands of local beer, many of them real ale. What part of the American beer market is held by real ale is difficult to assess; certainly, like Canada, its share is no more than one per cent. But the fact that reassures beer drinkers who are outraged at the inroads made by light ales is the international scope of the real ale movement. Britain's CAMRA has effected changes to the country's liquor laws; Canada's CAMRAC is growing in strength and prestige. For the beer drinker all is not pessimism and gloom. Even in the shadow of growing light ale sales, the beer lover can smile in the knowledge that time changes all things – time, and our basically reliable taste in beer – and that childish, fleeting fads will ultimately be swept away by tides of wholesome, genuine beer.

Bibliography

About Beer and the Brewing Industry. Brewers Association of Canada. Ottawa: 1985.

Ade, George. *The Old-Time Saloon*. New York: Ray Long & R. Smith, 1931.

Alberta Report, 2 September 1985.

Amis, Kingsley. *On Drink*. London: Jonathan Cape, 1972.

Baker, Oliver. *Black Jacks and Leather Bottells*. London: Privately printed, 1921.

Beebe, Lucius. *The Big Spenders*. New York: Doubleday & Company Inc., 1966.

Behan, Brendan. *Brendan Behan's Island: An Irish Sketchbook*. London: Hutchinson, 1962.

———. *Brendan Behan's New York*. London: Hutchinson, 1964.

Bemelmans, Ludwig. *La Bonne Table*, eds. Donald and Eleanor Friede. New York: Simon & Schuster, 1964.

Berry, George. *Taverns and Tokens of Pepys' London*. London: Seaby Publications, 1978.

Berton, Pierre. *Klondike*. Toronto: McClelland and Stewart, 1963.

——— and Janet Berton. *Canadian Food Guide*. Toronto: McClelland and Stewart, 1974.

Bickerdyke, John. *The Curiosities of Ale and Beer*. London: Spring Books, 1965. (First published in 1889.)

Bishop, George. *The Booze Reader*. Los Angeles: Sherbourne Press, 1965.

Boswell, James. *Everybody's Boswell: The Life of Samuel Johnson*, abridged. London: G. Bell, 1961.

———. *London Journal, 1762-1763*, eds. F. A. Pottle et al. London: The Reprint Society, 1952.

Brewing Review, Number 15, January, 1986 (London).

———, Number 17, February, 1987 (London).

Brillat-Savarin, Jean Anthelme. *The Physiology of Taste*, trans. M. F. K. Fisher. New York: Alfred A. Knopf, 1971.

British Columbia: A Centennial Anthology, ed. Reginald Eyre Watters. Toronto: McClelland and Stewart, 1958.

Bryant, Arthur. *The Age of Elegance 1812-1822*. London: Collins, 1950.

Chalfant, Fran C. *Ben Jonson's London*. Athens: University of Georgia Press, 1978.

Chase, A. W. *Dr Chase's Recipes, or Information for Everybody*. Ann Arbor: By the author, 1862.

Coffey, Thomas M. *The Long Thirst: Prohibition in America 1920-1933*. New York: W. W. Norton, 1975.

Cups and their customs. London: John van Voorst, 1869.

Dictionary of Canadian Biography. Toronto: University of Toronto Press, 1979.

Dictionary of Canadianisms, A. Toronto: W. J. Gage, 1967.

Doxat, John. *Drinks and Drinking*. London: Ward Lock, 1971.

Durant, Will and Ariel Durant. *The Story of Civilization*, 11 vols. New York: Simon & Schuster, 1935-1975.

Financial Post, The, 12 August 1978.

——, 13 October 1984.

——, 5 January 1985.

——, 16 March 1985.

——, 10 August 1985.

Fowler, Gene. *Beau James: The Life and Times of Jimmy Walker*. New York: Viking Press, 1949.

Fraser, Antonia. *King Charles II*. London: Weidenfeld and Nicolson, 1979.

Freeling, Nicolas. *The Kitchen*. New York: Harper & Row, 1970.

Frenchman, Michael. "Scotch Whisky: The Spirit of the Age." *Time Canada*, March 31, 1986.

Girouard, Mark. *Victorian Pubs*. London: Studio Vista, 1975.

Gray, James H. *Booze: The Impact of Whisky on the Prairie West*. Toronto: Macmillan, 1972.

——. *Red Lights on the Prairies*. Toronto: Macmillan, 1971.

——. *The Roar of the Twenties*. Toronto: Macmillan, 1975.

Great Canadian Beer Book, The, eds. Gerald Donaldson and Gerald Lampert. Toronto: McClelland and Stewart, 1975.

Gregson, Harry. *A History of Victoria 1842-1970*. Victoria: Victoria Observer Publishing Co., 1970.

Hackwood, Frederick W. *Good Cheer: The Romance of Food and Feasting*. Detroit: Singing Tree Press, 1968.

——. *Inns, Ales, and Drinking Customs of Old England*. London: Bracken Books, 1985.

Hallowell, Gerald A. *Prohibition in Ontario*. Ottawa: Ontario Historical Society, 1972.

Hennigar, Ted R. *The Rum Running Years*. Hantsport: Lancelot Press, 1984.

Higley, Dahn D. *O.P.P.: The History of the Ontario Provincial Police Force*. Toronto: The Queen's Printer, 1984.

Historical Essays of British Columbia, eds. J. Friesen and H. K. Ralston. Toronto: McClelland and Stewart, 1976.

Hughes, J. P. *How You Got Your Name*. London: Phoenix House, 1961.

Hunt, C.W. *Booze, Boats, and Billions*. Toronto: McClelland and Stewart, 1988.

Jackson, Michael. *The Pocket Guide to Beer*. Scarborough: Prentice-Hall, 1982.

Maclean's, 15 August 1983.

Marchant, W. T. *In Praise of Ale*. Detroit: Singing Tree Press, 1968.

Marketing, 23 January 1978.

Mayfield, Sara. *The Constant Circle*. New York: Delacorte, 1968.

Mencken, H. L. *Newspaper Days*. London: Kegan Paul, Trench, Trubner, 1942.

Minter, Roy. *The White Pass: Gateway to the Klondike*. Toronto: McClelland and Stewart, 1987.

Montagné, Prosper. *Larousse Gastronomique*. London: Paul Hamlyn, 1961.

Newman, Peter C. *Bronfman Dynasty*. Toronto: McClelland and Stewart, 1978.

Oliver, Peter, *G. Howard Ferguson: Ontario Tory*. Toronto: University of Toronto Press, 1977.

One Hundred Years of Brewing. New York: Arno Press, 1974.

Patton, Janice. *The Sinking of the I'm Alone*. Toronto: McClelland and Stewart, 1973.

Pepys, Samuel. *Passages from the Diary of Samuel Pepys*, ed. Richard Le Gallienne. New York: Boni & Liveright, 1921.

Pottle, Frederick A. *James Boswell: The Earlier Years*. New York: McGraw Hill, 1966.

Priestly, J. B. *The Prince of Pleasure and his Regency 1811-1820*. London: Heinemann, 1969.

Pub: A Celebration, ed. Angus McGill. London: Longmans, Green, 1969.

Rybczynski, Witold. *Home: A Short History of an Idea*. New York: Viking Penguin, 1986.

Sinclair, Andrew. *Prohibition: The Era of Excess*. Boston: Little, Brown, 1962.

Tavern Anecdotes ... & Reminiscences. Manchester: E. J. Morton, 1973.

Vista, No. 1, 1988.

Watney, John, *Beer is Best*. London: Peter Owen, 1974.

———. *Mother's Ruin: A History of Gin*. London: Peter Owen, 1976.

Weiner, M. *The Taster's Guide to Beer*. New York: Macmillan, 1977.

White, Elmer J. *'Stroller' White: Tales of a Klondike Newsman*, ed. R. N. De Armond. Vancouver: Mitchell Press, 1969.

Wilson, Edmund. *The Twenties*. New York: Farrar, Straus and Giroux, 1975.

Woods, Shirley E., Jr. *The Molson Saga*. Toronto: Doubleday, 1983.

World Guide to Beer, The, ed. Michael Jackson. London: New Burlington Books, 1982.

Yoder, Paton. *Taverns and Travelers: Inns of the Early Midwest*. Bloomington: Indiana University Press, 1969.

Young, Jimmy. *A Short History of Ale*. Newton Abbot: David & Charles, 1979.